WORLD TR
AND
LONDON LIFE BETWEEN THE WARS
(1924 - 1933)

Volume 5
of
THE COLOURFUL LIFE OF AN ENGINEER
Memoirs of Harry Chickall Lott MC

As Peter Scott wrote of himself, in his autobiography:
"I am, without question, the luckiest, and I believe, the happiest man I know."

Grosvenor House
Publishing Limited

This book is published by
Grosvenor House Publishing Ltd
Link House
140 The Broadway, Tolworth, Surrey, KT6 7HT.
www.grosvenorhousepublishing.co.uk

A CIP record for this book
is available from the British Library

ISBN 978-1-83975-620-7

About the Author

Harry was born in 1883, a descendant of the Lott family who, for 200 years, had farmed at the Valley Farm and Willy Lott's House in Flatford, made famous by Constable's paintings. In 1890 his father left farming and invested in a foundry business, Lott & Walne, in Dorchester where Harry attended Dorchester Grammar School and won a scholarship to study Engineering at the Central Technical College in London.

He first saw Canada on an Atlantic cable laying expedition in 1905 and emigrated there in 1907, where he worked as an inspector on the construction of bridges, buildings, and hydro-electric schemes in five provinces, living in Montreal, Toronto, and Winnipeg and in construction camps in the backwoods of Manitoba

He returned to England in 1914 to join up for WWI and served in the trenches with the 8th Battalion, Royal Sussex (Pioneer) Regiment. He was awarded the Military Cross for acts of exemplary bravery and promoted to the rank of Major after the battles of the Somme and Passchendaele where he was wounded. He was transferred to the Royal Engineers and, after the clearance of the battlefields in 1919, he was posted to the British Army of Occupation in Mesopotamia where he was appointed Lieutenant Colonel in charge of Mechanical & Electrical Services in Baghdad and Basra.

When he was demobilized in 1924 Harry sailed from Basra to Bombay where he joined the Empress of Canada's first round-the-world cruise to Vancouver and returned home from Montreal after visiting friends and relatives across Canada.

He joined Balfour Beatty & Co. in London for whom he worked as a consulting engineer for 30 years until he retired aged 72 in 1955. In the 1920s and 30s he carried out surveys for hydro-electric schemes for the East African Power and Lighting Company in Kenya and undertook assignments in India and Nigeria as well as another round-the-world trip, beginning with a journey to China on the Trans-Siberian Railway, to submit a bid for the Shanghai Municipal Electricity Department.

His memoirs describe a remarkable life full of adventure and good luck. He did not marry until he was 59 and had a son Brian, who has edited these memoirs, adding some historical background and other items of interest from the diaries which Harry kept from 1900 until he died in 1975 aged 91.

Preface

These memoirs were originally written or rather typed using an old-fashioned Smith-Corona typewriter by my father, Harry Lott, during his retirement from the late 1950's until a year before he died aged 91 in May 1975. He had kept daily diaries from 1900 until a week or so before his death as well as numerous personal papers, photographs, menus, cuttings, reports, and letters. These provided source material for the several volumes of memoirs he wrote covering his first 50 years, up to the mid-1930's, when he considered that the 'colourful' years of his life had come to an end. By then he had become somewhat frustrated that his company, Balfour Beatty, no longer sent him on interesting overseas assignments but instead kept him office bound in London, using his extensive international experience and engineering judgement to evaluate and comment on the various new projects and business opportunities which came their way.

Having essentially completed his memoirs he asked a writer and journalist, Peter Ford, for his opinion on their suitability for publication. Peter thought that they were full of interest and suggested that they would benefit from the inclusion of more personal comments on the various individuals mentioned and that some links to current events of the day would add context. As a consequence my father added many inserts into the text and extra pages of anecdotes and detail wherever he could, with the result that without the benefit of a word processor the memoirs became even more like a scrap-book which no-one would ever read.

I inherited his memoirs, 75 years of his diaries and a filing cabinet full of his papers, photograph albums and other memorabilia. Whilst sorting through all these documents for archiving or disposal I decided to edit his memoirs, put them on a word processor and prepare them for publication in the hope that they may be of interest to future generations. During this process I added some extra material from my father's diaries and personal papers and I also inserted some historical background details in places, however, the majority of the content is exactly as he wrote it.

In preparing these memoirs for publication I decided to split them into five separate volumes, each dealing with a different chapter of my father's life. All five parts, if published together, would result in a book of a size which would put off most readers. If edited to remove many of the details, then each part would be of less interest to anyone reading it as a historical document. I can imagine my children, grand-children and possibly their descendants being interested in picking up a particular volume on, say, Canada, Mesopotamia or World War I and reading that, whilst not being prepared to tackle all five volumes at any one time.

The second reason is that outside the family each volume has potentially a quite different readership. Some readers or historical researchers may be interested in one or two of the volumes but not in all of them. The following summary of the contents of each volume provides an over view of the memoirs as a whole and enables readers to determine their interest or otherwise in the other volumes.

My father was an engineer, an officer and always a gentleman. He had a remarkable life and an interesting and varied international career in engineering during the first half of the 20th century. After 59 years of independence as a bachelor, he married my mother in 1942; she was 25 years younger, and they enjoyed 32 years of very happily married life together before he died at the age of 91. In his last three decades he was a wise and wonderful father to me, despite being 60 years my senior.

This work is my tribute to him. It has been a real pleasure re-living his experiences, researching stories of the people he met, the places he visited and the engineering history he describes. I hope that it will be of some interest and inspiration to my family, his descendants, and future generations of engineers.

J Brian Lott OBE
London, 2020

The Colourful Life of an Engineer
Volumes 1 to 5

Contents

- Inspector of transmission line to Pointe du Bois power plant
- Hunting moose and caribou in Manitoba and Quebec
- Canoe trips on the Winnipeg River and later in Montreal
- Supervision of drilling for a dam on the North Saskatchewan River
- Consulting engineer in Montreal with T. Pringle & Son
- Survey for a hydro-electric scheme on St Maurice River
- Chief designer of a new factory for Kodak in Toronto
- Leaving Canada to join up for World War I in 1914
- Across Canada on return from Mesopotamia in 1924

Volume 3

The Life of a Pioneer and Engineer on the Western Front
(1914-1919)

- Joining the 8th Battalion, Royal Sussex (Pioneer) Regiment
- Training in England and arrival in France, July 1915
- Life and work in the trenches
- The Loos Show - September to October 1915
- Appointment as Captain in 'B' Company
- The Somme 1916 and award of the Military Cross
- Transfer to the Royal Engineers
- Commander of No.5 Army Tramway Company
- John English Lott - killed in action - May 1917
- The Battle of Passchendaele - July to Nov 1917
- Wounded and convalescence - Oct 1917 to Feb 1918
- Back to the Somme - the German Spring Offensive
- Controller of Foreways, 5th Army - promotion to Major
- Armistice Day and Spanish Flu - Nov/Dec 1918
- Clearance of the Battle Areas - 1919

Volume 4

Mesopotamia
(1919-1924)
The Story of an Engineer with the British Army of Occupation

- Transfer to Mesopotamia and journey to Baghdad in 1919
- Appointment as Assistant Director of Works in Baghdad
- Visit to Persia for Christmas 1919
- The Arab Revolt, 1920

The Colourful Life of an Engineer

Volume 5

World Travels
and
London Life between the Wars
(1924 – 1933)

Introduction

This is the last of the five volumes of my memoirs and covers the first nine years of my professional life as a consulting engineer with Balfour Beatty & Co. from 1924, when I returned home from Mesopotamia, until I turned 50 in 1933. During this period I undertook safaris in Kenya to identify and survey suitable sites for new hydro-electric schemes, made a round-the-world trip starting with a journey to Shanghai on the Trans-Siberian Railway, spent three months in negotiations with the Madras Government on a new hydro-electric scheme at Pykara Falls and three months in Nigeria preparing a report on their electricity supply and distribution system. Between these trips I enjoyed club life in London, entertaining friends to dinners and the theatre in London, making occasional visits to the Continent and spending time at weekends with my parents and relatives in the country. But before starting on that story I should summarise my life and career up to 1924 for those who have not had the chance to read the earlier volumes.

The first volume of my memoirs begins with my family background, visits to the Valley Farm and Willy Lott's Cottage in Flatford, where my ancestors had been yeoman farmers for 200 years, and describes our way of life in a typical East Anglian farmhouse 130 years ago.

Following the agricultural depression of the 1880s my father left farming and moved to Dorchester in 1890 where he invested in an iron foundry, Lott & Walne, which he thought would be more profitable than farming. So my schooldays were spent at Dorchester Grammar School from which I obtained a scholarship to study Electrical Engineering at the Central Technical College in London, later to become part of London University.

After three years in digs and at college in London, at a time when many new and exciting engineering developments were taking place, my first real engineering job, working for a firm of consulting engineers, was as an assistant engineer on the Atlantic cable laying expedition in 1905. During that trip whilst our ship was being repaired in Halifax, Nova Scotia, I made a brief visit to Montreal, Toronto, and Niagara Falls and fell in love with Canada. It was a young country full of opportunity and I decided to return to live and work there.

After eighteen months gaining practical experience in the workshops of Marshall's of Gainsborough, and having obtained my father's permission to emigrate, I left Liverpool in July 1907 aged 24 bound for Montreal on the SS Victorian. My experiences in Canada are described in Volume 2 which provides a glimpse of the early days in Canada before the First World War.

I landed in Montreal along with many other young immigrants, with only £10 in my pocket and no job to go to. Within a week I was working for the Allis Chalmers Bullock Company in their high-tension electrical testing department for 15 cents/hr. After 6 weeks I moved to a better job with the Canadian Inspection Company for whom I worked as an inspector of steelwork and bridge construction in Montreal, New Glasgow (NS) and St Casimir (PQ) before being sent to Winnipeg (MB) to supervise the erection of a bridge over the Red River.

After my first home leave in the summer of 1909 I returned to Canada and began an assignment for Smith, Kerry, and Chace, consulting engineers, working as an inspector on the construction of a 77 mile transmission line between Winnipeg and the new hydro-electric power plant being built at Pointe du Bois. The following two years, most of which were spent in construction camps in the backwoods north-east of Winnipeg, were some of the most colourful of my life. I lived in a tent during the harsh winters when the temperature fell to 40 degrees (all temperatures in Fahrenheit) below zero, and during the hot, midge-infested summers when the mercury rose to 100 degrees. Occasional visits to civilisation in Winnipeg to meet friends provided a welcome contrast to the rough conditions of camp life.

Weekend adventures included canoe trips with friends on Lac du Bonnet and the Winnipeg River and hunting expeditions for moose and caribou with Arthur Mitchell, a well-known local character, as a guide.

After Winnipeg I spent three months near Prince Albert supervising drilling work in the North Saskatchewan River to find a suitable location for a new dam and hydro-power plant to serve the city. We did not encounter bed-rock and advised against the construction of a dam, but the city engineers ignored our advice and went ahead, leaving Prince Albert with massive debts and the La Colle Falls dam half-finished a few years later.

I returned after a second visit to England to see my family, accompanied by Cyril Skinner whose mother had employed me to 'show him Canada' and help him find a job there. Having done that, I started work with T. Pringle & Son, consulting engineers in Montreal, and was sent to survey the site for a hydro-electric scheme on the St Maurice River near Grand-Piles. This was followed by design work in the Montreal office for some new buildings, including Kodak's large new factory in Toronto for which I was the Chief Designer; it was to be built in reinforced concrete in the early days of that form of construction.

When war broke out in Europe I joined the local Company of the Westmount Rifles and started training with them in the evenings. However, there seemed little prospect of an early commission and of going to France, so in December 1914 I threw up my job and paid my passage back to England to join up there. By this time my parents had sold up in Dorchester and had moved back to the family home at Wenham Place, near East Bergholt, where my father was farming again.

My experiences in the War are the subject of Volume 3. I joined the 8th Battalion, the Royal Sussex (Pioneer) Regiment, and had four months training in England before we went to France in July 1915. As a 2nd Lieutenant I had charge of a platoon of 40 'Pioneers' whose main work was digging trenches and dug-outs and building shelters and barricades close to the front line.

My War memoirs describe the ups and downs of the daily life of a middle-ranking officer and his men in one of Kitchener's new Pioneer Battalions, living and working alongside the Infantry and the Royal Engineers in the trenches and billets close to the front line. They are based on the detailed diaries I wrote at the time with the addition of short extracts from other sources to provide historical background and continuity, all enhanced by the vivid memories which remain and the reflections of 40 years of hindsight.

The memoirs include the major battles of the Somme in 1916/17 and Passchendaele in 1917 where I was wounded and are a personal story rather than a military description of the battles. Promotion came quickly as senior officers fell and those below took over command. By the end of the War I had been promoted to Captain in the 8th Royal Sussex Regiment and then to Major in the Royal Engineers where I was the Forward Area Officer in the Headquarters of the 5th Army, responsible for constructing and maintaining the light railways and tramways used to supply the troops at the front. I was Mentioned in Despatches three times and awarded the Military Cross in January 1917. The fact that I escaped serious injury for more than two years, until October 1917, despite numerous near misses, testifies to my extreme good luck.

Soon after the Armistice in November 1918 several of us caught Spanish Flu' and I spent three weeks in hospitals in Lille and Étaples before being sent to convalesce in the luxury of the Grand Hotel du Cap Martin, not far from Nice. I returned to the RE Headquarters staff at Loos, a suburb of Lille, in February 1919 and was Senior Construction Engineer during the clearance of the battlefields until August 1919 when the War Office asked me to transfer to Mesopotamia where the British Army of Occupation required engineers. The story of my next four years in Mesopotamia is the subject of Volume 4.

I arrived in Basra on 5th November 1919 via Bombay, thirty-six days after leaving Southampton, and sailed up the Tigris to Baghdad on a river steamer which had been used as a hospital ship. My appointment was as Assistant Director of Works and Director of Electrical and Mechanical (E&M) Services with the Mesopotamian Expeditionary Force. Soon after my arrival I was formally demobilized from Military Service and became a British Gazetted Official with the status of Lieutenant Colonel and a salary of 1600/- Rupees per month.

Besides a team of Army officers, all engineers, I also had up to 8,000 men, mostly Arab, Persian, and Baghdadi Jewish civilians, under my administration as well as some enrolled Indians from the Indian Army, including Hindus, Muslims, Sikhs, and Punjabis whom we used as electricians, wiremen, mechanics, clerks, and store-keepers.

Our work was to look after the electrical generating and water supply facilities and construct new ones to service the British garrisons and local residents in an area 800 miles from east to west and 300 miles from north to south around Baghdad. We also used refrigeration barges to produce ice and store frozen meat from Army bases in Malta and Britain.

During my inspection visits to our many units I became familiar with all the towns throughout the region from Mosul, Kirkuk and Tekrit in the north to Hillah and Dewaniyeh on the Euphrates, and to Kut and Amara on the Tigris in the south.

For Christmas that first year I visited our Persian lines of communication and Kermanshah where I stayed with Alfred and Emily Tayler. Alfred was a cousin of mine from East Anglia who had been wounded and lost a leg in the War. He had joined the Imperial Bank of Persia which sent him to the branch in Kermanshah where their daughter, Doris (Lessing), the future Nobel Prize-winning author was born.

The Arab Revolt dominated much of 1920 and caused us a great deal of anxiety and expense, reinforcing our units to ensure everyone's safety. Baghdad in summer was oppressive and the Arab unrest at the delays to their independence had boiled over in the 100 degree heat.

Fortunately, I was able to take 3 months leave during the following summer of 1921, leaving Baghdad at the end of March and spending a week in India visiting Delhi and Agra before sailing home from Bombay and returning by the same route at the end of July.

Life in Baghdad was a mixture of early rising and hard work during the day followed by relaxed evenings in 'The Work House', the name we gave to our mess in River Street. Guest nights sometimes included the ladies, officers' wives, and nurses from the military and civil hospitals. During autumn weekends we enjoyed shooting trips for duck on the river or for sand-grouse and partridge in the desert.

In January 1922 I was transferred to Basra to take over as Deputy Director of RE Services. My responsibilities covered an area as far north as Amara on the Tigris and Nasiriyeh on the Euphrates and my employees included 2,920 enrolled Indians and 500 enrolled Persians as well and several hundred Arab labourers.

In April that year responsibility for RE Services was transferred from the Army Command to the RAF and we constructed several facilities for the RAF including their new base and hospital at Hinaidi and their HQ, barracks, hospital, and rest camp in Basra, whilst continuing our regular work of maintaining the electrical and water supplies and ice works in the region.

Visits to Ur of the Chaldees, shooting trips in the Marshes, tennis parties at the Makina Club, becoming a Freemason and other social events added variety to the less comfortable life in the heat and humidity of Basra.

My task during those two years in Basra was to complete our projects whilst reducing our establishment to a fraction of the initial numbers, in line with the British Government's policy of cutting the cost of maintaining a presence in the region.

Feisal was appointed King of Iraq in 1921 and, in June 1923, when he paid his first official visit to his Southern Province, I attended three dinners which were arranged for him to meet local officials in Basra.

Towards the end of my time in Basra, in order to visit Nasiriyeh to inspect work there and give advice on the defences of the town and aerodrome, I used to go by air in a two-seater RAF de Havilland DH 9A from our air-strip at Shaiba. At the time I was working for Air Marshal Sir John Salmond who thanked me for staying on an extra 12 months at his request to continue the staff reductions before leaving the country and resuming my civilian career.

I was given a wonderful Farwell Dinner at the Makina Club and a Garden Party which was fully reported in the Times of Mesopotamia on 23rd February 1924 when I left Basra for Bombay on the SS Vasna. In Bombay I was lucky to obtain a birth on the Empress of Canada on its round-the-world cruise to Vancouver, from where I crossed Canada looking up relatives and friends on the way before returning home from Montreal. That trip and my subsequent world travels and life in London are the subject of this Volume 5.

Harry C. Lott

World Travels and London Life between the Wars (1924-1933)

Returning from Iraq around the World in 1924

From Basra to Bombay on the SS Vasna

The year 1924 was one of the most colourful and remarkable for my continued good luck and the opportunity for world travel. In February, at the age of 40, I was finally demobbed and handed over my responsibilities on the GHQ staff in Basra. After 4½ years in Mesopotamia with the temporary rank of Lieutenant Colonel I reverted to the rank of Major (late RE), and on returning to civilian life I dropped the use of a military title altogether, although many of my colleagues still insisted on addressing me as 'Colonel Lott'.

The War Office had agreed to defray the return costs to their starting point for volunteers who had travelled to England at their own expense, and I received a voucher worth £113 plus £500 for out of pocket expenses to return to Montreal from where I had set out in December 1914.

The normal way out of Iraq was by ship from Basra, although the Nairn Transport Company had just started a motor-car service across the desert to the West. I left Basra (the Bassorah of the 'Arabian Nights') for Bombay on a small slow steamship, the SS Vasna, on 23rd February.

Soldiers embarking on the SS Vasna in 1924

As we left, one of the RAF planes circled our ship and did some stunts whilst the band of the Rajputs, who were leaving with us, played us out. The journey took 5½ days, starting with our passage down the Shatt al-Arab waterway where, in those early days of the industry, oil pollution on the shore was visible. We stopped first at Abadan for 7 hours where we took on board 500 tons of fuel oil for the boilers and then made another stop at Bushire in Persia to take on passengers. Our final stop of 12 hours in Karachi gave me another opportunity to see this interesting desert city of 200,000 people. On the final leg of the voyage to Bombay the maximum speed of the ship was 15½ knots and we covered the 294 miles in 24 hours.

As we left Basra I did my accounts and calculated my worldly wealth to be £4,685, of which £815 was still in Rupee bank accounts in India and Iraq, £853 in my Lloyds bank account in London, £105 in Canada and £2,800 was invested in stocks and shares in London.

A journey in the past is mainly recollected by the memory of fellow passengers. Of course there is the general impression of comfort or discomfort, good meals or bad, smooth or rough seas and good or poor luck at auction bridge. But these fade into insignificance beside the recollection of certain interesting people whom one meets on one's travels.

This particular voyage was marked by the fact that the entire cargo space on board was occupied by a complete Indian Regiment commanded by a Canadian, Lt.Col. Rogers. The Regimental band enlivened every dinner and provided an hour's dance music afterwards. The 'Retreat', sounded at sunset, was a pleasant variant to the day's routine.

One passenger deserves special mention as having contributed most to my enjoyment and education during the voyage. Mr Fisher was an American, 54 years of age, who had been travelling the world on business for many years and had evidently enjoyed several side trips for pleasure. He claimed to have visited almost every country, the last being the Yukon last summer when he took a canoe from Alaska to the mouth of the Mackenzie River and thence to Herschel Island, well inside the Arctic Circle.

He admitted that all the money he had made had been derived from British possessions in Burma, the Solomon Islands, and Canada. When asked his impression of British occupation, particularly of the British rule in India where he had lived for several months each year, he said that the British Empire will stand as long as the British are honest and clean. He paid high tribute to the Indian Civil Service and to the Government of the Crown Colonies, mentioning Ceylon in particular. He had made a small fortune from the sale of land he had bought in Winnipeg in 1889 and was looking forward to the income from 1,000 acres of coconut trees in the Solomon Islands; they apparently take 8 years to mature and live for 60 or 70 years.

I also enjoyed the company of another interesting personality, the geologist Noel E Odell, a colourful character who was on leave from the Anglo-Persian Oil Company (APOC) and on his way to join the Bruce expedition as the 'oxygen officer' for the ascent of Mt Everest. *(George Mallory and Andrew Irvine both perished during their summit attempt on this expedition. Odell lived for two weeks above 23,000 ft and twice climbed to 26,800 ft without supplemental oxygen.)* Like me he had served in the Royal Engineers in the War and he had subsequently been the leader of the two 1921/23 Merton College Arctic expeditions to Spitzbergen to explore and map the East Coast and hinterland. We both subsequently became members of the Royal Geographical Society and met occasionally at their meetings in London.

Of the ladies on board there was Mrs Blackwood, a Dane, who said that Englishmen made the best husbands as they waited on their wives, whilst Continental husbands expected to be waited upon. Miss Manger was also good company and joined us to make up a bridge four in the evenings. Walton and I took her to lunch at the Carlton Hotel during our stop-over in Karachi; commenting on a rather unappetising orange she said that 'like women, it was much nicer inside'. After Karachi, Lady Saltmarsh was one of the new passengers at my table for dinner.

India

We arrived at Victoria Dock, Bombay, on Saturday morning 1st March and I booked into the Taj Mahal Hotel for a couple of nights. Some old friends from my previous visits were still in town as well as some officers from Mespot and we met up for drinks on the sea front at the Royal Bombay Yacht Club.

When I went to Thomas Cook's office to exchange my voucher for a ticket that would take me to Montreal, they informed me that the first 'round the world' cruise ship, the 'SS Empress of Canada' owned by Canadian Pacific (CP), had just docked in Bombay and had vacancies for a few extra passengers holding ordinary first-class tickets for the rest of the voyage to Vancouver. The total cost of the ticket was £160 and so, using my £113 voucher, I only had to pay £47 extra, little more than the cost of crossing the Atlantic to Southampton, my final destination.

It was another of the great strokes of luck in my life - all my dreams of visiting a few Eastern countries on my return journey were surpassed by reality. I saw several more countries than I had planned, at much less cost and under far more luxurious conditions than would have been possible had I been jumping off and on passenger ships at different ports, getting my luggage ashore and taken to a hotel (with all the associated problems and costs of porters) and waiting until the next passenger ship going East arrived for my onward journey.

There was just enough time for me to make my third and last dash into the heart of India to get better photographs of Delhi and the Taj Mahal at Agra. This 5-day trip started with a train to Delhi on the GIP railway which took 35 hours for the 865 miles, partly because of the slow climb up the Ghats to 2,000 ft and partly due to stops for meals at station restaurants on the way. For the journey I hired an Indian servant to travel with me and to look after me and my luggage. The trip, plus my previous two journeys to see and photograph the Mogul buildings, involved a total of 5,600 miles travel by rail.

One day in Delhi at the Cecil Hotel was sufficient for my photographing. After a visit to the Red Fort, Peter Low took me to see the progress of construction of Lutyens' New Delhi, including two new water pumping stations, the Viceroy's House and the Secretariat Building designed by Sir Herbert Baker. I then spent a night on the train to Agra, 130 miles further on. During two days in Agra at Laurie's Hotel I went twice to see the incomparable Taj Mahal and, with a few Americans, hired a motor car to take us to the deserted city of Fatehpur Sikri, 23 miles from Agra.

Fatehpur Sikri was founded in 1559 by the Mughal Emperor, Akbar the Great, the son of Humayan, to become the capital of his Mughal Empire. The wonderful buildings had been planned and constructed within a seven-mile perimeter wall and had taken 15 years to complete. However, the city was abandoned in 1585 only 10 years after it was completed, due to lack of water when the lake and spring dried up. It was also too close to Rajputana with which Akbar was at war, and he decided to move his capital further away to Lahore. Inside the quadrangle of the magnificent mosque was the tomb of a Sufi holy man, Selim Chisti, built of white marble with windows of exquisite, pierced tracery resembling frozen lace.

Taj Mahal, Agra – 1924

Fatehpur Sikri with the white marble mosque,
the tomb of Selim Chisti

SS Empress of Canada

On my return to Bombay I boarded the SS Empress of Canada which was to be my luxury floating hotel for the next 2½ months. I had paid the extra charges for shore excursions at all the ports of call and so, when going ashore for a few hours or a few days and nights, I could leave all my kit in my cabin taking ashore only hand luggage. As well as the opportunity to see several new countries, the voyage gave me an opportunity of making many interesting friends amongst my fellow first class passengers, mostly wealthy Americans or Canadians who had paid large sums for the first 'round the world' cruise.

That afternoon on board I was joined at tea by one of the older American couples, the Atherton Smiths; 'he deaf and she nice' I noted in my diary. After dinner in the evening another American woman accompanied me for a stroll around the deck; she was 'large, voluble and an intermittent student, thinking of doing a term at London University or a tour of Europe alone'; no doubt fishing for a potential companion. As a tall, fit 40 year old bachelor, still bronzed and burnished from the Iraqi sun, I was an obvious target for such single women. However, whilst enjoying their company and escorting them from time to time, I managed to remain unattached throughout the voyage.

The S.S. Empress of Canada – 21,517 tons,
653 ft ocean liner launched in 1922

My first visit the next morning was to the ship's barber shop for a haircut. I came away an hour later frustrated and longing for the speed and efficiency of the simple Arab barber with his scissors and none of the electrical devices and elaborate dressings, tonics, and treatments which the ship's barber used and for which he charged handsomely.

Thereafter mornings involved a 1 mile promenade 7 times around the deckhouse and a swim in the beautiful, white-tiled swimming pool followed by a spray and shower before changing into a tennis shirt and shorts. After lunch, to avoid the sticky heat of the day, I generally had a siesta in my cabin which I shared with a cabin-mate, Mr W. Willis.

Ceylon

Tea at the Lavinia Hotel, near Colombo, Ceylon

Our first port of call was Colombo where we disembarked and spent 3 days and nights in Ceylon. I joined three others, Mr Harron (Canadian), Miss Esther Richardson (American) and Miss Rosie Wingfield (English), on a 2 day sightseeing trip up-country through tropical forests to Kandy, the former capital, around tea plantations and factories, returning to Colombo and ending up for tea at the Mount Lavinia Hotel. The last day sightseeing in Colombo ended with us watching the dancing at the Galle Face Hotel before our ship departed for Calcutta during the night. I had never learned to dance and so on this and other similar occasions I did not take to the floor.

Calcutta

Our next stop was Calcutta where we spent 4 nights in the Grand Hotel. After docking at Diamond Harbour at the mouth of the River Hooghly, we went by paddle steamer on the 6½ hr journey up-river to Calcutta; it was hot and humid with a temperature of 100 degrees in the shade. I went to the Telegraph Office to post a dozen letters to England and Canada and then took Miss Wingfield and Miss Sears in a car to see the Black Hole of Calcutta, the bathing and burning ghats, the Marble Palace and Jain Temple. The next day the three of us took a car to Fort William, the Victoria Memorial, and the Botanical Gardens where we saw the banyan tree with a crown measuring 1,000 ft around its circumference. Locals celebrating the Hindu 'Holi' day added colour and charm with brilliant flowers in their clothes and hair. By contrast, one of the many depressing sights we saw was at the Kalighat Temple, a filthy place of sacrifices, beggars, a sacred tree (for barren women), flies, and filthy water coming from beneath the shrine. The sanitation in the city, and even in the Grand Hotel where rats could be seen running about at night, was appalling. An American, on returning to the ship, said he was 'glad to go - glad to be back - but wouldn't give 10 cents to go again'.

Before leaving Calcutta I went to the YWCA to trace Ada Atkins, my niece, whom I knew was in the city on her travels. I found her at 29 Park Lane and took her for an excellent dinner at Firpo's before taking her home and returning to the hotel where my room-mate, Avegno, crept in at 4.00 am.

Paddle steamer on the Hooghly River taking
us from our ship into Calcutta

Rangoon

After Calcutta we called at Rangoon (now Yangon) the capital of British Burma, where we had only 36 hours. The principal place of interest amongst the many shrines, mosques and pagodas, and the sellers of incense sticks, flowers, and prayer flags, was the golden-roofed Shwey Dagon Pagoda with its shimmering pillars of mirror mosaic built two thousand five hundred years ago. Walking, as we had to, without shoes or socks up the marble steps was burning if one stepped off the coir matting onto the marble.

Amongst my impressions of Rangoon, 'the greatest rice port in the world' with cockle-shell boats in the harbour, were the priests in copper coloured togas; Burmese women smoking cigars; Indians doing most of the labouring; Chinese girls being taken to free schools in motor-buses; street and house drainage in open channels; beautiful silk sarongs worn by both men and women and vaccination marks on the babies.

It was 'a most unpleasant day, extremely steamy' as we left Rangoon. One lady talked of the number of tins of talcum powder she had used in order to get her clothes on and off in the hot weather. In the afternoons, after tiffin, I generally went to my cabin to strip off and rest. We had lectures in the evenings on the places we were about to visit, and I joined in games of bridge and learned to play mah-jong, but sometimes retired to my cabin to read or write letters.

Singapore

The voyage from Rangoon to Singapore, over 1,100 miles, passed through the Straits of Malacca affording us wonderful views of Sumatra's mountain ranges rising to 11,800 feet.

Seeing the sights of Singapore in a rickshaw 31st March 1924

We spent 2 days in Singapore; at the southern end of the Malay Peninsula it was the chief entrepôt for the East India trade and had a population of only 300,000 in those days. We entered the beautiful harbour at sunrise where tin, rubber, spices, gums, rattan, and copra were the principal exports.

Our sightseeing included visits to rubber plantations and a rubber factory, a forest reserve, and the botanical gardens. In the evening there was a dinner dance at the famous Raffles Hotel where I acted as escort to three ladies. The evening ended by our being 'kidnapped' by some local rubber planters who took us for a midnight drive into the jungle as far as the 'Gap', returning us to the ship at 1.30 am after drinks at one of their bungalows.

On board ship between ports my only means of keeping fit and trying to maintain my weight (which was 177 lbs in a wet towel) was walking around the deck house and swimming in the pool. I preferred swimming in the early morning after chota hazari when it was cooler, and few other passengers were around. In the afternoons, the pool was crowded with ladies and occasionally, in the late afternoon after tea, a few of them persuaded me to support them in their attempts at swimming. It was still so hot at that time of day that I had no time to cool off before changing for the first sitting of dinner at 6.30 pm at which I was booked.

As well as the businessmen and millionaires, there were a number of single ladies on board with whom I walked and talked, swam, and had tea, or accompanied on shore excursions, normally two or three at a time – there was safety in numbers. Rosie Wingfield and Esther Richardson were my most regular companions; there was also a Miss Sears, Miss Taylor, Miss Metcalfe, and Miss Dodds.

Java, Indonesia

On 2nd April I got up early to witness our departure from Singapore; ours was the biggest ship which had ever visited the port. We crossed the equator at 6.00 am and that evening were entertained to a Carnival dinner with masks and fancy headdresses, certificates from Neptune, and dancing. Not feeling able to join in the dancing, I played bridge after dinner with Bob Riley, Charles Edbrook, and H. Pole Fletcher who became my regular bridge partner.

We arrived in Java the next day at the artificial harbour at Tanjung Prick, constructed in the 1880s. I joined W.H. Inglesby for a car trip around old Batavia and Welterveden, a residential port close to present day Jakarta with beautiful streets and canals, where we stayed in the Hotel des Indes.

During our 3-day visit we went by train to the Buitenzorg Palace, the former summer residence of the Governor General in Dutch colonial times, where we walked around the botanical gardens which had been established in 1817 and were one of the largest in the world. From there we took another train to Bandung, an up-hill journey of 7 hours, and were driven to Pene the next day to see tea gardens and a tea factory.

My companion in the car was Senator Nathaniel Curry, a large 73 year old with a white walrus moustache, who had started life as a carpenter in mining towns in Nevada. He had moved back to Nova Scotia where he had established a successful construction company and a company manufacturing railroad wagons before he entered politics and became Senator for Amherst.

On the way back we were driven terrifically fast down the mountainside on good, asphalted roads, passing what seemed an infinite number of terraces with village islands on the way. We scamped lunch at the hotel to catch the train to Garoet, passed the beautiful Plateau of Leles and visited Lake Begendit and the Lake of Leles which reminded me of the Trossachs. After a visit to hot springs and a mud volcano we caught a train back to the coast to rejoin our ship.

During our visit to the 'Garden of the East' I had tasted four new fruits: loquats, rambutans, mangosteens and durian, the latter smelling very strongly of onions and rotten eggs but considered a local delicacy. I had been impressed by the sense of peace and contentment, the absence of noise, no sign of religion and the fact that both sexes appeared to be equal.

Manila

We left Java at midnight on 8th April and headed for the Philippines, skirting the coast of Borneo, and reaching the capital Manila after 100 hours. During the voyage I had discussions on US politics with Senator Robert (Bob) O'Brien (Republican) who was an out and out roué, and Mr Hoxey who spoke of the rottenness of American politics, the graft and ignorance of the Shipping Board, and the saving quality of the common sense of the President and Cabinet.

We spent two days sightseeing in Manila and the surrounding neighbourhoods, returning to the ship at night. Before we left I was the guest of Sir Augustus and Lady Nanton and was seated on her right at their dinner party for 13 at the Manila Hotel. Sir Augustus Nanton was one of the principal investors and developers of Western Canada, notably Winnipeg, Calgary, and Vancouver. The town of Nanton, Alberta, was named after him as were streets in several other Canadian cities. He had brought his family on the voyage and I enjoyed conversations with him, his wife and his brother, Brig.Gen. H.C. Nanton. Winnipeg had been their home for 40 years; he knew the Coombes and I told him of my work on the construction of the transmission line to Pointe du Bois and my other adventures in Canada before the War.

After we left Manila another well-travelled American, Adolf L. Bernheimer, became very friendly and invited me to join his table for two for the remainder of the cruise. We had many long talks; he turned out to be a multi-millionaire, telling me of his two million dollar house, 'Yamashiro', meaning mountain palace, which he had built near Los Angeles in the style of 17th century Japanese architecture, with rooms especially designed to contain art treasures he had collected in China and Japan. He also showed me the designs for another house he intended to build on a tiny island he owned in San Francisco Bay. It was in the style of a 5-storey pagoda in which he would live on the top floor and his invalid brother on the floor below.

During the voyage from Manila to Hong Kong we listened to an address by Mr Curtis of Chicago, who proposed a resolution of 'appreciation' of American rule in the Philippines and particularly of the Governor General, Leonard Wood's administration. The

Philippines had been clamouring for independence which had been firmly rejected by President Coolidge.

Hong Kong

When we docked at Kowloon I was met by my cousin, Engineer Captain Harold Sears DSO, and his wife May. They took me to their house 'in the clouds' on the Peak where they employed 5 Chinese servants and arranged a dinner party for me, followed by some excellent bridge. Harold took me to the Submarine Depot Ship Ambrose in the Dockyard, showed me over L4 Submarine, and we went for tea in the Repulse Bay Hotel, 'the nicest I have seen'.

The next day Lt.Col. R.F.A. Butterworth, an old friend from Baghdad, showed me over HMS Carlisle, a 40,000 hp light-cruiser, introducing me to Capt. Dickens, a nephew of the novelist. He also introduced me to the Hong Kong Engineering and Construction Company and the Chief Engineer of Hong Kong, Col. Russel Brown. After driving me around the New Territories to the Fanling Golf Club and the Country Club, the Butterworths gave me a dinner party that evening. To repay them and my hosts, Harold and May Sears, for their hospitality, I gave them a special dinner party on board the ship before we departed. Harold was eventually promoted to Rear Admiral and left my son Brian a generous legacy in his will.

Visit to a Javanese tea garden with Senator Curry of Montreal

Sir Augustus Nanton

Yamashiro - Adolf Bernheimer's 'mountain palace' near Los Angeles

Floating homes in Aberdeen, Hong Kong

At the Temple of 500 Buddhas, Shanghai

Shanghai

On reaching Shanghai we anchored downstream at Woosung (Wosong) at the mouth of the Whangpoo (Huangpu) River, the 70 mile long man-made river which flows through Shanghai as the last tributary of the Yangtze. We passengers were taken by tender to the city; a journey of 1½ hours. Many, including myself, stayed one of the two nights in the Kalee Hotel to see the sights and experience the lively nightlife in the Chinese Quarter and the shows in the Great World entertainment complex.

Thinking of my need for a new job I called on Trollope & Colls for an interview with the Managing director, H. Richardson; 'a favourable impression was made by both parties.' I also called on Faber, an associate of my old college, in the Shanghai Municipal Council.

Japan

We arrived in Japan at the port of Kobe by way of the beautiful Inland Sea of Japan, a day long vista of islands and lovely scenery. I stayed a couple of nights in Kobe so that I could make a visit to the Sacred Park in Nara, travelling via Osaka, one of the largest cities in the world at that time.

I then took a train to Kyoto and stayed a few nights in the Miyako Hotel where Bernheimer was also staying to meet some Japanese art dealers and architects and discuss his next acquisitions. After his death, his mountain palace Yamashiro and its contents became a showplace for the public. From Kyoto there were excursions: to Kameoka where we shot the rapids to Arashiyama (of cherry blossom fame); to Lake Biwa and a 7 mile ride in a flat-bottomed boat through tunnels and a power canal; and to Uji tea gardens and bamboo plantation, followed by an evening at a Kabuki theatre in Kyoto.

We rejoined our ship in Kobe and travelled on to Yokohama where we disembarked. The city had been flattened by a devastating earthquake on 1st September the previous year so that hardly a single building was habitable. By chance, the SS Empress of Canada had been scheduled to stop at Yokohama in 1923, a few days after the earthquake, and she had assisted in evacuating many local people.

I spent another two nights in Japan, the first at the remarkable Imperial Hotel in Tokyo, one of Frank Lloyd Wright's most original designs which he claimed was earthquake proof. Nearly half of Tokyo had been destroyed by the 1923 earthquake but the Imperial Hotel had survived, helped no doubt by the fact that it was close to the edge of the devastated area. From Tokyo I travelled by train to see the temples at Nikko and stayed a night in the Kanaya Hotel. Besides visiting the temples, seeing their amazing lacquer work and the 'royal' bridge, we visited the Urami Falls and the ancient avenue of Cryptomeria (Japanese cedar) trees, planted hundreds of years ago when the temples were built.

One more day of sightseeing in Tokyo ended my twelve days in Japan before we left from the port of Yokohama for Honolulu on the Hawaiian island of Oahu.

In the Sacred Park at Nara

The view over Kyoto from the Miyako Hotel – 1924

Trip down the rapids to Arashiyama

Visiting a temple in Nikko in cherry blossom time

The Imperial Hotel, Tokyo, designed by Frank Lloyd Wright

Saying good-bye to Yokohama with coloured streamers and a floral welcome in Honolulu

Hawaii

The 8-day voyage from Japan to Honolulu was made miserable by rough seas and bad weather. 'Feel wretched from sea-sickness' – 'spent most of the day on my bunk' – 'lose my tea and miss dinner' – 'unable to appreciate the advantage of being alive'. It was a relief to arrive in Honolulu where we were given a traditional Hawaiian welcome and were garlanded with long wreaths of hibiscus flowers.

We spent two crowded days sightseeing in Honolulu and went by street-car to the world-famous Waikiki Beach to have lunch in the Moana Hotel and watch the surfboarders. There I noticed a guest receiving a telephone call at the table without getting up; the telephone was brought to the table and plugged into a socket in the floor – not something I had seen before.

The next day Rosie Wingfield, Esther Richardson and I were entertained by Harry von Holt, a Hawaiian American on the ship. The von Holts were a wealthy and prominent Hawaiian family. Harry had been born on the island and his son Ronald

Kamehameha von Holt gave us a Hawaiian lunch in his new house built on a mountain road with a spectacular view from its large picture window framed with a plain wide teak border. Four years after our visit Ronald and a partner bought the Kahua Ranch and made it into a successful tourist resort.

After lunch we were taken to a pineapple plantation and cannery with an adjacent factory delivering 12,000 tin cans per hour to the cannery. The cannery claimed a record production of 900,000 tins of pineapple in one day. The hygienic conditions were impressive with all the women workers wearing white overalls and rubber gloves so that the pineapples were never touched by human hands.

That afternoon we collected our swim suits from the ship, and I went with the two ladies for a ride in an out-rigger canoe paddled by two stalwart Hawaiians. They took us beyond the surf and then, riding the crest of a wave, we roared back onto the beach. After that we had a go ourselves with me in the bow, but with not the same success.

Paddling the out-rigger canoe ourselves with me in the bow

Honolulu came to the pier to see us depart

The Eruption of Mt Kilauea – Hawaii
17th May 1924

A large crowd came to see us off from Honolulu when we left on 16th May and steamed to the port of Hilo on the big island of Hawaii, the largest of the group. There we were driven 31 miles up to the top of the volcano, Mt Kilauea, shown on the map below.

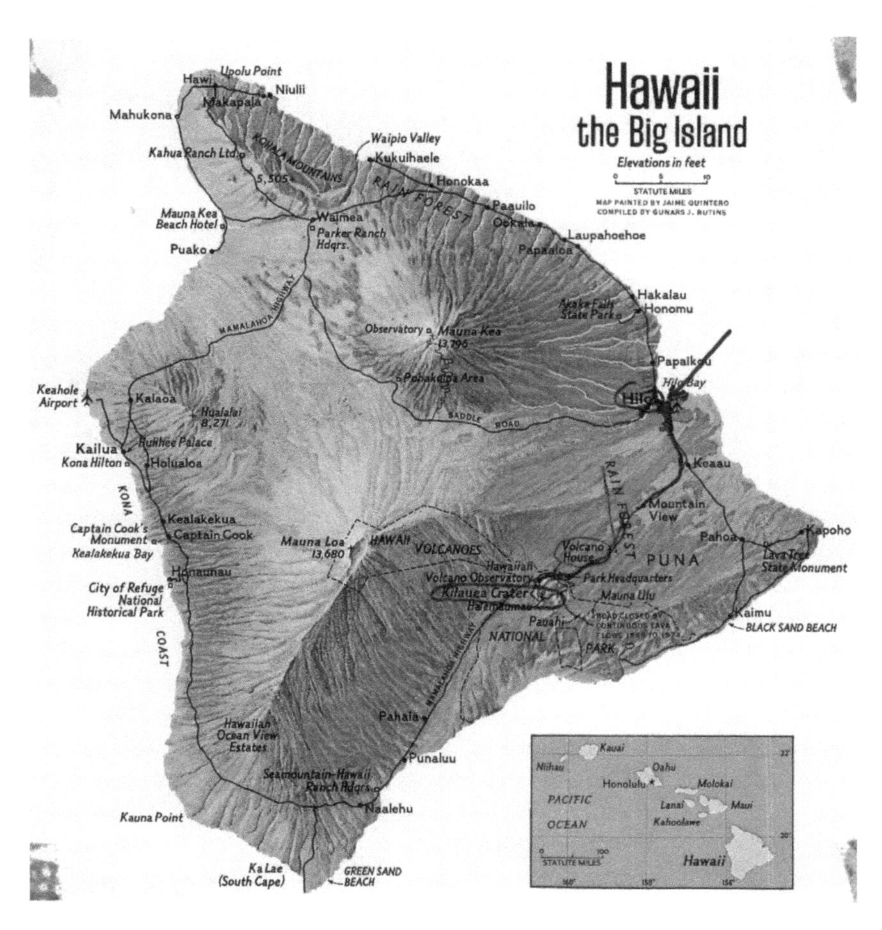

Photograph by R. W. Perkins

A PANORAMA OF THE CRATER OF KILAUEA, SHOWING THE FIERY PIT, OR "HOUSE OF EVERLASTING FIRE" (HALEMAUMAU), IN THE CENTER (SEE COLOR PLATES IV, V, AND VII)

A panorama of the crater showing the Halemaumau smoking

We passed Volcano House and reached the bluff where I descended the steep bank with Rosie Wingfield and six others to the floor of the huge crater. Augustus Curtis, Miss Green, and I then went to a lower terrace, closer to the 'fire pit' where we had a terrifying experience.

After a few quakes, the fire-pit (Halemaumau) erupted, sending rocks and ashes hundreds of feet into the air. At the top of their flight the rocks sent lightning flashes to the ground. One rock weighing 8 tons was later found 3,500 feet from the pit.

We were only about 300 yards from the pit ourselves at the time of the explosion and headed back immediately. I exposed the last two films in my camera before we began our climb back up to the rim of the crater, a few hundred feet above us. Breathless, we reached the top and were overjoyed to find a big car not far away with one of the cruise passengers who had prevented the Hawaiian driver from fleeing to safety and leaving us, or possibly our remains, behind.

In the crater just before the eruption

In the crater defying the Goddess Pele – until she protested

One of the last two photos of the eruption I was able to take from within the crater, before climbing the few hundred feet to the rim.

Life Member No. 1324

CERTIFICATE OF MEMBERSHIP

HUI O PELE HAWAII

Know All Men by these presents:

that Major H. C. Lott.

of London England

having visited the Volcano Kilauea, in Hawaii National Park on the Island of Hawaii, Hawaiian Islands, Territory of the United States of America, and having made offering acceptable to Pele, Goddess of Volcanoes, at her fiery palace Halemaumau, which is called House of Everlasting Fire, is entitled to full active life membership in the Hui o Pele Hawaii, and is hereby granted all rights, privileges and benefits appertaining thereto. In testimony thereof we have caused the seal of our Realm to be affixed.

PELE

Sealed by Fire

By the Goddess

Thomas Boles

KUHINA NUI

SUPERINTENDENT HAWAII NATIONAL PARK

Done in our Palace of Halemaumau this eleventh day of June 1924.

Hahuna

As we left the mountain a thunderstorm broke. The heavy rain falling through the great ash cloud came down as a smooth grey grout, a liquid cement. It weighed down the wonderful fronds of the tree ferns and covered our car with a ¾ inch layer of mud. Fortunately, the windscreen could be opened up for the driver to see between the two halves and so the greatest adventure of the cruise ended with the luckiest of escapes for us all in the crater party.

Lady Nanton and others watching from the Uwekahuna Bluff

The eruption as seen from Volcano House Hotel when we returned

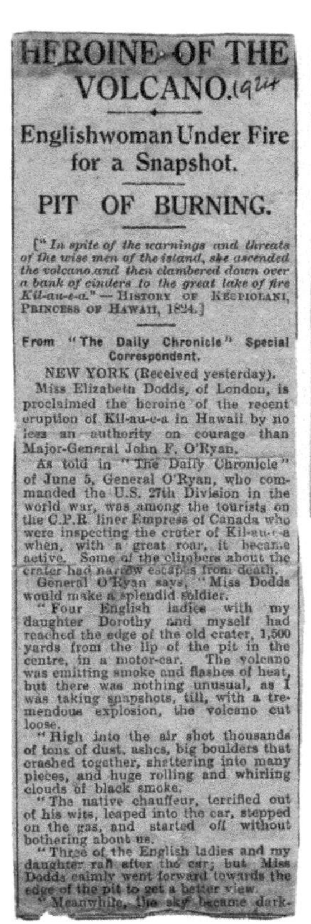

HEROINE OF THE VOLCANO. 1924

Englishwoman Under Fire for a Snapshot.

PIT OF BURNING.

[*"In spite of the warnings and threats of the wise men of the island, she ascended the volcano and then clambered down over a bank of cinders to the great lake of fire Kil-au-e-a."* — HISTORY OF KEEPIOLANI, PRINCESS OF HAWAII, 1824.]

From "The Daily Chronicle" Special Correspondent.

NEW YORK (Received yesterday).

Miss Elizabeth Dodds, of London, is proclaimed the heroine of the recent eruption of Kil-au-e-a in Hawaii by no less an authority on courage than Major-General John F. O'Ryan.

As told in "The Daily Chronicle" of June 5, General O'Ryan, who commanded the U.S. 27th Division in the world war, was among the tourists on the C.P.R. liner Empress of Canada who were inspecting the crater of Kil-au-e-a when, with a great roar, it became active. Some of the climbers about the crater had narrow escapes from death.

General O'Ryan says, "Miss Dodds would make a splendid soldier.

"Four English ladies with my daughter Dorothy and myself had reached the edge of the old crater, 1,500 yards from the lip of the pit in the centre, in a motor-car. The volcano was emitting smoke and flashes of heat, but there was nothing unusual, as I was taking snapshots, till, with a tremendous explosion, the volcano cut loose.

"High into the air shot thousands of tons of dust, ashes, big boulders that crashed together, shattering into many pieces, and huge rolling and whirling clouds of black smoke.

"The native chauffeur, terrified out of his wits, leaped into the car, stepped on the gas, and started off without bothering about us.

"Three of the English ladies and my daughter ran after the car; but Miss Dodds calmly went forward towards the edge of the pit to get a better view.

"Meanwhile, the sky became dark-

EXPLOSION OF KIL-AU-E-A ON HAWAII.

A striking photograph, taken by General O'Ryan, of the volcano of Kil-au-e-a in Hawaii, which suddenly burst into eruption while a party of visitors, including a London woman, were on the edge of the crater.

ened by clouds, from which presently came lightning flashes, with peals of thunder which rivalled the roaring that came from Kil-au-e-a's inferno.

"Miss Dodds did not seem to hear my shouts to her to come back. She kept right on. When I came up with her she was fitting a new roll of film into her camera. She said it was impossible for her to leave till she had taken her photograph.

"I persuaded her to retreat with me only by assuring her that I had taken what I believed to be an excellent snapshot, and would let her have a copy.

"Meanwhile our car had disappeared down the trail. Fortunately it was stopped by a jam of motors which had brought up others of the ship's party from Hilo, 35 miles away. And so we were able to overtake it."

This account by an American General of the bravery of Miss Dodds is rather exaggerated; she was on the rim of the crater more than 1500 yards from the pit whilst Miss Green and 7 men, including myself, were in the crater only a few hundred yards from the exploding pit.

The last eruption of Mt Kilauea of this kind – as distinct from the welling up and overflowing of molten lava – had been 134 years earlier in 1790 when a Hawaiian army marching against the great Kamehameha was annihilated. Over the following few days more eruptions took place caused by rocks avalanching down into the fire pit. My two photos, later exhibited at the Royal Geographical Society, were probably the closest taken during the 1924 eruptions.

After lunch on the ship I went by car with Misses Richardson and Wingfield to see the Rainbow Falls, lava tubes and boiling pots, and the town of Hilo before the SS Empress of Canada left for Vancouver, the final port of call on its world cruise.

Apart from the Kilauea eruption, my lasting memory of Hawaii is of the abundance of flowering plants and trees: 3000 varieties of hibiscus, plumeria (frangipani), bougainvillea, plumbago, begonia and canna lily. Also the food: breadfruit cooked as a vegetable when green and like sweet potato when ripe, stewed green mangoes, coconut milk cocktails, mullet cooked in ti-ki leaves, fried Hawaiian bananas, pineapple, and coconut cake.

We steamed away from Hilo across the Pacific sighting land and snow-capped mountains 6 days later on 23rd May as we arrived off Williams Head, Victoria. The sea was perfectly smooth for almost the whole 2,400 miles which we covered in record time.

I had made many new friends on board and, having become a Mason during my time in Basra, joined the 40 or so other passengers and crew in the ship's Masonic Club meeting. Wallace Thornycroft, a Scot, told me that he had paid £620 each for himself, his wife and two daughters for the whole trip, on top of which he had to pay extra for the shore excursions. I did not tell him that the voyage from India had only cost me £47.

There were the usual evening entertainments, musicals, and sing songs and of course games of bridge, mah-jong, and dominoes, the latter being Bernheimer's favourite game. My Arab Sheikh's costume which had been made for me in Basra came in very useful for fancy dress occasions. I wore it for the wonderful farewell dinner and Masquerade Ball on 21st May. By pure chance Rosie Wingfield came to the Ball as a Persian princess and we walked together in the Grand March, winning the first prize for the most descriptive costumes. The dance programme consisted of eight foxtrots interspersed with a few waltzes and I took to the floor for two of the waltzes with Rosie, receiving congratulations for my first attempts at dancing.

After a grand dinner provided by CPR at the Empress Hotel in Victoria, I said goodbye to Adolf Bernheimer, Esther Richardson, Rosie Wingfield, and the others and returned to the ship for the short trip to Vancouver where we docked the following morning.

I am standing in the centre of the third row wearing a bow tie

My fellow passengers on the SS Empress of Canada – I am in a safari jacket standing apart on the left against the upper deck

Visiting Friends and Relatives across Canada

Disembarking at Vancouver on 24th May I spent just over three weeks touring in Canada, visiting my aunt and cousins in British Columbia as well as many of the friends I had made during my seven years in the country before the War.

After a couple of nights in Vancouver where I met Pearson and Willis, I took the CPR train and stopped over at Kamloops to see Aunt Agnes and her husband Charlie Green at Rose Hill before going on to Notch Hill and then Blind Bay on Shushwap Lake to visit the Barnards. When I left, my cousin Arthur Barnard drove me from Blind Bay back to Notch Hill station in a 'Democrat' with two horses.

CPR train journey from Vancouver to Banff through the Rockies

There I caught the next CPR train for the 13-hour journey to Banff where I checked in for two nights in the world-famous Banff Springs Hotel, built and owned by the Canadian Pacific Railway company. It had a swimming pool in the forecourt heated by the hot springs and was famous for its 'million dollar view' over the Bow River valley.

I visited the hotel again forty years later for a couple of nights in September 1964 with my son Brian on our trip across Canada after he had finished three months' vacation work experience with Canadian Industries Ltd in Brownsburg, Quebec.

The journey across the Rockies was spectacular and has been described as like travelling through fifty Switzerlands rolled into one. I found the train as uncomfortably hot as the hotel in Vancouver had been, but it did have an observation platform where I was able to sit out until dark, only going in for meals.

The 'million dollar view' down the Bow River valley from Banff Springs Hotel – my photo taken in May 1924

Banff Springs Hotel brochure – September 1964

After Banff I travelled on to Winnipeg and stayed with the Clendenings, old friends from my pre-war days, visiting several others during the next 3 days, including J.G. Glassco, W.G. Chace, and P.V. Torrance and Marjorie, who gave me a wonderful welcome and lunch. A.L.G. Taylor was more than surprised when I phoned and invited him and his family to dine with me at the Royal Alexandra Hotel. He showed me a newspaper report that Captain Harry C. Lott had been murdered by an Indian in Alaska. Their son, Cyril Taylor, my godson, was then 10 years old and Conrad was 20.

Indian Charged With Murder

Juneau, Alaska, Aug. 8.—Willie Jackson, an Indian, was arrested here today charged with the murder of Captain Harry C. Lott. It is claimed that Jackson killed Lott because Lott would not give him home brew beer.

I also called on Sir Augustus and Lady Nanton and he arranged for me to visit the Great Falls hydro-electric project on the Winnipeg River where I spent my last night in Manitoba in the construction guest house. It revived old memories as I went by train to Red River, East Selkirk, and Lac du Bonnet, then by speeder along 'my' transmission line to have a conducted tour of the Pointe du Bois power plant before returning to Lac du Bonnet.

Sir Augustus died later that summer. I mention the sad fact because, at the dinner party given by the Nantons in Manila, he had been the first to get up from the table at which there happened to be thirteen people. Lady Nanton, answering my question at the time, said that he had probably gone to look for the missing guest. Thus his death supported the old superstition that the first person to rise from a party of 13 dies within the year.

From Lac du Bonnet I took a CPR train to Fort William, Ontario, and spent a night there at the Avenue Hotel before boarding a steamer to cross the Great Lakes. The hotel charged $5.50 a day 'American plan' or $2.75 for bed and breakfast. I had a small cabin on the SS Keewatin and 'a very enjoyable 45-hour passage with a break at Sault Sainte Marie for a walk through the town. We disembarked at Port Nicoll for the 3 hour train journey to Toronto.'

Transferring from the Great Lakes Steamer
to the train at Port McNicoll

In Toronto I was entertained by another old friend, Mrs Chace, before leaving for Montreal for further visits to more pre-war friends during my 8 days there.

Mrs Chace, my hostess in Toronto

I finally left Canada on 18th June from Quebec on the CP liner S.S. Empress of France for the voyage home across the Atlantic via Cherbourg to Southampton. A particularly interesting fellow engineer on board was H.G. Acres who pioneered the development of hydroelectric power in Canada and founded the engineering firm which bore his name.

SS Empress of France (formerly SS Alsatian); 18,481 tons, 571 feet in length – the ship was converted from coal to oil after my voyage in 1924

Of the £500 (all in £5 notes) which I had taken from Bombay for personal out-of-pocket expenses, I arrived back in England with £125. This money I invested in The Consolidated Mining and Smelting Company of Canada and sold the shares 15 months later for £537, thus recovering more than I had spent on my trip. In this very lucky gamble I had acted upon a tip given to me by a stranger on the train in BC, but against the advice of my Montreal friends who thought that the future had already been discounted in the price I paid for them.

Back in England - 1924

Europe was still unsettled in 1924. Stalin was well established as Secretary General of the Central Committee of the Bolshevik Government in Moscow and political movements in the aftermath of WWI brought the Fascists to power in Italy and caused the Second Republic to be formed in Greece. Hitler was arrested for High Treason - normally punishable by the death penalty - but the judge granted him clemency believing him to have good intentions. In January the Conservative Prime Minister, Stanley Baldwin, lost a vote of No Confidence in Westminster and resigned allowing Ramsay McDonald to form the first Labour Government for 24 years. However, his minority government only lasted until October when elections returned the Conservatives and Stanley Baldwin once again.

At home on the farm at Woodgates, East Bergholt

I arrived back in England at the end of June and stayed for several weeks at Woodgates with my parents whilst I was looking for my next job. Father was renting Woodgates Farm in East Bergholt from Mr Leslie Harris (of Wenham Priory), having had to leave Wenham Place when it was sold by the owner. He was also still renting the Hill House Farm in Gt Wenham, mainly in order that his sisters Clara and Alice could retain their comfortable home there in the fine old Tudor house now that Clara's husband Henry Batley had died.

Apart from the first 6 months of 1915 when I was training with the Royal Sussex Pioneers before leaving for France, it was 17 years since I had lived in England for any length of time. My parents and aunts were now in their 70's and I had returned as a very different person after my experiences in Canada, in France during the War and in Mesopotamia. East Bergholt and the nearby villages had hardly changed over those years and the quiet rural way of life was a complete contrast to the international life to which I had become accustomed. However, having kept in touch with family and friends with frequent letters and the occasional visits of a week or two on leave, I slipped back easily into the old environment albeit with a new detachment and objectivity. Everyone was keen to see the photographs of my travels and many evenings were spent looking through my albums and talking about my adventures.

My parents loved having the family around and my father's sisters, Clara and Alice, to whom he was very close were regular visitors, coming over from Wenham for 'tea, bridge, supper and mah-jong', often two or three times a week. My sister Clara who was living only 5 miles away at Sunnyside in Mistley with her husband Bob Fitch and young son John, my godson, was also a frequent visitor. Not so frequent but of course equally welcome visitors were my sister May, her husband Charlie Atkins and daughter Joyce (9) who lived in Harrow on the Hill, and my brother Charles, his wife Dot (née Lilian Parry) and their children Jack (15), Kitty (11) and Elsie (7) who came down from Lincolnshire occasionally. Whoever was visiting, evenings were always spent playing bridge or mah-jong, often before as well as after supper. When there were no visitors I would play three-handed bridge with Mother and Father and occasionally we had a game of mah-jong which I had taught them. When I hired a piano for 25/- per month to enable me to keep up my key-board skills we had musical evenings with Aunt Alice and my sister Clara, who were both accomplished pianists, playing their part in the entertainment.

Mother had not really recovered from the loss of her eldest son, English, in the War and seemed quiet and withdrawn. I felt that it was particularly important for me to spend some time with her, helping her in the garden, netting the strawberries and raspberries, picking blackberries, sloes, and other fruit, erecting a dovecot, and taking her to see Clara and her grandson John in Mistley and her friends in nearby villages. She said that she had lost her faith and would rarely join us when Father and I went to East Bergholt church on Sundays - sometimes to both matins and evensong. In August I gave her 1 dozen quarts of Harvest Burgundy (@ 4/6d) which she enjoyed and had been prescribed as a tonic – a habit which my sister Clara acquired later.

Woodgates Farm, East Bergholt

At Woodgates in 1924

With my niece Kitty Lott and
Bob Fitch & my sister Clara Fitch

My frequent walks with Father around the two farms, inspecting the crops and looking at the work to be done, gave us plenty of opportunity to talk about many things including his finances which were obviously worrying him. He was losing money on the farms and would not have been able to continue had it not been for the overdraft which my brother Charles and I had guaranteed for him at the bank. I promised him a further £150 to help out in addition to the £600 which I had already lent him. He farmed in an old-fashioned way, not only was he growing wheat, oats, barley, rye, beans, peas, potatoes, and trifolium (white clover), but he also kept sheep, cattle, pigs, and chickens. Occasionally, when he was not there, I would feed the pigs and get the calves and colts in.

The situation was not helped when 1924 turned out to be one of the wettest and worst harvests of his career; heavy rains, storms and dull weather had persisted throughout the summer causing meadows to flood on the farm and in many other parts of the country.

Whilst I was living at home from July to October I helped out whenever I could, going out with Father to shake up the stover after over-night rain and helping the men pull docks from the white clover field. I spent a day sharpening the knives on the mower and binder and helped to get the binder ready to harvest the oats. Once the harvest started we set up the sheaves into stooks and sometimes had to re-set them after storms had blown them about. Later, after the rains, we had to break up some of the sheaves to separate the grown and sprouting from those that were undamaged and to separate out the thistly sheaves.

The Hill House, Gt Wenham

Father managed to cart part of his trifolium crop, but part was spoilt by the rains. The wheat crop, which he finished cutting on 18th August between rain storms, was also poor. In September he was only able to sell 20 out of 39 sacks of wheat for which he received 53/- a quarter (equal to 2 sacks or 8 bushels or 504 lbs) making only £26.10s. The 19 sacks which were refused by the millers had to be dried before grinding. In October he sold 50 sacks of barley @ 50/- per qtr. and 50 sacks of rye @ 46/- per qtr. making a total of £120. By then he had threshed 38 sacks of wheat, 86 sacks of barley, 78 sacks of oats, 57 sacks of rye, 16 sacks of tares and some mustard seed. He had 60 bushels of tares to sell, getting only 6/9d a bushel compared to 9/6d the previous year, and 8 cwt of mustard seed which he sold for 34/- a cwt.

Having obtained a game licence from the local Post Office for £3, I was able to get some good rough shooting in the autumn walking around the farms with my gun and Father's dog, Prince. I generally returned with a brace of pheasants or partridges and a rabbit or hare for the dinner table. Father often joined me as did my brother Charles when he was staying.

Once or twice a week I walked over to Wenham to visit my aunts in the Hill House and stayed for lunch, or tea and cake, or for supper and bridge in the evening. Father would sometimes come too and join us for supper and bridge. Some Sundays I went over early to go to the service at Gt Wenham church with Aunt Alice where she was in the choir and I played the organ. The Hill House was where my books and papers had been stored in the attic whilst I was overseas, and I spent some time sorting through them. In October I helped to pick the rather poor crop of apples in the orchard and joined the men picking potatoes soon after the first white frost on 18th October. However, the Hill farm was partly the cause of Father's losses and before I left I managed to persuade him to give notice on the lease and to look for a house in East Bergholt for his sisters. He accepted the decision as an implied condition of my loan and my willingness to continue guaranteeing his overdraft.

Mistley was another of my regular destinations for a walk to see sister Clara, Bob, and John. We would have tea, supper and bridge and I would play with John, occasionally staying on a Saturday night and joining them at Mistley church on Sunday.

In July I made a trip to Lincolnshire to visit Charles and his family at Breezemount, his house in Kirton-in-Lindsey, where he was the manager of the Kirton Cement Works. Whilst there we went in his Chevrolet to Skegness to see his daughter, my niece Kitty, who was boarding at Parkside School and also to Brigg where my nephew Jack was at the Grammar School. I stayed for 10 days with Charles and Dot and we had a very social time, playing lots of tennis and bridge, meeting the Elmquists and several other friends as well as his in-laws, Charlie W. Parry and Tom Parry, both of whom were successful businessmen. Tom owned Redbourne Hall, and their names will crop up again later in my story.

Job-hunting in London

Since returning to England I had been actively looking for a job, writing letters and sending applications to various companies and consulting engineers. I made several visits to London, taking the train from Ipswich or Colchester to Liverpool Street, going for interviews and meeting old friends from my time in Canada, France, and Mesopotamia. If I was on my own for lunch I liked to go to the Trocadero (commonly referred to as the Troc) Grill Room where a good lunch cost 4/6d, or the Strand Corner House although that was often very crowded. When entertaining friends I chose the Hotel Waldorf, the Hotel Cecil, or the Howard Hotel in Norfolk Street, and we often went on to a show after dinner. At the Winter Garden Theatre in Drury Lane we saw Leslie Henson in 'Tonight's the Night', the show in which he had become an over-night star, and on another occasion we saw Douglas Fairbanks' new silent film 'The Thief of Baghdad'.

During one visit I called on Alfred and Emily Tayler who were staying at the Bayswater Hotel and saw Doris who was now 5 years old and her brother 2¾ year old Harry John Tayler, another godson of mine. I had stayed with them for Christmas 1919 when Alfred was a clerk with the Imperial Bank of Persia, and they were in living in Kermanshah. Sometimes I took the train to Harrow on the Hill to have dinner with sister May and Charlie Atkins at 129 Weldon Crescent and occasionally stayed the night there.

In June, the newspapers reported the death of Mallory and Irvine who were last seen 'going for the top' of Mt Everest by their team-mate Noel Odell whom I had met in February on board the SS Vasna on his way to join the expedition in India. On a happier note the headlines in July were of the Paris Olympics where

Harold Abrahams and Eric Liddell won gold medals in the 100m and 400m events, later made famous in the film 'Chariots of Fire'.

I spent a week job hunting in London in July staying at the Cannon Street Hotel; it was so busy that my first two nights were spent in a meeting room. During the week I went to the Air Ministry accounts department to claim £393 in outstanding pay and expenses, attended a Conversazione at the Institution of Civil Engineers, visited the Wembley Exhibition, and called on contacts at Trollope & Colls, Vickers, Kodak, Armstrong Whitworth, and the Foundation Company, but all to no avail; the depression in business was apparent.

The Roaring Twenties was a decade of boom and bust, of flappers and playboys, jazz and the Charleston, the General Strike, and the Wall Street Crash. The UK economy was not helped by the government's decision to maintain the value of the pound at $4.85. The over-valuation of sterling led to unemployment and labour unrest and wholesale prices fell by 25% between 1921 and 1929.

Whilst in London I used the Institution of Civil Engineers in Birdcage Walk as a base where I could read and write letters. Basil Mott was the President, and Sir Alexander Gibb and Sir Alex Binnie were two of the prominent members to whom I applied for a job. Binnie told me of an opportunity in Rangoon at £1,485 pa and Merz & McLellan also mentioned a possibility in Burma, but neither appealed to me.

Introduction to Balfour Beatty & Co. Ltd.

Eventually an old friend from Montreal days, J.M. Crabbe, introduced me to Balfour Beatty & Co. Ltd., a company that had been set up in 1909 by two Scotsmen: George Balfour, an engineer who had worked for a New York consulting company, and Andrew Beatty, an accountant. After World War I the company focused on the rapidly expanding electricity supply and transmission business and was heavily involved in establishing the

National Grid in Britain. In 1922 George Balfour and Andrew Beatty, together with some London financiers, set up a new company called Power Securities Corporation to finance and manage larger power projects overseas - William Shearer was its Managing Director and Balfour Beatty Co. Ltd. its wholly owned engineering subsidiary.

The East African Power & Lighting Company (EAP&L) based in Nairobi had been experiencing financial and administrative difficulties and in 1924, on the recommendation of friends in London, its Chairman, Major Hamilton 'Freddie' Ward, signed an agreement with Balfour Beatty & Co. under which it became the managers and engineers for the company. It was to be the first major overseas venture for Balfour Beatty and Power Securities Corporation, and they were looking for someone to handle it.

I wrote to Balfour Beatty on 3rd October with a summary of my training and experience as a civil and electrical engineer over the previous 23 years, asking to be considered for 'the next vacancy for a senior engineer or executive'. In my covering letter I explained that:

My experience statement also includes the names of persons to whom I would like you to refer as to my:

- *habits and general reliability;*
- *energy and unusual appetite for hard work;*
- *tact and personality in dealing with staff of various nationalities, getting the maximum results out of all kinds of labour;*
- *administrative ability and technical knowledge; and*
- *resourcefulness in overcoming local difficulties in the most economical way.*

My membership of the leading engineering societies has enabled me to keep up-to-date in both the technical and economic side of my profession.

In response, I received a 'wire' asking me to call at Balfour Beatty's office in the City on Monday 17th October 'for a meeting in the forenoon anytime between 11 am and 1 pm'. There I was introduced to the directors, William Shearer (Chairman), H.L. Williams (Chief Engineer), Sir Tom Callender, K.A. Scott-Moncrieff, J.G.B. Stone and finally George Balfour. Sir Tom Callender was a friend of Shearer and had established his Callender Cables & Construction Co. (later to become BICC) in 1896. Since 1904 he had been supplying electric cables to projects all over the world and had experience of overseas projects.

After several interviews, during which I told them of my work in Canada and four years in Iraq managing a public utility, supplying towns with electricity, water, and ice, they offered me an appointment at £100 per month on the staff of the East African Power and Lighting Co. under their recently signed management contract.

As nothing at all was known in London of the 'baby' company, I was to go to Kenya to obtain all the facts and figures and make a report for the new managers on the local management and operations and their proposed developments for which additional capital would be required. As a result I became the 'wet nurse' for EAP&L and remained the London manager with responsibility for that company until I retired over 30 years later.

There were discussions over several days in London on my terms of reference whilst I prepared for the assignment, reading up on the company and its projects, writing letters to the other companies to whom I had applied, and being fitted for two Palm Beach suits (8 guineas each) and a new light grey cashmere suit (7½ guineas). To relax in the evenings I went to see 'The Street Singer' at the Lyric Theatre starring Phyllis Dane and Harry Welchman, and to the Gaiety Theatre to see 'Poppy', 'a very ordinary musical, after which I stopped at the Strand Palace Hotel for a hot chocolate on the way back to my hotel'. One afternoon I walked to Piccadilly to buy cake and candies as presents before taking the train to

Harrow to visit my sister May. The following week I entertained her to dinner at the Regent Palace Hotel and we went on to the Adelphi Theatre to see 'Diplomacy' starring Gladys Cooper, Duncan Milward, Ian Hunter, and Lady (Mrs Beerbohm) Tree.

The letter confirming my contract dated 25th November said that a passage had been secured for me on the boat leaving Marseilles two days later and a ticket was enclosed for my rail journey to Marseilles and the boat from there to Mombasa. Also enclosed was a Letter of Credit for £250 to be accounted for on my return.

Christmas in Kenya - 1924
The East African Power and Lighting Company

Thus, on 26th November I took my baggage to Victoria Station, paid £3.5s.7d for excess baggage of 190 lbs over the 66 lbs allowance and left on the 11 am train for Marseilles. We reached Paris at 7.30 pm and Simone Gueschwind, my first real girl-friend with whose family I had been billeted in Lille during the War, came to spend an hour with me whilst we had dinner in the Gare de Lyon. I had the upper berth in a sleeping car and arrived in Marseilles at 10 am the next morning. There, after a good lunch in the Grand Hotel I embarked on the SS Azay le Rideau for the slow 20-day voyage to Mombasa.

Lady Howard de Walden

During that voyage I made several new friends including Miss Yate (we had mutual Canadian friends), Harrison Edwards, and Lord and Lady Howard de Walden. Lady Howard de Walden was a good amateur violinist and I used to accompany her on the piano when she and Miss Yate sang a few songs. The de Waldens' ancestral home was Audley End in Essex and Thomas Evelyn Scott-Ellis, the 8th Baron, told me of the substantial estate of central London properties which he had inherited from his grandfather.

He was three years older than me, and we had long talks on a wide range of topics including falconry, politics, war experiences, morality in business and the public school boys being recruited by Jardine Matheson. He said, 'I am not a snob, or at least I try not to be', but when we got to Nairobi he likened it to 'Surbiton aping Simla'. He told of a dinner he had given for the provost and bailee at an estate of his in Scotland when the leading bailee, somewhat the worse for wear, tried to make his exit from the hall after dinner by opening the door of the grandfather clock. Another story, told against himself, was of a safari he had been on in the Belgian Congo where he had had difficulty in getting people to take heed of his instructions for the provision of men and horses - 100 men had deserted en bloc.

The Hamoudi Mosque, Djibouti, French Somaliland

We all went ashore at Port Said for a few hours, had lemon squash at the Eastern Exchange Hotel and I posted 27 letters which I had written to family and friends during the voyage. After passing through the Suez Canal we went ashore again at Djibouti in French Somaliland, walking the ¾ mile into the town which at midnight in the bright moonlight was inexpressibly beautiful.

The central square of the Moorish town was lined with tall oleander bushes, their strong perfume pervading the air. After visiting the hotel for coffee and stamps, we walked to the serai and the Hamoudi mosque before returning to the ship and proceeding to Mombasa.

Mombasa, Kenya Colony – 1924

I told my fellow passengers that the only man I knew personally who had been to Kenya was killed by the natives in 1908 on his first day ashore, 20 miles north of Mombasa. His name was Tom London, a large, muscular man of 40-ish, with whom I had been on the Atlantic cable-laying expedition of 1905. We had worked together during the manufacture of the cable and we sat at the same table during the laying of the cable by the SS Colonia. He was the senior engineer of the cable manufacturer of which his father was the Managing Director.

In 1908 his company was about to lay another submarine cable across the Indian Ocean from Kenya. As usual, the heavy shore-end of the cable was to be landed in an unfrequented bay to avoid being damaged by ships' anchors and it was customary for one or two of the senior engineers to go ashore. Tom got separated from his companion in the bush and was killed by the local natives. A search party after the ship departed found his remains which were taken for burial to Mombasa where I saw the memorial to his memory. I was then told that 19 natives had been hanged for the crime – such was colonial 'justice' in those days.

Arriving in Mombasa on 16th December I was met by Charles Udall, the first Managing Director of EAP&L, with his Chief Engineer, Holmes. They drove me to Nairobi where they had booked a room for me in the New Stanley Hotel, just across the road from their office. I was astonished at the herds of kongoni (hartebeest), wildebeest, gazelles, and zebras which we saw on the way; none of them appearing frightened by our presence. I was shocked when some days later an American couple with a 9 year old child arrived at the hotel after a safari boasting that they had shot, amongst other animals, 9 elephants, the largest having 100 lb tusks.

I spent 44 days in Kenya on inspections, in conferences and talks with EAP&L staff and meetings with settlers and businessmen, copying agreements and collecting as much data as I could on the company. Besides gathering information in Nairobi and Mombasa, Udall drove me in his Hudson Super Six to Ruiru, Thika and Nakuru to inspect the installations there. A dam and a small hydro-electric plant at Ruiru had been built in the early 1900s and was generating 120 kW. In 1909 Udall, having made a survey of the Thika River, had begun construction of a hydro-electric scheme at Ndula with two turbines of 1,000 kW each which were in the process of being commissioned whilst I was there. The Thika scheme was needed to add to the power being generated by the three 120 kW locomobile steam sets at the Parklands station in Nairobi.

Avoiding the Nairobi crowds welcoming the Duke and Duchess of York on their Royal visit, I spent Christmas at Thika, living in a grass-thatched, mud-walled hut built for the engineers on the new project. Rats from the thatch often ran down the walls as we ate our meals.

Christmas Day 1924 at Thika and the Ndula construction camp

From Thika I went towards Fort Hall to look over the Maragua Co.'s plant (85ft head; 310 kVA; 570 volts; 750 rpm single runner turbine) and explored the river for further hydro-power sites before returning to Nairobi to write up my conclusions. Although my report was not going to be complimentary, before leaving I decided to read a carefully prepared draft of my observations and conclusions in front of the Directors of EAP&L. I thought that it would be politic to do so, and it would also ensure that any inaccuracies could be pointed out and corrected. Despite being highly critical of the management and the lack of any sales promotion policy, my observations were received with exceptionally good grace by Charles Udall who was at the time also Mayor of the City of Nairobi.

I left Nairobi by train on 23rd January and stayed at the Manor Hotel in Mombasa whilst waiting for the SS Azay le Rideau to return, 4 days late, from its trip to Madagascar and Mauritius. Udall wrote to me before I left and asked if I would meet and interview an Indian agent there who might act as a 'salesman' for EAP&L's electricity. He had calculated that if London were to send out a man to do the job it could cost £1,000 pa and he would have to sell 200,000 more units at 16 cents in order for the additional profit to just cover the costs.

Five years later, when giving evidence as expert witness to a Tribunal in Nairobi set up by Lord Passfield, the Colonial Secretary, I had to describe Udall's suggestions for another hydro-electric scheme at a site called Grand Falls on the Tana River as utterly impracticable. He was a very generous-minded man and bore me no ill-will and, to everyone's surprise, greeted me as an old friend when we met later in the Nairobi Club.

Incidentally, the Colonial Secretary, Sydney Webb, was an active social reformer, an early member of the Fabian Society and co-founder of the London School of Economics. He had reluctantly accepted a peerage as Lord Passfield.

From the heat of Mombasa the temperature fell as we steamed north to Suez; the men discarded their tropical clothes for tweeds and the ladies put on their fur-trimmed overcoats. During the voyage home, when I was not feeling sea-sick, I had time to assemble my notes and complete my report so that it was ready for the typist when I returned to the office on 18th February. In the evenings after dinner I passed the time reading, writing letters, chatting to other passengers, or playing vingt-et-un.

One of the passengers with whom I had long chats and kept in touch later was Commander William McClure Lunt, a naval officer 5 years older than me and a member of the Sports Club in St James Square. For reading, I was enjoying 'Simon called Peter', the 1921 best seller by Robert Keable, and its sequel 'Recompense'. Going ashore at Djibouti and Suez I met up with the Thomas Cook representatives there who gave me my mail, including letters from home and papers from the office.

Back in England, having completed my first assignment, I had several months of uncertainty as to my future position with the company. My visit had obviously been a success as Udall asked my boss Wm Shearer if I could be appointed as his Chief Engineer, and Major Ward wrote Shearer an appreciative letter saying:

Dear Sir,

'May I be allowed to offer a sincere word of congratulation upon the selection of Colonel Lott for the visit of inspection here.

Briefly, Colonel Lott has gained the respect of every member of the Company with whom he has come in touch, by his technical qualifications, ability, thoroughness, and tact.

I cannot say how thankful I am that I pressed - whether it influenced the Local Board or not I do not know – for a visit of inspection, such as has been made, rather than support the alternative suggestions, such as calling Udall home.'

In another letter from Major Ward to Mr Shearer, he wrote:

' ... Lott has done excellent work and has handled matters perfectly. It is impossible to say more; his services have been very much appreciated. He seems to confirm all that I told you in London and in stronger terms.'

My memories of that first visit to Kenya are vivid:

- There were only dirt roads; the 'murrum' (a clayey laterite) provided a hard surface but without any wearing quality. During most of the year cars raised a cloud of fine dust, even in the streets of Nairobi. To overtake a lorry on a country road meant penetrating a blinding dust-cloud hoping that there was space enough on the road ahead for passing. During the rainy season, the road surface first became slippery and eventually turned into a quagmire requiring chains.

- The lean, wry look of the pioneer with his sunburnt face, neck and knees and hairy forearm protruding from a simple pullover or combined short-sleeved shirt & jacket, belted but with blouse looseness, and his double terai hat.
- The black servants, at first appearing to the visitor as all identical, then gradually revealing vastly different faces, characters & capabilities. All of them, unlike the natives in India, exuded a stuffy odour to which one eventually grew accustomed.
- The sight of a line of natives using pangas to cut the grass on a lawn no bigger than a tennis court outside a Government office in Nairobi.
- The difference in the native garments between town and country dwellers. The latter picturesque in his one garment, a blanket fastened on one shoulder, revealing as he passes, a fine lean figure of which any white man of the same age would be proud.
- The complete lack of beggars, cripples or under-fed natives to be seen, in contrast to India with its fakirs and self-mutilated beggars who swarm the towns and villages.
- The native workmen on construction in the country districts who sometimes worked completely nude, putting on their blanket (looped to one shoulder) when the day's work was done. They seemed much happier than their more sophisticated friends in the towns and certainly had fewer worries than their European employers.

Kikuyus working at Thika on the hydro-electric scheme – 1924

Return to England in 1925

I needed a proper wardrobe for my new life in the City and on my first day back I purchased an overcoat (£9.9.0), shoes (£2.10.0), a hat (£1.7.6) and ordered a new suit.

During those first few months in London I stayed at the Norfolk Hotel, just below the Strand, before taking up residence at the West Side Country Club in Ealing in August. In London I lived well and dined out regularly, the Regent Palace Hotel being one of my favourite venues where I would often stay to read in the lounge after dinner. I was reading another of Keable's books, 'Numerous Treasure', having finished 'T.Tembaron', a sentimental story by Frances Hodgson Burnett. In June, my diary records that 'I did my first crossword puzzle'. Crossword puzzles had appeared for the first time in a British publication in 1922 in Pearson's Magazine.

Weekends at home in East Bergholt

At weekends I invariably escaped to the country, leaving the City after work at midday on Saturday and returning on Sunday evening or Monday morning. I usually went home to my parents at Woodgates and as soon as I arrived on a Saturday afternoon I changed into my country clothes and went for a walk around the farm with Father. The fresh country air was invigorating, and I was able to catch up with the family news and activities on the farm.

My sister Clara, the aunts and other members of the family were frequent visitors, and I joined them in the usual routine of tea, bridge, supper, and mah-jong in the evenings. At Easter I went with Father to East Bergholt church where we heard Steiner's Crucifixion conducted by my cousin Amy Lott, daughter of Stephen Lott of Wenham Grange.

In June I had the first wireless set installed at Woodgates; it was a 4-valve unit for which a wireless pole had to be erected. 'Listening in' became a regular habit for all of us and often replaced bridge or other activities in the evenings and on winter Sunday afternoons. We listened to wireless broadcasts of concerts from the leading orchestras and services from cathedrals and churches all over the country. There were also popular programmes such as Albert Sandler with his Eastbourne Grand Hotel orchestra and personalities such as Sir Harry Lauder singing 'Keep Right on to the End of the Road' and other old favourites. Mother's favourite news reader was Eric Dunston (32) who left to become manager of the Indian Broadcasting Company in 1926; according to the newspapers she was not the only one who had fallen in love with his voice. However, occasionally the wireless 'went dead' for no apparent reason and before it was repaired 'the evenings were very quiet'. I spent one evening 'renewing the wiring of the wireless set' myself.

The harvest began on Bank Holiday Monday 3rd August, and I watched the binder start on cutting the oat field at Woodgates and the beans at the Hill. By 22nd August, all the wheat, beans and oats had been carted on both farms and the fields nicely cleared before the rains; only the barley was left. The harvest at Woodgates was finished by 5th September and a day later at the Hill. After the harvest Parker and Pickus left us but Father retained Sid Madden, the new horseman, and took on Billy Brundel.

My brother Charles and his family had come down for the Bank holiday week from Lincolnshire and he and Jack (17) spent a couple of days with me in London where I entertained them and took them to the zoo, aquarium, museums, and some of the sights.

Father's lease of the Hill House Farm was coming to an end and in June the farm was put up for auction, but no bids were received for it. At the sale of his surplus stock in September he received £175 for the horses, £75 for other stock and £127 for the 'dead stock'; a total of £377. My aunts, Alice and Clara, then moved to Rybersdale (Miss Gissings), a 17th century house with a Georgian facade on Rectory Hill in East Bergholt.

For Christmas, in addition to a parcel of fruit, Christmas confectionary, wine and crackers, I gave Mother a cheque to help out with the family finances. She wrote me a wonderful letter thanking me for my 'great kindness in sending her such a handsome present and most liberal cheque'. I know that it was, as she said, 'a real blessing' as my father was still losing money on the farm and they had no capital to fall back on.

Father was only renting our house and the farm at Woodgates and could not afford to pay the £175 required for an electricity service line to be laid to the isolated property and for the house to be wired, nor would the landlord pay for it. So we continued to use paraffin lamps until we evacuated the house at the start of the war in 1939.

Weekdays in London

On Sunday evenings I generally caught the fast train back to Liverpool Street from Ipswich or Colchester and had dinner on the train before returning to the Norfolk Hotel in the Strand. Having completed my report on my visit to Kenya and made presentations and recommendations to Shearer, Ward, and the EAP&L Board, I was left to kill time in the office, working on the occasional technical report until they decided what to do with me and their new company. It was an unsettling time as I was still only on a monthly contract and needed something more permanent. With little to challenge me in the office, I contacted as many old friends and potential employers as I could and invited them to join me for a lunch or dinner.

Dining out and the London theatre scene

Consequently I was far more often the host than the guest and an evening without company was so much the exception that it was recorded in my diary. Entertaining friends and business colleagues was the rule, most of them I had met during my years overseas.

For lunch I generally booked a table at the Constitutional Club or the Regent Palace Hotel and sometimes had dinner there too.

However, more often in the evenings I would dine at popular restaurants, my favourites being the Trocadero, the Café Royal and the Piccadilly Hotel Grill Room where the well-known violinist, de Groot, directed the Piccadilly Orchestra. For a special evening I entertained my guests at the Savoy Hotel where dinner for three cost £5. On such an occasion we would have a short drink before dinner, a bottle of champagne (25 shillings) at the meal and brandies afterwards. The Savoy table d'hôte menu was priced at 15/6d making a total of £4.9s.6d. for three, plus a tip of 10/6d, bringing it up to £5 (equivalent to £300 today).

Having spent a long time living in mostly remote or unsophisticated surroundings, I made full use of the opportunities which London offered for entertainment in the evenings. Two or three times a week after dinner, either alone or with friends, I would go to the theatre to see the latest plays and musical comedies or the Variety shows at the Alhambra in Leicester Square.

My diary entries for four days at the end of April illustrate the very social lifestyle I was leading at that time:

Monday 27th: Dinner with Painter at Regent Palace – then to Playhouse to see 'White Cargo' for second time - Brian Aherne and Doris Sawyer in the leading roles - sit in front row of Upper Circle.

Tuesday 28th: After office, meet Commander Lunt at the Trocadero where I give him dinner and take him to the Alhambra afterwards - drink at Lyons Oyster Bar - walk back by midnight.

Wednesday 29th: Dinner at Regent Palace Hotel with ex-Governor of Nigeria who lived in East Africa for 25 years.

Thursday 30th: Meet Comdr. Lunt & Miss Skrine at Scott's for lunch – am persuaded to learn dancing. In evening return to hotel to change and then go to Regent Palace Hotel to dine with Mr & Mrs Ferguson (ex-Baghdad) & Peggie.

One evening I entertained my sister May and Charlie Atkins to dinner at the Regent Palace Hotel and then took them to the

Drury Lane Theatre to see the wonderful musical 'Rose Marie' which suited all tastes. I did the same for my other sister Clara and Bob Fitch, and then again for the Aunts. Following the same pattern for other guests too, I saw the show eight times.

Looking back at my diary I must have been to most of the plays which were on in London at the time, including 'Fata Morgana' starring Tom Douglas, 'It Pays to Adventure' at the Aldwych with Ralph Lyons and Tom Wells, 'Beggar on Horseback' at the Queens Theatre, 'Just Married' at the Criterion and 'The Farmer's Wife' at the Royal Court amongst many others. At the Lyceum I saw the Carl Rosa Company perform the operas Cavalleria Rusticana, Pagliacci and Madam Butterfly. I also saw Charlie Chaplin's movie 'Gold Rush' soon after it was released at the Tivoli which had opened as a silent cinema in 1923 on the site of the music-hall of the same name.

The Capitol Cinema Theatre had opened in the Haymarket in February 1925 as the latest of London's new super-cinemas. It was no ordinary cinema and had a super-restaurant, a dance club, and an organ, the first I had seen like the old Imperial in Montreal. I went there to hear Vincent Lopez and his band; it was 'a cacophonous performance which was enthusiastically applauded'. Lopez, a 29 year old pianist and leader of his orchestra, had made his name in New York playing jazz and dance music in hotels. In need of money to finance his extravagant life-style, he had left New York 'pursued by creditors' and accepted an invitation to play at the opening of the Kit-Cat Club in London in May, followed by performances at the Capitol Theatre.

Later that month several of us visited the British Empire Exhibition at Wembley and watched the spectacular air show 'London Defended'. In June we went to see the Royal Tournament at Olympia, and in September we went to the Wembley Torchlight Tattoo on the evening that it was attended by the King (George V), Queen (Mary of Teck), Princess Mary, and the Queen of Norway.

Although my entertaining cost me about £250 per year - a sizeable portion of my salary - it was well worthwhile for I was able to enjoy the company of many friends and relatives who would not have been able to afford a similar return of hospitality. However, one who could and did return my hospitality was Cyril Skinner whom I had tutored for his Cambridge entrance exams and taken around Canada. He drove me in his Sunbeam Super 6 to his home at 100a Knightsbridge where he and Nina gave me an excellent dinner; his mother also invited me to her dinner parties at Bolton Gardens from time to time.

Offer of a job in the Punjab

In my search for permanent employment I exchanged letters with Lt.Col. Basil C. Battye DSO, under whom I had served as a Field Engineer in the 5th Army in France in 1918. Battye was a truly remarkable man of tremendous energy who was a splendid boss, although some of his ideas and gadgets were not only unconventional but to many people they seemed ridiculous. He came from a well-known family who had served India for generations. After the war, in 1922-24, he had undertaken a survey of the hydro-electric potential of the Punjab province and recommended a 48 MW scheme on the Uhl River in the Mandi district.

Lt.Col. Basil Battye DSO

The British Government approved his scheme in May 1925 and Battye was appointed Chief Engineer. He had sent me details of the project which he set about staffing as soon as it had been approved. Thus, on 21st July I received from the Indian High Commissioner in London an offer of an appointment in the Punjab as Superintending Engineer for the Mandi hydro-electric scheme. The offer involved a four-year contract on a salary of Rps.1760 per month, equivalent to £1,575 pa, rising to £1,850 pa, including first class passages to and from India, generous leave terms and a matching Government contribution to the Provident Fund of 1/12th of my salary.

The Start of my 30 Year Career with Balfour Beatty & Co.

The Indian offer brought matters to a head when I discussed it with Shearer, with the result that a few days later I received an offer of a permanent position with Balfour Beatty. Although the initial salary of £800 pa was a drop of £400 on my temporary position with the EAP&L, Shearer promised me a 25% increase to £1,000 pa in January and I decided to accept his offer. Battye cabled saying 'tremendously disappointed, is this irreversible?', but I knew that I could not work happily carrying out some of his designs, even though the salary would be more than twice what I was accepting in London. Also, now in my early 40's, I was enjoying London life and was looking forward to living in England again after nearly twenty years of working overseas. Thus started my 30-year career in a very progressive firm which, although slow to give increases in salary, offered considerable variety in work and location.

The West Side Country Club, Ealing

It was hot in London in June; the temperature reached 87 degrees and I was finding living at the Norfolk Hotel claustrophobic. One evening I went to Buckhurst Hill to look at the Old Roebuck Hotel near Epping Forest as a possible alternative but decided on the West Side Country Club at Eaton Rise in Ealing instead, and took up residence there on 4th August. Although it took me an hour or so to get to the office in the morning, the club had tennis courts and I found the outdoor space a welcome antidote to a day in the office.

When I first arrived at the club my evenings were spent alone, going for walks after dinner, reading and writing letters. However, I soon got to know some of the other inmates and had long chats with them, joining them for bridge after dinner and sometimes not turning in until after midnight. Leslie Harcourt West, Phillip Allard, and a chap we called 'Dam-it-all' became my most regular companions at the Club, but Squires, Miss Crowther and the Misses Thomas often joined us for bridge too; the latter lived nearby and sometimes invited us to bridge at their house. During a chat one evening with Squires about the pros and cons of Empire, he quoted the late Abyssinian Emperor's description of the British occupation saying, 'It comes down on us as lightly as snow but freezes as hard as ice'.

Quite often, when I wanted to relax in a home environment after work, I went to Harrow for an evening with my sister May, Charlie, and Joyce, returning to the Club at Ealing for the night. The Club became particularly busy in early October when, each year, it hosted a Ladies Tennis Tournament.

Speculations on the Stock Market

My total assets in June 1925 were £410 cash in the bank, £4,560 in stocks and shares, plus a loan to my father of £750, to which I added £280 as an estimate of my personal effects making a total of £6,000 (≈ £367,000 today).

The decade that followed the First World War was a time of excess and the rising stock market led to much speculation. Now that I was back in London I began to take an active interest in investing, or more accurately in joining the speculation on the market. Following discussions with Leslie West and others at the Club, I invested about 40% of my portfolio in nine different rubber companies, putting amounts of £50 to £300 (≈ £3,000 to £18,000 today) into shares in each of Luboko, Escots, Toegoesari, Castlefields, Kepong, Dunlop, Patani Para, Dusan Durian, and Roya Muso.

With the increasing demand for rubber for tyres in the fast expanding automobile industry, I thought that the price of rubber would continue to rise and reach a peak in about two years' time. Not only my savings but also a £700 bank overdraft went into these speculations. The spot price of rubber reached 4/10d per lb in 1925 and on 23rd November I recorded 'an exciting day on the Stock Exchange in rubber shares'; the next day I noted 'rubbers are easier - peak of boom apparently passed'. I should have taken the advice of a friend who recommended taking early profits. However, I did not, and I lost money when the price fell to 2/8d in January 1926 and collapsed to 1/7½d in November. West became very depressed with his losses.

My other speculations were mostly in infrastructure companies involved with railways, the oil industry or power generation, such as Leopoldina Terminals (Brazilian railways), Canadian Pacific Railways, International Railways of South America, Callender Cables, APOC and Burmah Corporation. For income I bought 6% Austrian bonds, 7½ % Hungarian bonds and Tanganyika Concessions 10% Preference shares. Fortunately, several of these 'punts' paid off handsomely; I doubled my investment of £450 in Manila Electricity, sold most of my Consolidated Mining & Smelting shares at their peak of $247 having bought them for $40, and also made a profit of 20% when I sold my 6% Austrian Government bonds for £300.

The experience, sometimes dearly bought, kept me in touch with the markets and enabled me the better to report on financial propositions put up to my firm and on which I had to write memoranda for the directors after a careful study of the projects we were offered.

Weekend excursions out of London with Capt. Inglis

AC 12 hp 'Royal' car – 1925

Capt. F.C. Inglis, a colleague from Basra, contacted me when he arrived in London on leave in June and I entertained him to several dinners and evenings at the theatre. One weekend he drove me home to Woodgates in his AC 12 hp 'Royal' car and took my parents on drives to Felixstowe and Harwich. Later, the two of us had a couple of weekend outings to the coast. In July we drove 85 miles to Canterbury and Margate, putting up at the St George's Hotel, Cliftonville, where we dined and watched the dancing - the Charleston had just become the new dance craze and the floor was packed with Charlestoners.

On another fine, hot weekend in August we drove to Rye and Pevensey, then through Hastings and Bexhill, finishing up at Eastbourne at the Queens Hotel for Saturday night where, again, we watched the dancing after dinner and went for a walk on Beachy Head. We drove back through Tunbridge Wells, staying Sunday night at the Spa Hotel. On Monday 'after sampling the chalybeate waters in the Pump Room we motor to London. Car running badly on BP - at Reigate we take on Shell - fast run on Great West Road near Ealing. Lunch near Ewell and go through Richmond Park, cross the river at Kew and motor to the Engineers Club in Piccadilly.' That afternoon we went on to the British Empire Exhibition at Wembley and visited the Malaya, Australian and New Zealand exhibits, the Amusement Park, and a Palmist.

It was at the Engineers Club later in the year that I heard an 'optimistic speech by Winston Churchill', the Chancellor of the Exchequer, who had decided in his April budget to return the pound to its pre-War value against gold, a disastrous decision which led to the subsequent financial crisis and the General Strike in 1926.

The week before Inglis left London to return to Baghdad there were reports of an attack on the Nairn Transport Company in Damascus. In 1923 the company had pioneered the trans-desert route from Beirut, Haifa and Damascus to Baghdad which became known as 'The Nairn Way'. I gave Inglis dinner at the Troc Grill Room, and we went on to the Palace Theatre where I had booked box seats to see 'No, No, Nanette'; the show had been packed out for months. The next day we went to Maidenhead for lunch at Skindles (5/-), renowned for its celebrity guests and its reputation as a place for adulterous relationships; we spent the afternoon there in a punt on the river (10/-). I did not see Inglis again after that visit; he was killed in an air crash in Iraq in 1927.

Membership of the Royal Geographical Society and the Kosmos Club

In November I was elected a Fellow of the Royal Geographical Society (RGS) upon the recommendation of two old Iraqi friends, Maj. Gen. Sir Percy Cox, and Capt. R.E. Cheesman, both famous names in the Arab world. Robert Cheesman had been Private Secretary to Sir Percy Cox when he was High Commissioner in Iraq and was an explorer and ornithologist as well as a military officer. He was credited with being the first to map the Arabian coast from the Gulf of Salwah to Uqair and with discovering Cheesman's gerbil.

By attending the Monday evening lectures and becoming a member of the Kosmos Club, the dining club of the RGS which was limited to the most travelled Fellows of the Society, I met many other interesting people. After listening to a lecture on the glaciers of Karakorum (Mongolia) one evening, I met Noel Odell again not long after his return from the tragic Mt Everest expedition and we had lunch together at Simpsons.

Amongst the others I met there was Mr Ronald Giblin, a retired Surveyor-General of Siam, who was working on a History of Tasmania, to which country an ancestor of his had emigrated in the 1830's. His subsequent book on the Giblin family contained a photograph of his father which exactly resembled a photograph, taken about the same year (1878), of my grandfather Charles Giblin of Ridgewell Hall, Essex. When Lloyd Giblin, a relative of Ronald, came with his wife to visit us in Wivenhoe in 1971, on first seeing me she exclaimed, 'Look Lloyd, there is your father!' There is no doubt whatsoever that his family and our line of Giblins had a common ancestor; their similar facial characteristics and those of the previous generations clearly show the mark of heredity, even though there had been no blood connection between the families for over 150 years.

I also had a chance to talk to Leonard Woolley at the RGS when he gave a lecture on 'Ur of the Chaldees'. During his excavations there in 1923 he had shown a group of us over the site from which my collection of Babylonian tablets had originated.

Christmas 1925 in Paris

On Thursday 24th December both Leslie West and I left the Club for our Christmas holidays, he to Madeira and I to 'Gay Paris' (gay having its original meaning then) for the long weekend. I took the Pullman boat train from Victoria at 10.45 am and arrived at the Hotel du Louvre in Paris at 6.45 pm, the first class return ticket costing me £5.16s.2d. I spent the evening with my old friend Simone Gueschwind and visited her family at 117 Boulevard Haussmann on the Tuesday before I left for the boat train home. During that weekend I walked miles, visiting all the major sights, attending a Christmas High Mass at La Madeleine, and going to L'Anglers on the Champs Elysées for 'thé dansant'.

For entertainment in the evenings I went to the famous shows at the Moulin Rouge and the Folies Bergère which were much more fun and risqué than anything in London. On Sunday I met up with a cousin, Miss Lucy Howard, and dined with her the next day at the Café de Paris, after which we went to the Casino de Paris to see a spectacular show starring the Dolly Sisters, the Tiller Girls and Maurice Chevalier. My diary notes that good champagne cost 9/- (shillings) a bottle and a good Chablis only 9d (pence) a half bottle. The Channel was windy and rough on Tuesday and I was terribly ill on the ferry back to Folkestone, getting soaked with spray as I stood on deck for the fresh air.

Life in London in 1926

The Constitutional Club

In January I was elected a member of the Constitutional Club in Northumberland Avenue and remained a member for almost 30 years until I retired from Balfour Beatty in 1955. The Club had been founded for Conservatives and I had chosen to join it, rather than any of the other West End clubs, because of its easy accessibility to the Embankment Underground station from which I could take the Tube to Cannon Street, a short walk from my office at 66 Queen Street. Initially I used it just for entertaining guests at lunch and sometimes in the evenings too. However, it was so convenient that I eventually took a room there and used it as my residence during the week instead of the West Side Country Club.

The Constitutional Club in Northumberland Avenue

On the first occasion of dining there I met Mr E.R. Wood of East Bergholt, one of the original founder members in 1883. The Club was known for its large cellars which extended under the pavements of Northumberland Avenue; its charges for wines at the meals were extremely reasonable. The selection ranged from the cheapest South African Hock costing only 2/6d a bottle to the finest vintage port or old brandy. When port ceased to be in general demand after dinner the Club began to sell to its members some of the 30,000 bottles in its cellar and I bought a couple of dozen bottles to take home.

The Club was not normally very busy but when I took Malcolm Gunn there in December I noted that it was 'inconveniently crowded' as it was 'Baron of Beef' day. Each year just before Christmas the Constitutional Club held its Baron of Beef day; one of the annual celebrations of Clubland. The 'baron' this year weighed 398 lbs. They put it on the 'jack' at 9 am on Saturday morning and kept it turning until 6 pm. A ton and a half of coal was used keeping the fire going. The Mansion House also had a jack, but the Lord Mayor had to have his baron cut in two; only in the kitchen of the Constitutional Club was there a jack big enough for roasting a baron whole. The basting, which was most important, was done in relays by men wielding giant ladles.

The Club hit the headlines in February 1932 by breaking with tradition and opening a real cocktail bar; an innovation which caused shock amongst many of the older members. In comparison to other rendezvous in the Club, the cocktail bar was almost cheeky. It was bright and modern and decorated in a charming fashion, as if it belonged to a new hotel rather than a gentlemen's club.

I also joined the Royal Automobile Club in Pall Mall in order to use its lovely Roman-style swimming pool and because of its spacious dining room where one could entertain lady guests. It was years before the Constitutional Club arranged accommodation in the basement where members could entertain lady friends to lunch or dinner.

London Clubs provided me with a life of extreme comfort and even luxury. Not only the members but also the many stewards (waiters) who provided a most efficient service were all men, including of course the Hall Porter and the valet who looked after my clothes, brought me early morning tea, and got my bath ready. However the exclusiveness of these clubs where no one of colour was admitted, even as a guest at a meal, was the cause of much criticism, embarrassment, and bitter feeling. In those days even a Maharajah of immense wealth could not be a guest of a Britisher whom he had just entertained most royally at his palace.

I had been a guest at several such clubs during my travels, including the Bombay Yacht Club, the Madras, Adyar and Ooty Clubs in Southern India, two clubs in Shanghai and two in Nairobi; one of them, the Muthaiga Country Club, being probably the most famous and snobbish in Africa, but none of them would have been so unwelcoming to a foreign prince or dignitary.

Dancing lessons

In March 1926 I started taking lessons in ballroom dancing from Miss 'Gee' Skrine and paid her £3.17.6 for a series of 10 lessons. I had been introduced to her by Commander Lunt whom I had met on board ship returning from Mombasa. The three of us were dining at Scott's one evening when they persuaded me that I should learn to dance. However, I was a slow learner and signed up for a second series of 10 lessons before making my debut in public at a dinner dance at the Savoy Hotel where we danced several foxtrots and a waltz. Later that evening some young debutantes arrived in the Savoy restaurant in their feathered head-dresses, having come straight from being presented at Court in Buckingham Palace. On another occasion there, we were on the floor with the Duke of Gloucester who was entertaining and dancing with a very pretty, fair-haired girl. Towards the end of the year I had a third series of lessons with Miss Skrine; I enjoyed her company and was still not very proficient on the dance floor.

My Work in the London office for Balfour Beatty

The 1920s were a time of post-war expansion when British engineering companies like Balfour Beatty were world leaders in the financing, design, and construction of industrial and infrastructure projects such as the new transportation and electricity generation and distribution schemes being built around the world. Amongst the many and varied schemes seeking capital for development which I had to analyse and on which I prepared reports and recommendations for my 'big boss' Wm Shearer in 1925/26 were the following:

- ***Mondego coal mines, lime kiln and cement plant near Figueira da Fez in Portugal:*** The shareholders had lost most of their investment and were looking for a purchaser to buy them out and finance an expansion of the coal mines and cement plant.

- ***Taranto Tramways and Electricity Supply Co, Italy***: The company had been floated in 1919 with a capital of £250,000 to build and operate a power plant and a tramway between the old and new towns of Taranto. The power plant had not been built and the tramway was losing money. For a payment of £20k for the shares, £10k for debt repayment and expenditure of £50k to build the power plant, the purchaser would receive a 55 year concession for the electricity supply and a monopoly of public transport in Taranto.

- ***Lacroze Underground Tram subway in Buenos Aires, Argentina:*** In a brief report based on the very limited information provided I identified several flaws in the proposal and recommended against pursuing it further.

- ***Pulp & Paper Project at Lake St John in Quebec, Canada:*** My Canadian experience enabled me to produce a detailed 12 page report on this C$10 million scheme which included the acquisition of 1,500 sq. miles of virgin forest, construction of a 20,000 hp hydro-electric plant, a 60,000 tpa newsprint mill, river improvements and a town site development. I estimated a return on capital of 4.3% and pointed out that the pulp and paper industry in Canada was expanding fast, competition would be intense, and the price of paper may continue to fall, despite the rapidly growing demand for newsprint in the USA.

- *Steirische Hydro & Electricity Co Ltd, Graz, Austria:* This Styrian company was offering new shares to pay for the completion of the Teigitsche Power Station, a long distance transmission line to Ternitz, an auxiliary power station at Armstein and a hydro-electric development on the Mur south of Bruck to supply the whole of Styria. Austria was embarking on a policy of water power development and electrification of the railways and had passed legislation to make investment in these schemes attractive and reduce imports of inferior quality coal. The political and industrial environment was stable, and I concluded that the project had favourable prospects.

- *Hydro-electric projects and Transmission Lines for Compania Hydro-Electric Mexicana SA:* David Shepherd, a cousin of Shearer who was working for a Canadian firm, was proposing hydro-projects on two rivers in NE Mexico, the Rio Blanco (22,500 hp) and the Rio Naranjos (26,000 hp), with a total of 653 miles of transmission lines, giving a yield of 11% on the estimated cost of £3.5 million. After researching rainfall and run-off data in papers of the American Society of Civil Engineers, I wrote to David explaining that we could not support the schemes as we believed he had over-estimated the run-off percentage of rainfall and the value of pondage in the Rio Blanco scheme.

- *The Electrification of the Grand Duchy of Luxembourg:* The preferred bidder for the Concession to supply the

Duchy with electricity was a Mr Legrand, who was seeking finance for his technically elegant scheme involving a battery of coke ovens to produce 290,000 tpa coke to be sold to the iron and steel industry, a 15kW power station using the gases from the coke ovens, 750 miles of electric transmission lines and 12.5 miles of gas supply mains. The project was to be financed by £1.5 million of bonds guaranteed by the British Government to cover the supply of British equipment, plus £800k of Preference shares for the balance of the funding. After a meeting with the financier Edward de Stein in Pinner's Hall, Austin Friars, I concluded that the estimates were too optimistic and were vulnerable to a fall in the value of the Belgian franc and so recommended against Balfour Beatty involvement.

Other financial propositions which I studied and reported on to Shearer included:

- Electric power supply in Romania;
- Irrigation and hydro-electric projects on the east coast of Spain; and
- Cuba Railway proposition requiring finance for 243 miles of main-line railway estimated to cost £3,300 per mile.

In assessing these schemes I had to produce estimates and investigate the legal, technical, and financial aspects of the projects for which my experience of schemes in Canada and Mesopotamia was invaluable. I prided myself on my reports which were thorough and summarised the issues clearly and concisely for Shearer and his fellow directors before they made an offer or investment decision.

The Perak River Hydro-Electric Scheme

In June Shearer gave me just one weekend in which to make a quick, intensive study of the Perak River Hydro-electric Scheme. The considerable file of papers he gave me to review contained reports with conflicting estimates of the capital cost and the expected revenue from the scheme. My memorandum resulted in his decision not to participate unless Balfour Beatty carried out an independent survey.

The scheme had been the brain-child of Frederick Bolton, a hydro-electric engineer who had been hired by the Federated Malay States (FMS) Government to improve the power supply to Kuala Lumpur and the tin mines in the Kinta Valley. After much negotiation between the High Commissioner of British Malaya (Sir Laurence Guillemard), the Chief Secretary of the FMS (Sir George Maxwell) and Sultan Iskander of Perak, an agreement was reached on the structure of a company and they were trying to raise finance for the scheme in London. When Shearer declined involvement on my recommendation, Sir Montagu Barlow of Armstrong-Whitworth agreed to participate, and the company was floated on the London Exchange in July 1926.

The scheme's Chenderoh dam was built on schedule in 1927-1930 but the company ran into financial difficulties with the onset of the Great Depression. In 1932 Armstrong-Whitworth bowed out and were replaced by their arch rivals, the Balfour Beatty group. The principal holders of the debentures and preference shares, the British and Malayan Governments respectively, had begged our chairman, George Balfour MP, to become Chairman of a new Board of Directors to take over and manage the scheme. Unfortunately, it was my rival in the company, Eric Bergstrom, whose baby it became and who had developed it into a thriving £5.5 million concern by 1961.

City Livery Dinners

In April I had my first of many experiences of dining as a guest of a City Livery Company. My host who entertained me at Mercers' Hall was Lt. Colonel W.B. Lane, another old friend from Baghdad. He had been a member of our GHQ mess which we called 'The Work House', for we said that those of us who lived there did all the work. He became Master of the Mercers' Company following a long family tradition and I was fortunate in being one of his regular guests.

City dinners in those days had up to 9 courses and were served with a gamut of wines. The menu that evening consisted of plover's eggs (sherry), turtle soup, salmon (hock), devilled whitebait, saddle of mutton, asparagus (champagne), roast duckling & peas, Westmorland ham & salad (burgundy), iced orange soufflé (brandy), maids of honour, strawberries & cream, and coffee (port). The dinner menu and guest list were included in a booklet which outlined the history of the Mercers' Company and its role in the development of Northern Ireland which was not generally known.

Queen Elizabeth I, as part of a plan to settle ongoing disputes between the O'Neills and O'Dohertys, had invited the City of London to finance the establishment of a plantation or colony in Ulster and people it with English and Scottish settlers. After she died in 1603, her successor James I established the Honourable Irish Society and persuaded each of the twelve principal Livery Companies to contribute £8,333 for which they were given a twelfth part of that portion of the County of Londonderry which he had vested in the Irish Society. The names such as Londonderry and Draperstown derive from those days.

My first Motor Car

I had been contemplating buying my first car for a few months and had discussed the merits of various models with Cyril Skinner and my friends at the Club. I decided on a 13 hp Clyno tourer for which I paid

The Clyno Tourer

Rootes £260 and took delivery of it in April 1926. The Clyno company had been formed in 1909 to manufacture motorcycles; it flourished during the First World War producing motorcycles with machine gun attachments. Soon after the war the company went into liquidation but was re-formed and produced its first car in 1922, becoming the third largest British car manufacturer after Austin and Morris. The 13 hp model had been released in October 1925 and proved very popular. In 1926 Clyno slashed prices and increased sales by 260%; they were producing 350 cars per week, working night and day. However, the company got into financial trouble again, losing out to Morris in the price war, and eventually went into liquidation in the depression of 1929.

Together with my taxi-driver friend, Charles H. Painter, who as Private Painter No.10 (MT.RASC) had driven me in my 5th Army HQ Sunbeam car in France in 1918, we drove the new car home from London to East Bergholt, Painter taking the wheel through the towns. He came with me on the Sunday for a 75 mile practice drive in the new car to Clacton and Colchester where my diary notes that we had 'two minor incidents'.

At first I kept the car at the Rootes garage in the West End where it was given a free inspection service every month for the first 3 months. At the second inspection on 1st June, after I had had the car for just over 7 weeks, I noted that I had done 1,341 miles. Painter gave me two or three driving lessons, meeting me at the garage and taking me around the West End and out to Harrow and Ealing. Occasionally West came out with me for a drive and took over on the way back. By June I felt confident enough to drive home to East Bergholt at weekends; the 76 mile journey took just over 3 hours and meant that on Monday mornings I had to leave Woodgates between 4 and 5 am in order to be back in my Ealing Club in time to change, have breakfast and catch a train to the City, 18 stopping stations away.

During those first few months of driving I experienced a few teething troubles. On one trip home 'I went via Cambridge Road and Chipping Ongar – a bad route – reached home after 4¼ hrs and vicissitudes – rain and a broken windscreen spindle'. On another occasion, after I had dropped Painter off at Chelmsford, I ran out of petrol near Colchester. And in August I had my first puncture after the car had done 2,336 miles.

Entertaining Friends in Town

Now that I was established in London my friends from around the world always got in touch when they were in town. I generally entertained them to lunch or dinner and sometimes to a show in the evenings. Many of them were colleagues from the War or from my time in Mesopotamia, including Brig.Gen. Glasgow, Col. Symonds, Col. Carey, Col. Bridcut, Col. Mousley DSO, Maj. Galloway, Maj. Wilson, Capt. Inglis and, of course, C.H. Painter, my driver. After taking Mousley to dinner at the Club and then to see 'The Student Prince' at His Majesty's one evening, I wrote rather uncharitably in my diary 'a virtuous but inexpressibly dull man; saving against a rainy day which, in his case, will never come'. He was engaged to Dorothy Pease, the daughter of the baronet Sir Arthur Pease, and married her in 1927.

From Canada there was A.L. Cavanagh (Winnipeg) and W.H. Lowe (Montreal), and in November Mrs Coombes and Marjorie (now Mrs Torrance) arrived from Winnipeg. After dining with them at Queen Anne's Mansions I took them to see 'Rookery Nook', a farce by Ben Travers which had recently opened at the Aldwych.

I also attended Old Centralians' dinners which were held at the Colony Club. The Centralians were the former students from the Central Technical College, and I met several whom I had not seen for 20 years.

During that autumn I was elected a vice-president of the Old Grammarians Club, the Dorchester Grammar School old boys' association, together with Vice-Admiral Sir Michael Hodges and Mr Thomas Hardy OM. I had met Hardy when we lived in

Dorchester. He and his wife attended the church we used to go to, and I once knocked him down on the ice as we were both learning to skate; I was then a teenager and he was pushing a chair.

Weekends with the Family in East Bergholt

My weekends at home in Suffolk were relaxing and much the same as ever, with walks around the farm, visits to the aunts, my sister Clara and her family in Mistley and to various cousins and family friends. In January I went skating at Flatford where the local farmer had flooded 13 acres of meadow and about 100 people had come to have fun on the ice that weekend. I sometimes went with Father to East Bergholt church on Sundays and very occasionally Mother came too. I enjoyed playing the organ and stood in for the organist, Mrs Storrs, at the morning and evening services on some Sundays in the summer when she was nursing her son.

On the farm in March, Father's 99 ewes produced 166 lambs which he sold in July for 'only 39 shillings each, £1 less than last year'. In June I helped 'pulling docks in the wheat crop which was showing luxuriant growth and the 'singling' of the sugar beet was practically complete'. Father had started to grow sugar beet and had sold the 40 tons from last year's crop for £115.

On August Bank holiday weekend I drove Mother and Father to Newmarket and to Carlton Grange to spend the day with 88 year old Aunt Jessie and Walter Boggis. They had married in 1890 when Walter was the 26 year old 'farm pupil' at Ridgewell Hall and Jessie was 52. After 36 years they still got on well although she was now an invalid and he had had a number of affairs. Walter was the Agent and manager of the Six Mile Bottom Estate and had been employed by Sir Ernest Cassel, a financier and friend of King George V. On several occasions Sir Ernest had invited the King and the Royal princes, together with other members of the aristocracy, to shooting parties on the estate which Walter managed and Jessie provided lunch for them at Carlton Grange. Walter was also a respected breeder and judge of sheep and livestock and had been commissioned in 1919 by the Government's Committee for Agricultural Relief of the Allies to purchase livestock to be sent to France and Belgium for re-stocking their farms after the War. We got back to Woodgates at 8.15 pm that evening; the 102 mile round-trip had been the longest car journey Mother had made.

A week or so before Christmas I took my parents to Ridgewell Hall to see Uncle Joe Boldero, Mother's brother-in-law, who was 78 years old and very frail; I thought he looked ten years older than Father who was a similar age. He produced a decanter of port and some mince pies, no doubt made by Miss Maud Manfield who also joined us; she had been employed by him for 23 years since her sister Claire Manfield had left to get married.

On New Year's Eve I went with my sister Clara and Bob Fitch to a dance at Brantham given by her friends Mrs Burrows and Mrs Foster Sproxton, whose husband was a director and chief chemist at the British Xylonite Company works at Brantham.

Bridge, Tennis and Friends at the West Side Country Club

If I arrived back at the Club in time after work, I would often join Leslie West and others to play a couple of rubbers of bridge in the evening. The others included Dutfield, D'Avigdor, Pizarro, Foster, Mr and Mrs Waley, Mrs Grant, the Misses Crowther, Miss Ida Williams, and Miss Gertie Thomson. Occasionally we were invited to the Waleys' or Mrs Grant's for a bridge party at their homes instead.

In the spring I started playing tennis at the Club with Carlos Brandes, a new member who had recently arrived from Brazil. We used to play at 7 am for half an hour before breakfast; he usually beat me, but we became good friends and went to the Continent together later in the year.

However, Leslie West was my most regular companion; he also worked in the City and we used to lunch together at Falstaff's in Eastcheap; it was on the site of Falstaff's Boar's Head Inn mentioned in Shakespeare's play Henry IV. After work he and I often had dinner at the Constitutional Club or one of our other favourite restaurants and would then go on to a show before returning to Ealing. We saw 'The Unfair Sex' at the Coliseum, the 'Blue Kitten' at the Gaiety, Leslie Henson in 'Kid Boots' at the Winter Garden Theatre and listened to a good band play the 1812 Overture at the Plaza cinema soon after it opened.

In May I entertained West to a special dinner with Bollinger 1917 (21/-) at my Club before we went on to the Comedy Theatre to see 'The Rescue Party' by Arthur Rattigan starring Aubrey Mather as the clergyman. He reciprocated by entertaining me to dinner at Café Monico after which we went to see Marie Tempest in Noel Coward's 'Hay Fever' at the Criterion. Occasionally he would come with me to one of the lectures I liked to attend at the RGS, the Institution of Civil Engineers or Central Hall Westminster.

Some weekends I stayed in town instead of going home to Woodgates. After dinner one Saturday in February, West and I went to Park Mansions in Knightsbridge to join Gordon and Vera Grindley for the evening, and we ended up playing vingt-et-un until 2.30 am. The next day we drove in Gordon's Peugeot to Little Gaddesden to visit Ashridge Park and Castle and have lunch and tea at the Bridgewater Arms. We dressed up for these outings and I changed into plus fours when West took us for a run to Bagshot and Virginia Water, 'damaging the car a little en route' I noted afterwards.

West was friendly with 'the Guinness crowd' and used to go to dances with them at the Rembrandt Rooms. That Easter he and I went for a grand tour of the south coast in his Vinot car. We picked up Judy Guinness from Queens Gate and drove to Bournemouth, had lunch at Romsey on the way and dropped Judy off at her destination. We stayed the night at the Highcliffe Hotel and on the Saturday had cocktails at the Royal Bath Hotel in Bournemouth, lunch at the Grand Hotel in Lyndhurst, tea in Chichester and finished up at the Royal Hotel in Bognor Regis where we went to the theatre and a dance and stayed the night. On Easter Sunday we had cocktails at the Metropole Hotel in Brighton and lunch at the Old Ship Inn before going on to Seaford to stay with Mr and Mrs W.M. Lovell. We spent Monday with the Lovells in Eastbourne, listened to the band on the promenade and had cocktails, lunch and tea at the Grand Hotel where the orchestra was playing, before returning to their house for dinner and bridge in the evening. Leaving Seaford before 7.00 am on Tuesday, we stopped for breakfast in East Grinstead and arrived at the Cannon Street Hotel in time for lunch. I went into the office for an hour or two before having a driving lesson near Marble Arch and returning to the Club for a good night's sleep.

We drove down to Seaford again to stay with the Lovells one August weekend, driving through 'the lovely Ashdown Forest' on the way. We played bowls after tea and bridge after dinner and, on Sunday morning, we took the Lovells to Eastbourne for cocktails at the Grand Hotel before returning for lunch and tennis in the afternoon. It was Lovell who had warned me in July that 'now is the time to sell rubber shares, not buy them', despite Kepong having just announced a 20% interim dividend. I was still a bull of the shares, but Lovell tried to change my mind, and in November he was proved right.

Membership of Engineering Institutions

I was keen to enhance my engineering credentials and keep up to date with the latest technical developments and had been an Associate Member of the Institution of Civil Engineers since 1909, giving me the right under its Royal Charter to be called Chartered Civil Engineer. I had also become an Associate Member of the Engineering Institute of Canada in 1913 and a full Member of the American Society of Civil Engineers in 1920.

In June I was elected a full Member of the American Institute of Electrical Engineers of which I had been an Associate since 1911. Chace, my former employer in Canada, who had endorsed my application, wrote to say that on my recommendation Battye had offered him the post in India which I had turned down. After World War II, when dollars for the annual subscriptions became much more expensive, I resigned from the Canadian and American societies as they were no longer important for my work.

The evening lectures at the Institution of Civil Engineers were interesting and one of the formal occasions I attended was the Annual Dinner at which HRH The Prince of Wales was the principal guest along with Sir Joseph Thomson FRS (1856-1940). J.J. Thomson was the eminent Cambridge physicist who had discovered the electron, the first sub-atomic particle, in 1897 for which he was awarded the Nobel Prize for Physics in 1906. He gave a tediously long speech in contrast to the excellent 15 minute speech which the Prince delivered in great style. Academic brilliance does not necessarily produce a good after-dinner speaker.

The Political Scene and the 1926 General Strike

The 1920s were turbulent years in Europe which was still adjusting to the aftermath of the First World War. In 1926 Benito Mussolini dissolved the Italian parliament, disbanded the Italian socialist parties, and declared himself dictator. Leon Trotsky resigned as Chairman of the Russian Revolutionary Military Council as he and Joseph Stalin battled for power in Russia following the death of Lenin. Stalin eventually took over control in Russia in 1927, and in Germany Adolf Hitler published 'Mein Kampf', resurrecting the NSDAP party in Munich. There were also uprisings and changes of Government in Greece, Spain, and Austria.

In March, the Electricity (Supply) Bill was debated in Parliament and George Balfour took part, warning of the serious implication it would have for the electricity supply companies. However, despite Conservative opposition to what was seen as nationalisation, the bill was eventually passed, and the Central Electricity Board was established to manage the supply and distribution of electricity across the country and resolve some of the problems which had disrupted supplies during the previous ten years.

The unions were increasingly talking of striking and we watched an Anti-Strike procession of 20,000 women pass through central London on 17th April; the only bad impression to the working class crowds being created by the society ladies on horse-back. However, the opposition of working class women did not prevent the General Strike from starting at midnight on Monday 3rd May when all the unions went on strike in sympathy with the Miners who would not agree to a reduction in pay and longer hours. The Strike lasted 8 days during which there were clashes between the police and strikers in cities across the country.

The next morning it took 2½ hrs for West and me to drive from Ealing to the City as the streets were packed with motor and other vehicles. We decided not to go home in rush hour; instead, we went to see 'Mercenary Mary' at the Hippodrome and then had dinner at the Troc Grill Room where we had a 'jolly evening watching a cabaret' before driving back to Ealing 'at top speed at 1.30 am after an Oxo at a coffee stall'. By Wednesday 'the traffic was a little easier on roads to the City and there was no molestation in the West End area'.

On Saturday 8th May I went with West and Brandes to the Underground Electric Railways Company of London (UERL) where they both volunteered as 'motor-men', but with no luck. So we went on to Chiswick where I left them getting jobs as a bus-driver and conductor for the London General Omnibus Company (LGOC) whilst I walked back to the Club. I had dinner with West on Monday and 'he was full of his bus driving experience' telling me how he and Brandes had spent the day keeping a bus route going for the LGOC. I had been to the office as usual, travelling to and from the City on the Central London Railway which was also run by volunteers. On Tuesday 11th May I noted that 'transport services were improving everywhere and there were 700 LGOC buses on the streets.'

The Strike was called off by the TUC at 1.00 pm on 12th May to the surprise of many of their members, leaving the miners to fight their own battle with the mine owners. The miners held out until November when they gave up their struggle and accepted the pay cut of 13% and an extension to the length of shifts from seven to eight hours imposed by the mine owners.

Visits to the Continent and the World Power Conference in Basle

During the summer of 1926 I spent several 'bachelor weekends' on the Continent. In June, having bought £3 worth of French francs @165 francs/£1 for the weekend, I went with Leslie West to Ostend. We stayed at the Osborne Hotel, listened to a splendid concert at the Kursaal, and went on to the Casino where we won £4.4.0 and celebrated with Leroy champagne and cognac. Back in Folkestone on Sunday evening we spent a night at the Burlington Hotel before driving to the office early on Monday morning.

In July, on my 43rd birthday, West and I went to Folkestone again and bought a weekend return ticket to Boulogne for £1.0.6. There we took a taxi to Le Touquet and Paris-Plage, checked in to the Hotel des Anglais and spent the evening in the Casino, attending the theatre, gambling, dancing, and drinking until 3.00 am, apparently 'all in strict moderation' according to my diary. On the Sunday we took a fiacre (18 francs/hr) for a drive round Le Touquet before going to the Casino for the afternoon where we 'had tea and a few minutes in the 'Bonk' room' before leaving by taxi to catch the 7.10 pm ferry back to Folkestone.

In September I accompanied Peter Low to Paris, en route to Basle where we attended the 1926 World Power Conference. In Paris we stayed at the Hotel Moderne (60 francs/night), went to the Casino de Paris, saw some of the sights, went to Le Laurent in the

Champs-Elysées for the thé dansant, and then dined at the Café de Paris followed by 'an excellent show' at the Folies Bergère. After attending part of High Mass at Notre Dame on Sunday I met up with Simone Gueschwind and her family again before Low and I went to dinner in Montmartre and a show at the Moulin Rouge.

The train from Paris arrived in Basle at 5.50 pm on the Monday and after a quick passage through customs we checked into the Metropole Hotel. The next morning we attended the opening meeting of the World Power Conference and toured the Exhibition Hall before changing into white tie and tails for the Official Banquet in the evening at which there was entertainment and dancing. During the next few days we took part in discussions on the latest developments in power generation and railroad electrification and visited the low-head hydro-electric plant at Augst, the Gosgen power plant and the Brown Boveri works at Baden.

In Zurich we visited the Escher Wyss works and were shown their 15,000 kW steam turbines and some extra high pressure turbines, before going by charabanc to Waggital to see the two power houses and 109 metre high dam, completed in 1924, which had created the Wägitalersee as a reservoir for pumped-storage hydroelectricity.

Having been well entertained during the week by several Swiss cities and cantons with receptions and banquets, we left Basle by train for Mainz on Friday; the French army were still in occupation there and army guards and personnel were much in evidence on the streets. The Holland Hotel provided an excellent dinner with which we enjoyed a 1921 Laubenheimer Reisling (5/6d a bottle) and the next day took the river steamer down the Rhine to Cologne to stay at the Dom Hotel for a few days. During our time there we attended a service in Cologne Cathedral, saw performances of Der Rosenkavalier and Cavalleria Rusticana at the Opera House, and visited the 100,000 kW Fortuna II power station, designed to burn lignite (brown coal). Then, after a day in Dusseldorf at the Exhibition, we continued our journey downstream to Rotterdam and took the ferry home to Harwich from the Hook of Holland.

Autumn 1926

I had cancelled my room at the West Side Country Club in Ealing when I left for the World Power Conference and on my return I stayed at the Constitutional Club for a week before joining West at the Norman Hotel in Putney where I took a room for £3.5.0. per week. It was not far from Putney Bridge Station, so relatively convenient for the City, and I stayed there until early November when I moved back to Ealing.

West and I repaid the hospitality of Mr and Mrs Lovell by entertaining them to dinner at the Savoy and taking them to 'Rose Marie' at Drury Lane, ending up back at the Savoy for sandwiches and a round of drinks. Lovell continued to try to convince me not buy any more rubber shares – I already had £2,100 invested in rubber companies and had recently bought shares in Biting Rubber and Yam Seng Rubber as I thought the price of rubber would soon recover from its low of 1/7 per lb.

At the Institution of Civil Engineers in October I saw Sir Charles Parsons presented with the Kelvin Medal and heard Senator Marconi deliver the James Forest Lecture on 'Radio Communications'. The Post Office had just inaugurated a new wireless service to Canada using the Marconi beam system with a 26m wave-length from a 20kW station at Bodmin and were charging 2/6d for 20 words (1½ d per word).

Letter writing

During my travels and years overseas I had always kept in touch with friends and family by writing letters, sometimes writing as many as five or six in an evening. As an example, one evening I wrote to Miss Skrine (London), Allard (Egypt), McLure Lunt (Kenya), Chace (Canada), Inglis (Mespot) and the Honolulu Volcano Research Association (Hawaii). I continued this in London and during my weekends at home with the old folk at Woodgates.

About this time I also developed the habit of writing (or rather typing) letters to newspapers and to those in authority on subjects about which I felt strongly, getting grievances or criticisms off my chest. I wrote one of the first of such letters to the Very Reverend Dean Inge at St Paul's Cathedral and also one to his counterpart at Westminster Abbey in similar terms. In each case before writing, I checked my facts and asked policemen on their beats close to the Cathedral and the Abbey how long the 'derelict' scaffolding with torn and flapping tarpaulins had been in position and each had said 'for years'.

Dear Sir

May I as an Englishman who returns to this country at intervals, express my personal sadness at the extraordinary lack of interest being taken in the care of the exterior of your great cathedral, which for dirt and general untidiness rivals many temples in Ceylon, Java, and the Far East where worship is still being carried on.

For years the Southern Transept has been disfigured by two unsightly scaffolds which appear to have been abandoned by a bankrupt contractor. It is difficult to believe that any self-respecting householder would allow such a ghastly disfigurement to remain upon his private house or business premises for a single month longer than absolutely necessary.

It must seem strange to foreign visitors that Westminster Abbey and St Paul's appear to be the most neglected structures in the metropolis, contractors being allowed to take as many years over repair works which should take only as many weeks or months, or perhaps be excused the trouble and expense of removing their scaffolds.

Yours very truly

Dean Inge, as a result of my letter to which he did not reply, soon instituted a mechanical arrangement of piping and hose which cleaned the dirt from the windows. The abandoned scaffolding was dismantled and removed without any further use being made of it – it had apparently been forgotten. In 1966, just 40 years later, I noted that a large sum had just been collected and spent on cleaning – with high pressure water – the dirt of centuries from all the exterior stonework of St Paul's and the addition of flood-lighting had enormously improved the effect of this when seen at night.

The Dean of Westminster replied most courteously to my letter explaining that only as funds became available was it possible to continue the maintenance and necessary repairs to the exterior fabric and he feared that it might take years to complete the restoration of the stonework.

Offer of Job as General Manager of Anticosti Island, Quebec, Canada

Gold was discovered in Johannesburg in 1926 and the consequent gold rush was followed the next year by the Kimberley diamond rush when one or two of my friends decided to try their luck in South Africa. There were plenty of opportunities for ex-Army officers to find interesting jobs abroad and Col. J.D.W. Holmes, my friend from the Royal Engineers, went to Mexico City as General Manager of Mexican Railways at a salary of £5,000 pa.

In August I received an offer from the Canadian financier C.R. Whitehead to visit Canada, all expenses paid, and be interviewed for the post of General Manager of the newly formed Anticosti Corporation.

Whitehead, who was President of the Wayagamack Pulp & Paper Company, had become very friendly after my survey and diving adventures for one of his companies in Quebec on the St Maurice River in 1912. During that survey for a projected hydro-electric scheme at Grandes-Piles he had had my activities watched, unbeknown to me, by one of his forestry engineers.

As a result, shortly afterwards, he had offered me the post of Manager of the Log-driving and Boom Association which every year, after the ice moved out of the St Maurice River, 'helped' 10 million logs move downstream to the various mills which owned them. The War and my part in it, had forced me to decline the offer but Whitehead continued to write to me regularly and visited me at my Club whenever he was in London.

The Anticosti Corporation had been formed by three companies, the St Maurice Valley Corporation, the Wayagamack Pulp and Paper Company and the Port Alfred Pulp and Paper Corporation with the objective of obtaining a permanent source of freehold pulpwood for their mills, thus relieving the owners from paying a C$1.40 stumpage to the Province of Quebec on their leasehold properties.

The new company had just bought Anticosti Island for C$6 million from Gaston Menier, the brother of Henri Menier, the chocolate millionaire, whose magnificent château would be the home and office of the new manager. For 30 years preceding his death in 1914 Henri Menier had owned and run Anticosti Island as his private hunting and fishing preserve, his social and economic experimental station and his almost feudal seignory; the largest and most curiously administered private domain in the world. Previously there had been only a few settlements on the island, mainly trappers and fishermen and their families living along the shores.

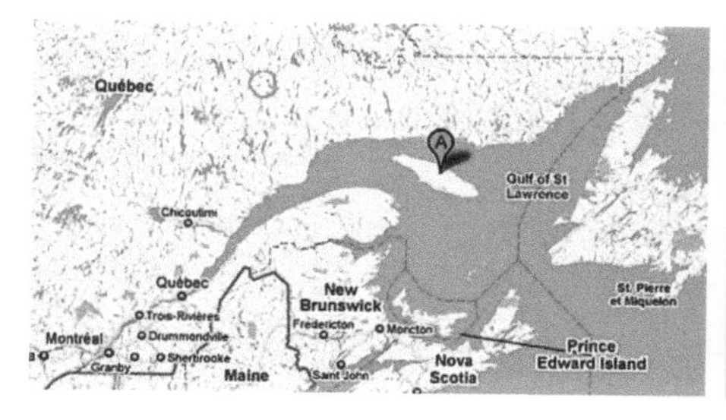

Anticosti Island in the Gulf of St Lawrence

The island, 135 miles long and a maximum of 35 miles wide, lay in the Gulf of the St Lawrence River, 150 miles west of

Newfoundland and 13 miles from the north shore of the river and was totally isolated from December for two or three months until the ice melted. It was a little larger than Puerto Rico and Menier had made it his own 'country' of which he was 'king'. He had established a pulp-wood business, a lobster and salmon canning factory and also a sealing operation, but he only spent a couple of months a year there himself.

The Anticosti Island opportunity was, at first sight, one of the really exciting opportunities for a civil engineer. The manager would be responsible for the development and exploitation of the timber in the 3,000 sq. miles of virgin forest, an un-surveyed nature reserve teeming with game and with salmon rivers. In his letter Whitehead said, 'There would be engineering connected with the job, dams, piers, wharves, railways, etc, as well as the lumbering operations and care of the town-sites; altogether a very interesting job.'

He went on to say, 'All I want to know is – are you available for such a position and, if it is going, could you run across and see us provided we pay your passage and expenses to Canada and back? Please cable back saying I can (or cannot) visit you, Lott.'

The initial work would involve the construction and importation of housing for possibly thousands of lumbermen and labourers and their families, almost certainly largely French Canadians. The manager would have almost sovereign powers over the population as the island was not administered by any Canadian Province.

The early days of occupation with the survey and construction of a railway through the dense woods and the planning of the timber areas and the fire-breaks would have been intensely interesting, and I was loath to throw away this opportunity of a new adventure. However, I realised from my earlier Canadian bush life, the terrible risk of forest fires before adequate firebreaks could be cut, and the impossibility of preventing lumbermen from smoking. Also, I could not speak French Canadian patois and felt that I would have been very much alone and out of place as their General Manager in a remote location.

So I declined the offer and settled for the more varied and international life as a consulting engineer based in London. In my letter to Whitehead thanking him for the offer I explained that I had recently joined Balfour Beatty and had committed to stay with them. Although I realised that considerable patience would be necessary, I explained that they were becoming recognised specialists in the finance, construction, and management of utility corporations at home and abroad with offices and major projects in several countries and I suggested that Balfour Beatty might even be of assistance to him in the future.

I recommended, as a possible candidate for the position, W.G. Chace in Winnipeg, under whom I had worked in 1909-1912 when he was responsible for the construction of the Winnipeg City Hydro-Electric Scheme. I congratulated Whitehead on his foresight and enterprise in acquiring Anticosti and sent him a copy of an article on his project which had just been published in the Financial Times.

In the closing paragraph I said, 'I propose leaving for Switzerland at the end of this month for a business-cum-pleasure trip during my holidays, attending the International Power Conference in Basle and visiting some of the more recent developments in that go-ahead little country.' It was my way of saying that I already had a satisfying job in London with an interesting future.

My finances

Having been brought up by parents with a very limited budget, I was in the habit of keeping detailed accounts of all my assets and expenditure. In my analysis at the end of 1926 my assets amounted to a total of £6,285, made up of investments valued at £5,873 (about £200 less than the previous year), cash in hand of £11 (≈ £670 today) and a loan to Father of £750 (≈ £ 45,000) less my overdraft of £349. I was lucky not to have lost more on my holdings in rubber shares.

My record of expenditure during the year totalled £1,254. 11. 4., although I very much doubt it was quite that precise. It was made up of:

General expenses	£ 631. 8. 0
Clubs and Societies	£ 33. 18. 6
Insurances	£ 14. 13. 6
Bookcase (for the office)	£ 34. 15. 6
Dancing lessons	£ 11. 12. 6
Doctor (7/6) and Dentist (£21)	£ 21. 7. 6
Presents – Xmas	£ 107. 15. 0
Income tax on salary	£ 118. 0. 4
	£ 973. 10. 10
Clyno car	£ 281. 0. 6
Total	£1,254. 11. 4

Safaris in Kenya in 1927 and 1930

The highlight of 1927 was my trip to Kenya. On 9th April Shearer ordered me to go to Kenya 'by the next boat' for a 3 month visit to settle the question of hydro-electric power expansions for the East African Power & Lighting Company. I had been spending most of my time in the office dealing with their engineering, operational and financial matters as the London manager for the company.

Journey to Kenya in April 1927

The next few days were spent packing and preparing for the trip and finishing off my work in the office. I bought a safari suit and topee and went to the dentist to have some fillings - carried out using cocaine as the analgesic. Painter took 3 heavy pieces of luggage to Tilbury docks for me to be put on board the SS Mulbera, a ship of the British India Line which I would join later in Marseilles. On 20th April Malcolm Gunn drove me to Victoria Station where we left the rest of my baggage in the luggage room to remain there overnight. Then, after a final briefing from Shearer the next morning, I returned to Victoria and boarded the 'Bombay Express', a train with Pullman carriages run by P&O, the largest shipping company in the world at the time. Harrison Edwards came to the station to see me off and gave me T.E. Lawrence's book 'Revolt in the Desert' to read on my trip. The train seemed to be only about a quarter full and I had a compartment all to myself.

Reflecting on the journey at the time I wrote in my diary:

'All the adventure and much of the romance has departed from present day travel. Speed, efficiency, and comfort have combined to make a long train journey or sea voyage a rest or relaxation to be desired rather than a perilous undertaking to be dreaded. Scenes on the departure platforms at Victoria are quite ordinary affairs – no fuss, no tears, nobody even worried about their luggage and yet most are starting on a journey of thousands of miles involving an absence of years for those who are leaving to take up posts in India.

'On the special train to Dover the Pullman car attendants are very lordly and condescending compared with the natural courtesy of the ordinary dining car waiters. Perhaps their more expensive (but less comfortable) cars make them feel superior to the ordinary persons upon whom they have to wait.

'The journey across France is, as usual, accompanied by much dirt from the poor coal used, spasms of very high speed alternating occasionally with long waits, particularly around Paris. The meals are good and expensive; 45 francs for lunch or dinner, with wine at say 12 francs for a good white wine, and a 10% tip plus coffee brings up the total for such a meal to 65 francs, or approximately 10 shillings (£1 being worth 122 francs then).

'Café complet the next morning cost 8 francs plus a tip and was a pleasant variant to the stereotyped English breakfast. Marseilles presented the inevitable small problem of tips and payments to baggage porters.'

There was no comparison between this voyage East, with its many incidents and sights, and the cold dreary wastes of an Atlantic crossing. The sea was calm and the weather beautiful as we entered the Strait of Bonifacio and saw the small island volcano Stromboli with its little village of square white flat-topped houses clinging to the hillside. Vineyards and olive trees extended far up the slope on the safe side, whilst a small stream of lava crept down towards the sea on the other side. An hour or so later Etna came into view, snow-covered with white 'smoke' issuing from its peak.

Our entry to the Strait of Messina on Sunday was held up until the skipper and congregation left the on-board service; meanwhile the ship circled quietly – fortunately, there was no whirlpool effect as in the Greek legend of Scylla & Charybdis. I passed the time walking on deck, chatting to some of the passengers, watching deck tennis and, in the evenings, playing bridge and taking part in the occasional informal dance to gramophone music.

When we reached Port Said the ship tied up at the APOC wharf and discharged explosives and other cargo. Several of us took a motor boat into town; I had a haircut, did some shopping, and posted 18 letters which I had written to family and friends. We had drinks and dinner at the Casino Palace before returning to the ship which set sail again at midnight.

After leaving Suez, where we unloaded a consignment of soap, we went on to Port Sudan, designed by Kitchener after the Sudanese war some 18 years earlier. Its buildings of cut coral stone gave it an air of permanence, almost extravagance. The streets were wide, even in the Indian bazaar where the individual dukas were large single rooms in buildings entirely surrounded by arcaded verandas in stone. The only soil seemed to have been imported from the hills behind the town. The shade temperature had risen, and I had changed to wearing shorts. I went ashore with Penn, McIntyre, and Bergstein for a walk through the town and a drink at the hotel where we listened to a piano recital before returning to the ship and watching the coolies at work. They were an extraordinarily fine bunch of men, mostly Sudanese. As in Kenya, there were practically no beggars.

We were given TAB inoculations before reaching Aden which was exceedingly hot and sticky. I walked along the shopping district to look at the dugongs and was disgusted by everything I saw on the streets. After we left Aden there was the usual ceremony at which his Aquatic Majesty Neptune came on board to initiate those 'landlubbers and greenhorns' who had not previously crossed the Equator. The initiation consisted of a trial and sentence delivered by a pseudo-parson before the initiates were branded with black paint, lathered with a soapy whitewash, and shaved before being ducked 3 or 4 times in the pool. Neptune and Neptune's wife (the lady engineer) and all the court were also ducked eventually.

In the evenings after dinner there was more bridge at which I often won several shillings, and there were dances and a fancy dress ball for which I wore my Arab costume. Of the several young ladies on board, Miss Laws, Miss Pratt, and Miss Cobham became my regular dance partners, as well as Mrs Stratton who was joining her husband in Nairobi where he had bought a partnership in a law firm.

On arrival in Mombasa on 11th May I was met by Commander Lunt, W.T. Kerr, and Josh Holmes; they showed me around the Kilindini Harbour sheds, the sub-station and wireless station, the Khalfan Soap works (the first modern two-storey factory in Mombasa built about 1920 and equipped with Krupp machinery) and the Sheriff Dewji premises (a large trading company which later became the MJ Group).

Nairobi and the Muthaiga Club

The next day we took a train up to Nairobi (elevation 5,460 ft) where the weather was pleasanter and cooler, and I checked into the Muthaiga Club which was to be my abode and headquarters; 'the most luxurious and comfortable one between here and Johannesburg'.

At the EAP&L office the next day I had a meeting with Maj. Hamilton F. Ward (Chairman), Charles A. Udall (General Manager) and J.J. Haines (Chief Engineer), from whom I collected my first batch of information on the company's power generating, supply and distribution systems. During the following three weeks I was shown round the existing power plants and sub-stations in the Nairobi area and reviewed the calculations for the growing power demand as well as the plans for the new hydro-electric schemes at Thika, Maragua and Ndula.

We normally took our lunch across the road from the office at the New Stanley Hotel and on one occasion there I met and had a long chat with W.T. Barry. He was the owner of Donyo Sabuk, a large estate 60 miles from Nairobi near Thika, made famous by a decorated American soldier Lord William Northrop Macmillan and his wife Lucy who had settled there in 1901. Macmillan and his wife had no children and built a castle at Donyo Sabuk in which they lived in one half during the summer and the other half during the winter. During the First World War the Lord's Castle, as it was called, had been used as a military hospital for British officers. Wild parties were held there under the maverick Colonel Ewart Grogan who led the wine tossing and wife swapping orgies of the Happy Valley Set. Macmillan had died in 1925 and Barry had bought the estate for £6,000. He employed 100 men who, with their wives and children, made up a squatter colony of 300 on the estate and ensured that he was never short of labour. Barry told me that one of his small coffee shambas (plantations) which was 15 years old yielded 9 tons from 11 acres. Davidson and Scott, whom I also met at the hotel, had not had such yields from their coffee shambas.

The Muthaiga Club was out of town and so in the mornings and evenings I was driven to and from the EAP&L office in Nairobi by G.G. Bompas in his 7 hp Austin. As well as running EAP&L, Ward and Udall were both elected members of the Kenya Colony Legislative Council and represented Nairobi North. Ward arranged several dinners at the Club to introduce me to other members of the Legislative Council including Robert Robertson-Eustace (Coast), Walter MacLean Wilson (Kikuyu), Helmuth Schwartze (Nairobi South) and Hugh Cholmondeley (Rift Valley). He also introduced me to Walter Huggard (Attorney General), Godfrey Rhodes (GM of Kenya and Uganda Railways), Gerald Maxwell (Chief Native Commissioner) and Commander Robinson (of Kenya Colony Wireless). Robinson was a resident at the Club too and became one of my regular companions; we often played tennis and spent the evenings talking after dinner or playing bridge with Ward, Eustace, and the others. On Saturday and Sunday evenings the Club held dances to which the local residents came for their weekend entertainment. I usually took the floor with one of the ladies and, when she was there, with Miss Stella Pratt whom I had met on the Mulbera.

Nairobi was full of interesting characters one of whom was Colonel Marcuswell Maxwell who had a distinguished war record and became well known as a big-game photographer in East Africa. He and his wife invited me to dinner with several others one evening and we ended up playing three rubbers of bridge at which I lost 2 shillings.

On another occasion I had dinner with Admiral Vincent Molteno, born in South Africa, the son of the Prime Minister of Cape Colony, who had distinguished himself in the Battle of Jutland in 1916. He told tales of his meetings with Winston Churchill whom he thought to be a poor judge of character but a prodigious worker, producing a memo between 2.30 am and breakfast on the value of the naval base at Rosyth - but then leaving some of his papers in Molteno's car.

My stay at the Muthaiga Club for 25 days cost me 777 East African shillings, net of my winnings and losses at cards. That figure was made up of membership at 25 shillings a week, board and lodging at 24 shillings a day and the balance being my drinks bill.

My first Safari

The prime objective of my journey to Kenya was to determine the extent of the river power available at the various possible sites for a hydro-electric development and to choose the most suitable reaches of the river for the next scheme. As this involved locating and surveying waterfalls on the two or three rivers within economical transmission distance of Nairobi, safaris were arranged for me, at least one of which was more of an exploration than a reconnaissance.

My first safari was to the confluence of the Maragua and Tana Rivers with a 17 year old apprentice, Denis Ker, who drove us there in a safari-body Hupmobile car. We set out on 7th June, called in at Ruiru to pick up a tent and camp bed on the way, and spent the first night at the Thika Blue Posts Hotel in a circular room built of reeds with a conical thatched roof.

On our second day out we called on the local District Commissioner and he lent us a tribal retainer from Fort Hall to accompany us on our survey and assist us liaising with the local tribespeople. He was a native who, for an obvious reason, we named 'Smiley' - he was tall and striking with make-up and trappings which I described in my diary:

'... his woolly hair was thickly plastered with a greasy looking mud which gave a matted curl appearance. Globules of the mud hung from the bottom edge of his wool, exactly like large red beads. The lobes of his ears had been pierced and the holes enlarged in the usual fashion, so that extended lobes would hang downwards, almost reaching his shoulders but, by looping them over the tops of his ears, the part that hung down carried metal ear-rings. Other metal discs were fastened to the top of each ear, perhaps to keep the looped-up lobe in place.'

'Around his neck were two tight necklaces, one like a dog-collar of beads on a one-inch wide strip. On his upper arm white metal rings were clamped tightly, with a polished brass ring encircling his right arm just above the elbow. Several more clamped rings, of aluminium and copper alternately, were worn as bangles. On each thumb a ring. Behind his neck hung a shaped piece of ivory attached to a thong, making a third necklet. A long brass chain of small links hung across his bare shoulder; on the other shoulder was looped the blanket – his only garment. The chain was fastened at his kipande (identification document). On each ankle he wore several chains of such varying lengths that they formed a brass band 3 to 4 inches high.'

With Smiley as my only companion I spent a day making a preliminary walk-over survey of the junction of the two rivers. Just before dark we were joined by W.T. Kerr and Chief Engineer Haines and they helped us make camp that night close to the

Maragua River at an altitude of 3,800 ft, some 1,600 feet lower than Nairobi. The next day we took two passing natives (Wakambas) as porters. Their only garment was their blanket looped over one shoulder, but they differed from the Kikuyu in having their teeth filed to resemble saw-teeth; a relic perhaps of the days when the Wakambas were reputed to be cannibals.

Our porters with locals at the confluence
of the Maragua and Tana Rivers.

In this photo the two natives standing were the Wakambas whom I employed as porters to carry rod, haversacks, and rifle; the rest, sitting and feeding, were local Kikuyus not objecting to being photographed.

The Tana River rapids

We forded the Maragua tributary at the foot of the steep rapids which later we found to drop a total of 248 ft from our camp level. Then, climbing up the Tana riverbank, we viewed its rapids with a fall of about 200 ft. My main objective was to locate a dam on the Tana, which, together with a canal and pipeline, would utilise this head of water and at the same time bring water from the Maragua to the same powerhouse.

The temperature that day was 93 degrees in the shade - the equator was only 45 miles away - and we were very tired by the time we returned to the fording place. Here we found that the water had risen so that it was now chest deep, making the crossing to the other bank distinctly hazardous with the rocky bottom very slippery and uneven. When we arrived back at the tents we were ready for our camp meal of soup, bully beef, fig pudding and tinned guavas.

The next morning the great cloud which generally obscured Mt Kenya (over 17,000 ft high) lowered slowly so that we saw its rocky and snow-covered pinnacles greet the rising sun. However, after two hours the mountain disappeared from view again; such glimpses were not an everyday experience.

With Smiley I made another walk-over survey of the terrain for a power canal before walking across country to Fort Hall (elevation 4,500 ft) where I was picked up by Bompas, the acting manager. The 60 mile drive back to Nairobi was the most nerve-racking experience I had had since the war. The car was heavy, the roads appalling and Ker's inexperienced steering most wild. He expressed great surprise that Balfour Beatty had not insured my life, for it was the custom of the FCO to insure every man who leaves England, not only in the interests of his family but to compensate for the loss of his services. After this trip the luxury of the Muthaiga Country Club was never more welcome.

We had learned much from this short survey which we used to good effect when making our next trip to the Seven Forks rapids on the lower Tana River, 150 miles by road and trail from Nairobi. For this longer safari we first proposed to take as leader of the expedition a local farmer-surveyor, but as his regular fee was £5.5s per day plus expenses we decided to take a 'white hunter', Hubert Stanton, at £50 a month on a daily rate basis. Hubert Stanton and his wife Jane later became great friends of mine and I arranged for my son, Brian, his wife and two small girls to stay with the old couple at their 'Bushwackers' game lodge on their way back from Zambia in December 1972.

With Stanton's 1 ton Chevrolet truck, a wonderful vehicle on bad roads, and the Hupmobile with its box-body – one to pull the other out of trouble – we set off to explore the Seven Forks reaches of the Tana. Our party included young Ker, Haines and his private servant, a cook, a gun-bearer of Stanton's, and a couple more servants, all local Africans of superior intelligence.

I accompanied Haines in the Hupmobile, and we set out at 7.15 am on 24th June, stopping at Fort Hall and again at Embu to call on the District Commissioner. We told him of our intentions, and he lent us a tribal retainer who had a long pig-tail. Because of his smart and somewhat dandyish appearance we called him Algy, but he was not a humourist, perhaps being weighed down with his responsibility as liaison officer with the local tribes to prove that our demand for local porters had government backing. We also took on 5 natives to act as porters initially. All the natives we saw around were carrying spears or bows and arrows.

We reached Kimbo's old village site at about 4 pm where we stopped to reconnoitre for a suitable camp site. With help of a local native Haines found an old track down to the base camp made by Cook, a surveyor who had been paid £1,400 the previous year by EAP&L for a useless survey of the area. So, at our first camp we had the luxury of a grass thatched open shelter for our meals instead of having to eat in our two small tents or out in the open. Haines and I walked about a mile down to the river, returning around 7 pm in time for sundowners with sardines as canapes. That was followed by dinner with lobster, beef, beans, and asparagus, all from tins. I turned in with a Mauser rifle, one of Stanton's, alongside me. The journey from Nairobi had taken us about 8 hours on roads which were in good condition.

On the following day we fixed up our small collapsible canoe in order to get the 5 natives and ourselves across the river for our first walk-over power survey. It took five hazardous journeys to complete the crossing. The natives had never been in a canoe before and were liable by any sudden movement to capsize it and throw the occupants into the crocodile infested water.

Our 'current ferry' across the Tana River

For the return crossing at the end of the day I devised a 'current ferry', first getting a rope across the river and then using box spanners to act as pulleys - one attached with a long rope to the bow and the other with a short rope to the stern. The current acting on the boat, askew with the line of current, sent it quietly across to the other side. By reversing the long and the short ropes, the current took the boat back again for the next load. The movement of the craft was much less than with a man using a paddle and the crossing was thereby much safer.

Thus the power of the Tana River did its first useful work for the white man. Some 30 years later its waterfalls and rapids were eventually harnessed to supply electricity to the city of Nairobi.

We walked upstream along the north bank to a place that had been identified as a possible dam site and on towards the Thiba-Tana confluence. We returned along the river and went downstream to a series of low rapids, named Split Rock Rapids after the character of one large rock in mid-stream. There was very little fall in the 3 mile stretch of river and we were not impressed by Cook's proposal to site a dam and a power scheme there.

With our porters ready to make camp

Algy showing Haines how to use a bow and arrow

During the day we saw Sykes monkeys (named after the Director of Public Works), black ibis with green iridescent wings and also water-buck as well as the tracks of many other animals including lion, buffalo, elephant, rhino, and zebra.

Stanton shot an impala, and we had a haunch of it for dinner, roasted with slices of fat bacon inserted in cuts across the meat, making a delicious change from tinned food. In the very brief twilight – we were only a few miles from the Equator – Algy gave us a little practice with a bow and arrow. Before turning in we bathed in a basin of water; crocs, as well as the generally harmless hippos, abounded in the river.

The Tana gorge and rapids

On Sunday 26th June day we crossed the river again in the canvas canoe. I explored up and downstream and came across a series of rapids with a total fall of about 100 ft within half a mile. We had lunch near the falls and, having spotted fresh elephants spoor nearby, I called them 'Elephant Falls', a name by which they were still known at the Tribunal in 1930.

We saw little dik-dik, the smallest of the antelope family, which, like a cat, scrapes earth over its droppings unless it uses the communal latrine. Back at camp across the river both Stanton and Kerr had a swim, with Haines on guard on the bank with a rifle in case of crocodiles. The next day we struck camp and proceeded to Cook's camp No 2. As Algy had failed to bring the expected porters, Stanton, Kerr, and Haines went to round some up leaving me alone with Algy and a 0.47 rifle. Not far from the camp I was charged by a bush-buck, an experience which I subsequently learned was quite common. Besides a score of larger water-buck (not good eating), red duiker, many monkeys, a hyrax (or rock rabbit) and some partridges, we encountered tracks of rhino and one of lion.

Algy and I reached the new camp at 3.45 pm to find Stanton and Kerr already there and ready for another tramp along the riverbank before dark. As usual, I took my evening bath at the riverside, sitting or standing on a rock and sponging myself down there (indicated by the arrow in the photo). A monkey on a nearby tree watched me with interest – probably his first view of a naked white man.

On Tuesday camp was struck again and Stanton and I must have walked almost 20 miles along the river inspecting the long series of rapids, whilst Haines and Kerr went about 12 miles along Cook's survey line with the porters carrying the camp equipment and food to camp No 6, four miles north of the river.

This was a very arid part of Kenya and all the trees and bushes, almost without exception, were armed with so-called 'wait-a-bit' thorns, so barbed that one could not easily withdraw from them. I had two drill shirts torn to rags and a pair of strong canvas trousers also suffered badly. During the six days of the safari I must have covered about 80 miles, indicating how very fit I must have been, though I should not have liked to carry a heavy gun in addition to my camera which was my only load. Frequently one had to stoop, almost into a crawling position, to pass under the bushes. Unfortunately, the paths left by hippos and rhinos were too low-roofed although comfortably wide, and they generally led away from the river instead of following the bank as we needed to. The four natives who accompanied us were carrying loads of blankets and food; unable often to walk upright in places they had to carry their loads under their arms.

Walking down to one of the several forks of the river I met a rhino at 25 yards; it was also walking to the water's edge. We both decided that we did not like the look of each other and so both turned tail and retired. I learned later that rhinos are extremely short-sighted beasts but very bad-tempered and charge at anything of which they get a smell down-wind.

Darkness fell before Stanton and I neared 'home' and we had difficulty finding the camp. We climbed a conical hill (myself on hands and knees as no amount of slicing at the leather soles of my shoes would make them grip on the slippery dry grass) and Stanton fired shots until 'camp' replied. Further rifle shots from camp every 15 minutes led us in the right direction. But progress through the thorn bushes was desperately difficult and we were extremely thirsty. Fortunately, we found a water hole in a dry gully under some rocks where the animals congregated at night. After we pushed aside the thick green scum, we found the water quite palatable and we each drank it with relish.

Eventually, when it was too dark to see, a boy who had been sent to find us with a hurricane lamp, led us to camp and a much-needed whisky. Never did I enjoy a supper of venison stew with fresh vegetables, which was served a little later, so much. Had we not found the camp we would have had to spend the night up a tree as there was abundant evidence of elephant, rhino, and other animals in the bush.

I told Haines that we had located a big power concentration in the Seven Forks reach, by far the most important one on the river, and that we had recorded the position by taking the bearings of the Kiambere and Kindaruma hills. He naturally wanted to see this for himself and so on Wednesday we rose at daybreak and, after breakfast, arranged for the whole party to proceed by the best route to the ford on the Kitui road. With the 40 porters all loaded, using long strips of bark as tump-lines or to tie up packages for head-loads, we reached the fording place where we camped for the night.

The next day the main safari returned along the Kitui road to the DC's camp at Embu whilst Haines, Stanton and I walked back upstream to Camp No.2, keeping close to the river and taking levels with an aneroid barometer along the way. After a few miles we came to a quiet stretch of the river before arriving at the foot of the Seven Forks reach where my aneroid gave a level of 2,600 ft. At the head of the Seven Forks rapids, 3 miles or so upstream, the aneroid reading was 2,900 ft. As these readings were recorded within a little under two hours, with no apparent change in atmospheric conditions, it was reasonable to assume that the 300 ft head was correct.

In the Seven Forks area the river split into several streams and little of it could be seen as the intervening ground was hilly and covered in dense scrub. We estimated that about 20,000 kW would be available here and could probably be doubled at peak load conditions by pondage of the river. It was a much more favourable site, and the dam and canal works would cost little more than the smaller Ikindi Rapids scheme identified earlier by Cook.

Using brushwood to get the vehicles across the stream

The safari team standing lt to rt: Haines, Algy, Kerr and Stanton

One of the branches of the Seven Forks rapids on the Tana River

Stanton generally led the way on our treks through the bush carrying his elephant gun (double barrelled and very powerful) whilst his gun-bearer carried his Express rifle for use with smaller game. During this reconnaissance we saw a pair of rhinos about 50 yards away, both females having slender pointed horns. We scared them off but a little later we noticed two full grown males wallowing in the mud not more than 70 yards away. Being to leeward of them we stood and watched them. One rhino became suspicious and, with the other following, walked towards us. We shouted and whistled until they also hurriedly departed. Once, when we had just stepped from a rhino path to photograph some rapids, a rhino charged by, too fast for me to turn and snap him as he passed.

We camped that night in the open having taken enough food and a canteen for the evening and early morning meal. The boys cut away all the grass in an open space and prepared beds for us with leaves and twigs before making a good fire for tea. This fire was maintained throughout the night, being replenished mostly by myself at 1½ hour intervals. It blazed finely and its warmth was welcome as we were travelling light and the night was cool.

Just before dawn I climbed down the steep slope to the river for a wash and to fill our canteen for our breakfast tea. The night had been quiet. We had slept with our rifles beside us for the district abounded in big game. Not only were there rhinos but elephants and buffalos, the latter being the most dangerous.

Starting from our bivouac as soon as the day broke at 6 am, we walked 8 or 9 miles and reached Camp No.2 where the cars had been left. Here we were delayed by a couple of hours before we could start them by juggling with the wires; Stanton had left the ignition keys with Ker who had gone on to the DC's camp the previous evening. After lunch, when we had paid off the boys, Haines and I set off for the 136 mile drive back to Nairobi - but then our troubles began.

Upon reaching the road, thorns collected in the bush penetrated the tyres and we had four punctures which took hours to mend as we only had a hand pump. Torrential rains and slippery roads forced us to stop for the night in a 'duka' (shop) at Fort Hall where the Indian shopkeeper lent us two camp beds for sleeping out on his veranda. He gave us breakfast of bread and cheese and tea at 6 am before we proceeded on to Nairobi covered in the red dust of the murrum. We arrived in Nairobi about 9.30 am after an absence of 8 days; Haines and I had a wash and shave, and I collected my mail and the newspapers before going back to the Muthaiga Club.

Over the next few days I worked on my Tana survey report and prepared estimates and comparative statistics for the Thika Scheme for presentation to the next EAP&L board meeting. Having received several letters from home and being keen to catch the next out-going English mail on 5th July, I took the opportunity of writing at length to my parents telling them of my experiences over the previous couple of weeks.

'Dearest Home-ones

The last two mails from England which arrived during my absence on the Tana River contained many welcome letters; in fact, I seem to have heard from everybody and I feel wonderfully grateful for them. Honours of course to you Mother and Father for very delightful letters, and then May and Clara, Charlie, and Bob, besides Nellie and Bessie Baker and Malcom Gunn.

I returned to Nairobi on 2nd July after an absence of 8 days – for we were wonderfully lucky in having an excellent white hunter who fell in with our desires to see as much as possible in as short a time as possible. Stanton was therefore a great help and worth his pay; I also found him a delightful companion on the one or two tramps that he and I took (with natives, of course, to carry things)........ A detailed description of my adventures in the bush followed......

Yesterday the local magistrate asked me to have lunch with a General S.H. Charrington. I had a delightful hour or so walking around his house full of hunting trophies and works of art, and the gardens some of the prettiest I have seen. It was Sunday and I returned here to laze in my room to read the bundles of newspapers that have come in the last two weeks.

This week I am likely to be entertaining Mr and Mrs Vernon to dinner and bridge at this club. And for the weekend I have asked Mr and Mrs Jack Oulton to come here from Thika. They are a young couple who put me up at his father's house a few weeks ago and they will be present at a dance on Saturday evening. I must also think of doing some more entertaining for I owe some in return to one or two others.

It is now 7.45 pm and I must change for dinner which is at 8 pm. Last evening the Hon. Cyril Ward (son of the Earl of Dudley) entertained Robinson and me for a few minutes as we sat at dinner; he had just driven in in rough clothes and coughing with the dust he had swallowed – or that was his excuse. He described himself – and almost correctly too – as the biggest stiff in Kenya. He is a retired naval captain, has been bankrupt once, and has now sold his farm out here.

After dinner Robinson and I went for a short stroll before turning in. We discussed the total eclipse which northern Europe had experienced on 29th June. I was sorry to have missed it, though my trip to the Tana had been some compensation.

Life at the Club was as sociable as ever; Robinson was still there and told me that he was falling in love with Miss Clark. After dinner and bridge with him, Carnelly, Schwartze and Hirst (an old timer) we discussed the qualifications for good wives. A few days later he announced his engagement and I entertained him and Mr and Mrs Gilbert Vernon to a dinner during which we had cocktails, sherry, champagne (Pol Roger 1919 at 25 shillings a bottle) followed by whisky pegs later. Another evening after dinner with Robertson-Eustace we watched the dancing at which 57 year old Lord Delamere was still a very active participant.

Before leaving Kenya I made more walk-over surveys taking levels of the Tana River near its confluence with the Maragua and of possible pipeline routes. By using the collapsible canoe we avoided the hazardous fording of the Maragua river each day. For two nights I slept out in the bush alone, for Ker had gone to Nairobi in the safari car. The two natives we had brought with us took refuge each night in a nearby native hut. Fortunately, only the calls of hyenas broke the stillness of the nights. Up at 5.45 am I made tea and had breakfast of porridge, bacon and fried-bread and marmalade before going out with Kithanga and one of the boys to take more land-level readings down an alternative pipeline route.

Our difficulty in getting more native help as 'axemen' was in spite of good pay offers. One strapping young fellow agreed to come despite being taunted by his lay-about friends who said that his knees bent whenever he carried a small bundle of grass for his goats. When alone I found that my ignorance of Swahili (I only had about 8 words) was a real handicap.

When Ker returned he brought a tent-shelter to sleep under in case of rain. European settlers on this strip of land between the Thaba Tana and Maragua Rivers were surprised that we had not been 'bothered by lions' for they had been called out at night by natives whose bomas (compounds for humans and cattle) had recently been attacked.

I must have been bitten by malarial mosquitoes during one of our expeditions as I had a mild attack with a temperature of 102 degrees for a few days; anti-malarial tablets were not available in those days and one relied on strong doses of quinine in gin with lots of tonic.

An interesting dinner at which I was the guest of Commander Lawford at his lovely home near the Thika River is worth mentioning. His white man-servant, his former naval orderly, waited at table and served us an excellent meal accompanied by champagne. Before the meal I had asked whether he changed for dinner. 'Oh yes' he said, 'into pyjamas.' Fortunately, I had a smart and clean suit of them with me.

Between safaris I held discussions with the Government's Director of Public Works and other officials and settlers who helped me with local costs for preparing my project estimates.

On 7th August a cablegram from London was delivered to our camp by a Sikh messenger. It required me to be in London with my report by 5th September so that it could be discussed by Balfour Beatty with EAP&L's Chairman, H.F. Ward, before he returned to Kenya. So, two days later, I was on my way by train to Mombasa having had a final lunch with Udall, W.T. Kerr, and Bompas at the Norfolk Hotel. During the journey, which was one of the dirtiest and dustiest, my companions were a consumptive settler who had been crippled in a fight with a leopard and the principal of Kenton College who was going to the Seychelles.

In Mombasa I was met by Lunt and Penn and on 10th August I boarded an Italian ship for Genoa. Before leaving I had drinks with Robertson-Eustace who had come to see Charles Huberich and his wife off. I spent several evenings talking to Huberich and once, when his charming wife, Nina, joined us, she forecast 'a disturbed future for me on arrival in London – a woman (in business) is to put matters right.' That led the following evening to us having a long talk on philosophy, religion, and life after death, and I later realised what she had meant.

We stopped for a few hours in Aden; the humidity was oppressively high and the temperature 96 degrees. When I changed for dinner into a modified evening dress my shirt became saturated within half an hour. At Suez I left the ship in Cook's tender for a trip (£7.12s.) to Cairo together with Charles and Nina Huberich – but more of them and this trip later. During the remainder of the journey home from Port Said via Beirut to Genoa it was not so hot, and I was able to work on my report and estimates for the Maragua-Tana dam scheme. In Beirut we spent an afternoon being driven to see rocks, inscriptions and monuments of Rameses III, the Hittites, Napoleon III and the French, before embarking for the last leg of our voyage to Genoa. The final dinner on board consisted of caviar on ice, real turtle soup, salmon & sauce, tournedos, pullet with peas and lettuce, bomb (illuminated with the lights out), cheese and fruit.

The 1st Class train ticket to London from Genoa cost £8. I went to Milan first with Major Ronald Munro to see the cathedral and then boarded the Orient Express, a train-de-lux, to Paris where I was told that my luggage had been held up at the Italian frontier. I paid Cooks 350 francs (£3) to recover it and then Munro and I went to the Gard du Nord to catch the boat-train to London, arriving there at 5.20 pm. I went straight to the Constitutional Club and thence to Regent Street to buy a ready-made suit (£6.16.6) before meeting Malcolm Gunn for dinner.

MARAGUA TANA SCHEME

Preliminary estimate Maragua Development
(dated 12th Sept. 1927.)

			£.
1.	DAM. Excavation, river handling & Concrete		1,200
2.	CANAL. Approx. 6000 cub.yds., assuming hard rock excavation at 5/- per cub.yd.	1,500	
	ADD: for aqueduct across ravine	500	2,000
3.	Sluice gates and canal entrance		
	Concrete Work £600	600	
	3 gates at £100 f.o.b. English Port	300	
	ADD: £100 for sea and rail freight	100	1,000
4.	HEAD POND. Retaining walls, excavation sluice gates and screens		3,500
5.	PIPE LINE. 700ft. long 100 tons erected at £50 per ton		5,000
6.	PIPE LINE SUPPORTS. Excavation, say £250		
	20 supports at 140 cub.ft.		
	2 supports at 600 " " = 185 cub.yds.		
	at £4 per cub.yd. =	£750	1,000
7.	POWER HOUSE buildings and foundation for 4,000 KW station		8,000
8.	EXCAVATION OF TAIL RACE 150ft. long x 500 sq.ft. - 2800 cub.yds. @ 4/- £560 say.	£600	600
9.	POWER HOUSE MACHINERY		
	2 turbines at £2800		
	2 alternators at 3500 c.i.f. Mombasa		12,600
10.	OVERHEAD CRANE c.i.f. Mombasa		400
11.	RAIL FREIGHT, transport and erection of all power house plant including crane		4,600
12.	TWO STEP-UP transformers (2500 KVA each) and local service transformer, erected say.		4,000
13.	SWITCHGEAR erected, say		2,500
14.	LAND DAMAGES	£250	
	Local Expenses	3500	
	Staff Quarters	2000	5,750
			52,150
	Engineering 5%, contingencies and insurance 10% ...		7,830
			£59,980

Contractors' profit is included in the various items

i.e. £60,000

My estimate for the Maragua-Tana Scheme

Reflecting on my time in Kenya it seemed to me that a happy native in Nairobi was one who at intervals could disappear to the Reserve, discard the few European clothes he possessed, and do exactly as he pleased, put red mud on his hair, make his body shine with grease, watch his wives do all the work and put them in the family way before he returned to town.

I recall a drive through an estate where the native riding in the back of our safari car jumped out to open a gate. After holding the gate open to allow the car to pass, he forgot to go through it himself, so he closed it and climbed over it to rejoin us.

Another story is also indicative of a native's mind. A house-boy returning to his master's bungalow found the back door locked. So he deposited his load of groceries, went round to the front door which he knew was unlocked, walked through the house to unlock the back door, and then walked back through the house and round the outside to pick up his parcels and take them in through the back door.

On my return to the office in London I finalised the report and estimate for my proposal to develop the Magarua-Tana Scheme. I also produced a further report with alternatives, including a 1,500 kW Maragua scheme costing £85k, and a second stage 4,000 kW Tana scheme costing £125k which would treble the EAP&L's generating capacity by 1933 to meet the anticipated demand.

Back in Kenya in 1930 for the Tribunal

In February 1930 Shearer asked me to return to Kenya on my way back from an assignment in India. He wanted me to review the alternative sites available for a hydro-power scheme in view of the local political difficulties which had arisen with the Maragua-Tana scheme I had proposed. The scheme had been put to a Government Tribunal to decide whether or not EAP&L should be given a concession to develop it.

Upon arrival in Nairobi I checked into the New Stanley Hotel and went to the office to meet the Chairman, H.F. Ward. He told me that the company had failed in the first of three meetings of the Tribunal to make a good case for the scheme because it involved the flooding and therefore the expropriation of some land belonging to the Kikuyu tribe, in spite of the very generous compensation land of better quality and larger area which had been offered in exchange.

Before the next meeting of the Tribunal, which had been delayed until my arrival in Kenya, the Tribunal Chairman, who was the Chief Justice of Kenya, asked me to inspect a possible alternative water-power site many miles lower down the Tana River, twice as far from Nairobi as the scheme we had proposed.

After a week studying the evidence and working up plans for possible alternatives I finalised arrangements for a further survey safari. With my usual good luck I was able to engage as our 'white hunter' and leader of the party, Hubert Stanton, who happened to be free and able to make similar arrangements for us as he had done in 1927.

This safari, like my previous ones, was full of adventure and we had similar difficulties in getting our two 30-cwt Chevrolet trucks across small rivers with sandy bottoms and through black cotton bogs with the help of piles of brushwood, using one truck to pull the other out of trouble. As in 1927 we encountered scores of animals: rhinos, hippos galore, crocodiles, zebras, baboons, water buck, impala, dik-dik, duiker, hyenas, and giraffes as well as the fresh spores of buffalo and elephant.

Thunderstorms in the afternoons and evenings were a nuisance as were the tsetse flies until dark. During that week in the bush we visited the original Ndula scheme, made a walk-over survey of the Seven Forks reach and the Maragua-Tana site and visited the Thika scheme as well as various smaller project sites. Of all these, the largest potential capacity was at the Seven Forks reach and the Maragua-Tana site. Both could produce approximately 10,000 kilowatts in an extremely dry season, which was our projection of the demand in 10 years' time, assuming the Colony developed faster than was usual in Europe.

With EAP&L staff on a walk-over survey at Seven Forks in 1930 lt to rt:
A. Sehoff, mains engineer who later died of leprosy, Harry Lott,
J.H. Odam (General Manager), and Murrell
(Government Hydraulic Engineer)

Tribunal in Nairobi on 17th March 1930

Our safari confirmed our earlier conclusion that the Maragua-Tana scheme would be far superior in cost and efficiency to the proposed alternative and I made this clear in my 'expert' evidence to the Tribunal on 17th March.

The Tribunal was concerned to establish that the proposed scheme would be in the public interest by keeping the price of power down. The power was required by flour and sisal mills and saw-mills as well as by the public. As all the schemes proposed were in native reserves, Ward, on behalf of EAP&L, had offered 2,700 acres of better value land in lieu of the 1,600 acres required by the scheme, to ensure that the natives were adequately compensated and that commercial interests would not profit excessively.

Ward, Odam and Dr Matthews attended the Tribunal with me, and I started my evidence by giving my credentials and that of my company, Balfour Beatty, who were in the forefront of power engineers in the world. I mentioned that I had just returned from India where the State of Madras had appointed us as their agents for a large hydro-power scheme in that State. I told the Tribunal that a hydro-power scheme would be the most cost effective and appropriate method of generation for Nairobi, advising against steam generation in view of the high cost of coal and its transportation from the coast. With its capital cost fixed, the average cost of power from a hydro scheme reduced as the power demand increased, whereas a coal or oil-fired power station's costs rose in proportion to the demand.

I gave several reasons for my recommendation of the Maragua-Tana site. Firstly, the available head was so much higher at 240 ft compared with 160 ft at Seven Forks. Secondly, the distance from the power company's system of supply was approximately 12½ miles compared with 44 miles from Seven Forks. Thirdly, the cost, which for both the above reasons favoured the Maragua-Tana site. It would cost approximately £200,000 to get 10,000 kW from the Maragua-Tana site to Nairobi compared to about £400,000 to get the same amount of power from Seven Forks. Furthermore the Maragua-Tana site could be developed more quickly and in stages. I pointed out that cheap power was an important factor in leading to economic prosperity in many countries and quoted the examples of Switzerland, Canada, and the USA.

The Tribunal hearing that day was all over by 12.30 pm having only lasted 2½ hours, and in the evening I entertained Hubert Stanton, his fiancée Miss Rosemary Riches and Miss Davis to dinner and dancing at Torrs Hotel which had recently opened across the road from the New Stanley Hotel where I was staying.

The New Stanley Hotel, Nairobi – 1930

Torrs Hotel, Nairobi – 1927

The following day the Tribunal proceedings were fully reported in the East African Standard, including my comment that I thought the memorandum and evidence given by C. Udall, the Mayor of Nairobi, was 'ludicrous'. That evening I met him for a chat over drinks in the lounge at the Nairobi Club; he was good company and bore me no grudge.

In August 1930 we were informed that Lord Passfield had vetoed our Maragua-Tana Scheme and it was a matter of grief to me that twenty eight years were to elapse before the much larger 8,000 kW Low Tana Scheme at Seven Forks was completed in 1955 at the site which I had recommended in 1927. In the meantime the EAP&L in Nairobi was forced to add large numbers of oil engines and to rely on power from Owen Falls, 253 miles away in Uganda, to meet the growth in demand for electricity.

After the Tribunal I spent several days in Nairobi finalising my report and evidence. Feeling poorly I went to bed early with a high temperature; the next morning the doctor diagnosed malaria and prescribed 27/30 grains of quinine for 4 days followed by 15 grains for a week.

Odam was also in bed with malaria which we had probably caught at Seven Forks. The quinine worked and we both felt well enough to go on another safari with Haines to revisit the other sites on the Maragua which were potentially suitable for a dam, power-house, pipelines, and head-works, taking measurements of levels, water flows and velocities along the way.

Government Road, Nairobi – 1927

Final Days in East Africa - April 1930

Before leaving Nairobi, when I had finished giving evidence before the Lord Passfield Tribunal, I paid brief visits to Eldoret and Nakuru to visit the sites where, later, we provided electricity generating stations and distributions systems.

Then, on 6th April, I ended my mission in East Africa by flying to Tanganyika with Tom Campbell Black in his 2-seater de Havilland Gipsy Moth, 'Knight of the Mist', with its 4-cylinder engine. It was a bumpy ride and I suffered from air-sickness, alleviated by a brandy at the hotel when we refuelled at Moshi. We landed a couple of hours later on a small, improvised landing ground at Kirogwe where we were apparently the first aeroplane to land.

Waiting for my pilot, Campbell Black, at Nairobi airport – April 1930

This was the prelude to a day's visit to the Great Pangani Falls on the Pangani River. The flight of 340 miles, my first in Africa, took nearly 4 hours and took us past Mt Kilimanjaro and Mt Meru. The cost of chartering the plane, an air-taxi of the East African Airways Company, was 2/6d per mile. Campbell Black had just piloted the Prince of Wales in the same plane during his safari in Kenya. Before returning to Nairobi he flew on to the island of Zanzibar where his was apparently the first plane ever to land.

Pangani Falls, Tanganyika

Watkins met me at Kirogwe and took me to his bungalow for dinner and the night. The next day we drove to Herr von Ditfurth's place where we hired a native guide who took us on one of the most strenuous walks I have experienced, several miles through tropical bush from Makinyumbi to Pangani Falls and back in torrential rain.

At the Great Falls I descended and twice climbed the 330 ft escarpment to view and photograph the cascades. Prickly heat quickly spread all over my body from my neck to my ankles and drove me almost desperate. Having no remedy to hand I stripped off my clothes and rubbed myself with a lemon which eased the irritation somewhat. Getting soaked in a tropical downpour during the long tramp back was refreshing. The only umbrella which one of our party (another European and two natives) had was carried by one of the natives to protect the rolls of film that I had exposed. My photographs proved invaluable later when Power Securities Corporation secured the concession from the Tanganyika Government to harness the Great Falls; they helped during the planning of the surveys which were a necessary preliminary to our design proposals.

My photographs of the Pangani falls were 'stitched' together by Kodak and made into a picture which later hung over the fireplace in the breakfast room of my home in Wivenhoe.

Having recovered from my trek of the day before, I was driven for four hours on a muddy road to Tanga to embark on a ship for Mombasa. Over lunch in Tanga I was introduced to several local business people and was driven to inspect a sisal factory at Kange before boarding the SS Dumra, a small coastal steamer of the British India line bound for Mombasa.

Returning Home

I spent 3½ days in Mombasa before embarking on another British India ship, the SS Matiana, bound for London via Marseilles. On the voyage home I became friendly with J.B. Ryan, a young American millionaire, son of the Ryan tobacco family, who was taking a tame zebra back home to America. Also I had discussions with Capt. Glen Kidston, another millionaire and well known in the racing and flying world, and we exchanged stories of our various safaris. He died in an air-crash in May 1931 after flying from London to Cape Town in 6½ days.

Leaving the ship at Suez with Ryan and others, we had a very cold early morning drive across the desert to Cairo, reaching Shepheard's Hotel in time for breakfast. We motored to the Pyramids and visited Tutankhamun's treasures in the Cairo Museum before leaving by train for Port Said and rejoining our ship.

Several of us disembarked in Marseilles and I travelled with Glen Kidston and Ryan on the luxurious Blue Train to Paris and thence to Calais and Dover, arriving a week earlier than if we had remained on-board.

When Mr. "Tom" Campbell Black was farming in Kenya his name was known only locally; within a few months it had become known throughout the English-speaking world. There can be few cases of a settler's name achieving such rapid prominence.

Born in 1897, and educated at Brighton College, Mr. Black served during the War with the R.N.A.S. and R.A.F. After flying a Handley-Page to Egypt, he and a brother took up land at Rongai, but he soon joined two other settlers in purchasing an aeroplane, with which they gave "joy-flights" in Nakuru. Becoming managing director of Wilson Airways, Ltd., a company formed in Kenya by Mrs. F. K. Wilson, of Nanyuki, Mr. Black has since flown repeatedly between Africa and Europe, and has done a great deal of pioneer flying throughout East Africa.

In 1929 he was awarded the Robinson Trophy for the most meritorious flight in East Africa during the year, he was the first to fly from Nairobi to Mombasa and back in a day, the first to land in Zanzibar, and the first to fly non-stop from Zanzibar to Nairobi and from Dar es Salaam to Nairobi. During the second visit of the Prince of Wales to East Africa Mr. Black acted as pilot to His Royal Highness whilst he was on "safari." His chief recreation is riding, and he is often seen in the saddle on Kenya racecourses and at polo.

Arrival of the first aeroplane to land in Zanzibar, Wilson Airways' "Knight of the Mist," piloted by Mr. T. Campbell Black. April 6 1930
after flying H.C.Lorr from Nairobi to Kirogwe (Tanganyika) Photo: D'Lord, Zanzibar.

When Campbell Black landed his DH Gypsy Moth on the golf course, his was the first aeroplane to land in Zanzibar – April 1930

Friends and Acquaintances made in Kenya

During the months I had spent in Kenya in the previous three or four years I made several friends and many interesting acquaintances in addition to my colleagues in the East African Power & Lighting Company. Of these, Hubert Stanton and Denis Ker were the two Kenyans with whom I kept in touch every Christmas. Ker and his partner later set up the safari firm Ker and Downey.

Col. Wellington Furlong

Another of the friends I made whilst staying at the Muthaiga Country Club in Nairobi was Colonel Wellington Furlong, an American who was starting a long safari escorting the young Guggenheim, the copper millionaire's son. He was employing Stanton as his white hunter and organiser and we became good friends. We began an annual correspondence and I entertained him at my Club in London. After I retired he and his wife visited us at home in Wivenhoe. He was the most versatile American I ever met; he had served in Turkey during the First World War as a Major in the US Army Intelligence Service and went to the Versailles Peace Conference at the end of the War as a Special Military Aide to President Wilson. He was also an author who illustrated his own works, an explorer who had visited Tierra del Fuego, a lecturer, and an accomplished mouth organ player.

I met many other interesting and well-known people in the Club. No one could have been bossier, telling the dance band what dances suited him, than Lord Delamere, 'the uncrowned king of the British settlers', who acted as a sort of dictator.

I had long talks with Sir Pyers Mostyn, 11th Baronet of Talacre, Flintshire, and we spent some time inspecting each other's travel photographs. He had inherited the baronetcy and the Talacre Estate from his cousin who had been killed in the War in 1917. Sadly, he also died young, at the age of 44, only 7 years after we met, and the Estate had to be sold.

The Hon. Denys Finch Hatton, the English aristocrat, big-game hunter, and lover of Baroness Karen Blixen was a director of EAP&L, as was Colonel Marcuswell Maxwell whose wife I met again in London a year or so later; she told me that during her husband's absences from home she kept a loaded revolver under her pillow so that she was ready to fire if anyone tampered with the screen covering the open window. But personal danger from the natives in Kenya was not serious in those days – in fact not until the Mau Mau troubles many years later.

The Hon. Cyril Ward, son of the 1st Earl of Dudley, whom I had met at the Club when he had just sold his farm, was killed together with his native servant in an air crash in 1930 not long after I returned to London; he was only 53. Finch Hatton also died, burnt to death in an aeroplane accident at Voi in Kenya in May 1931.

Others I met were Lord Carbery and Major Conrad Walsh as well as Mr Charles Huberich and his young wife, Princess Nina Mdivani of Georgia.

As the London manager with responsibility for EAP&L projects I kept in touch with the company throughout my time in Balfour Beatty and Eddie Rollo, the General Manager in the 1960s, sent me copies of the company magazine describing the progress being made on electricity supply in Kenya, Uganda, and Tanganyika.

The picture here shows the first stage of the £37 million, 100 MW Kindaruma scheme at Seven Forks which was inaugurated in March 1965 by President Kenyatta. Charles Udall, then 90 years old, attended the ceremony and, in his address, the Balfour Beatty Chairman, Sir Andrew MacTaggart, said he had received a message of goodwill and prosperity for the Project from 'another young spirit, Mr H.C. Lott, junior to Mr Udall by a mere seven years, and going strong in a lively retirement'. It had taken 37 years from my initial walk-over surveys of the Tana for this huge scheme to become a reality. During these years, the designs had been altered and improved many times, the political winds had changed, and the necessary capital had eventually been raised.

The Kindaruma Hydro-Electric Power Scheme
at Seven Forks on the Tana River

The staff newspaper of the East African Power & Lighting Company gave me a warm send-off when I retired on 11th November 1955. In their March 1956 issue, Don Small expressed the great regret of the older members of the company's staff in hearing of the retirement of Colonel Harry C Lott, MC, AMICE, and wrote:

'Harry Lott had a distinguished record in the First World War in the Royal Engineers and, prior to that, had wide experience of transmission line and hydro-electric work, particularly in Canada. Joining Balfour Beatty shortly after the War he has been continuously in charge of East African engineering affairs in the London office. During that time he was of inestimable service to the East African Undertakings and in particular to the Management as a guide and friend, and it is fitting that the debt of the Undertakings to him should be fully acknowledged.

He was always particularly good with young people, had a gift for putting them at their ease and thereby getting the best out of them.

He will be missed by many of us during our infrequent visits to the London office.'

Extracts from the Balfour Beatty Review in March 1965 following the opening of the Kindaruma dam and the first stage of the Seven Forks Project

*** *FRONTISPIECE*

LOTT'S ROAD

IT ALL BEGAN in 1927, *when Balfour Beatty (then a teenager) in the person of Mr. H. C. Lott, made a first reconnaissance of the proposed Seven Forks, Kenya, Hydro-Electric Scheme. On foot, accompanied by* 36 *porters and a white hunter, Lott set out on his hazardous task. There were no roads, no tracks, except for those of the animals. Meeting rhino, lion, ~~tiger~~, elephant, other creatures, fierce and gentle, of the jungle the party cut their way through* 100 *miles of bush. Prospecting, surveying, noting.*

There followed years of effort to secure ways and means of launching the massive undertaking. Far-sighted Kenyans co-operated energetically with Power Securities Corporation, the East African Power and Lighting Company. In 66 *Queen Street, more recently Bow Bells House, blue prints in their scores came off the Balfour Beatty drawing boards; to be critically assessed, set aside, revised, superseded as the exciting ideas of gifted engineers changed and improved. Like Lott's initial journey, the way continued hard. But the Chairman, with the Government of Kenya, refused to abandon a purpose the successful pursuit of which would benefit so abundantly a young, expanding nation.*

In 1964 *their faith and energy were rewarded. The preliminary monetary target achieved, there came the signal to begin.*

* * *

If you still doubt the association of happiness with hard work, look long and contemplatively overleaf. On March 5, 1965 *at Kindaruma, on the site of the dam wall which will contain the waters of the Tana River, President Kenyatta inaugurated the first stage of the Seven Forks Project.*

In one of the happiest pictures it has ever been the privilege of the REVIEW to print are His Excellency the Honourable Jomo Kenyatta, President of Kenya, the Chairman, and the Minister for Works, Communications and Power, the Hon. Dawson Mwanyumba, M.P. The President has detonated the first shot. The gigantic Scheme is afoot. 'Happiness,' David Grayson observed, 'I have discovered is nearly always a rebound from hard work.' Our picture (from the camera of Ines May) is a shining proof.

When we talk of Visions, let us remember Seven Forks. Thirty-seven years of envisagement, of courage and of hope: thirty-seven million pounds. Our toast is, 'All success to one of the world's greatest engineering projects.'

2

Balfour Beatty Review 1956

MR. HARRY C. LOTT

THE seventy-two-year life of Colonel Harry C. Lott, M.C., A.M.I.C.E., who retired from the service of the Company on November 11, 1955, has been a colourful one.

He came down from London University in 1904 and his first real job was the inspection of the manufacture and subsequent laying of the 1905 Atlantic Cable. Then, having had a glimpse of Canada, he decided to emigrate. He did, landing in Montreal in 1907 with £7 in pocket and no job. He spent seven wonderful years on engineering projects in five different provinces, working for consulting engineers on hydro-electric surveys (including diving) dams and power plants, as well as working on transmission line construction. On the line he spent 2½ years in a tent in Northern Manitoba, under much rougher conditions than would be allowed or tolerated today. In Montreal in 1912 he met Mr. J. M. Crabbe, who was then working for the same consultants. In 1914 he threw up his job to join the Army at home, and was in the trenches in France within 3½ months of donning uniform. He had four years in France, where he won the Military Cross, followed by 4½ years in Mespot (Iraq) and N.W. Persia. As Director of the E. & M. Services he was responsible for the supply of electricity, water and ice in Baghdad, Basrah, Mosul and many other towns, also for the final construction of a new 350-mile road over three mountain ranges in Persia, from Quaraitu to Kasvin.

Charles Huberich and Princess Nina Mdivani 'almost an affair'

Returning from my Kenyan trip in August 1927, on board the ship in Mombasa bound for Genoa I found that Mr Charles H. Huberich and his wife, Nina, were fellow passengers. I had met and become very friendly with them both whilst staying at the Muthaiga Club. Charles Huberich was an international lawyer with an office in New York. He had married the young Princess Nina Mdivani, his second wife, two years before we met as guests at a dinner at the Club given by Major Robertson-Eustace, MP for Mombasa.

Princess Nina Mdivani

After the dinner, the Princess read my palms and those of another guest, Capt. Robinson of the newly formed Kenyan Broadcasting Corporation. Both of us were greatly impressed by the extraordinary accuracy of her prediction that Robinson was likely to fall in love with a sick woman. This strange remark was in fact true, for, apparently unbeknown to her, Robinson was visiting a lady in hospital where she was being treated for tuberculosis and she became his fiancée.

During the voyage from Mombasa to Genoa I spent much time with Charles and Nina and at Suez we disembarked together and went to Cairo by train. There we three took a car to the Mena House Hotel and thence, on camels, to the Sphinx, which had only recently been fully excavated.

Charles Huberich and Nina on camels at Giza

On camels to see the Sphinx and Pyramids at Giza

The Nile at Cairo in 1927

At the Pyramids we watched a man run up to the top of the Great Pyramid in 5 minutes and back in 3 minutes. That night, which was too noisy and too hot to sleep, we put up at the Continental Savoy Hotel in the centre of Cairo. On our last morning there, the three of us visited the Cairo Museum and saw the marvellous Tutankhamun treasures before leaving by train for Port Said and rejoining the ship.

Princess Nina Mdivani was 23 when she married the 59 year old Charles Huberich in 1925. The Mdivani's were an aristocratic Georgian family who had fled to Paris in 1921 after the Soviets invaded Georgia. Nina, who had three younger brothers, was charming and I got on particularly well with her; there was a frisson between us. Our conversations on board were many and interesting, however

Sir Henri Deterding & Lydia (Kondoyoroff)

I detected some loss of interest in me when she learnt that I was 44 years old; 15 years older than she thought – or so she said.

Nevertheless, we met again in London on several occasions in the 1930's. Nina entertained me and her friend Lady Lydia Deterding, the Russian wife of the oil magnate Sir Henri Deterding, to lunch at the Berkeley Hotel in Knightsbridge. As neither of their husbands was present, I realised that I was the gigolo of the party.

At one stage during the lunch Nina, seizing a bit of paper, scribbled a note on it:

'*To a disappointing, hard to get heart bachelor, but we are married women and love.... don't be so cold.*'

Jose Maria Sert (1874-1945)

Determined to meet her husband again for a semi-business talk, I invited the Princess and Charles Huberich to a dinner-dance at the Savoy Hotel. Previously, with Santorelli the maître d'hôtel, I had arranged that the menu for the meal would include something never before served in London – mango fool. I am not sure that Nina noticed the intentional 'double entendre'. She turned up in a remarkable black dress with a feathered bodice and a new hairdo, both the result of a visit to Paris. I therefore found myself dancing with the most elegant and distinguished looking woman on the floor. Between dances I discussed an East African business prospect with Huberich who seemed interested.

On another occasion, over cocktails at her hotel, she suggested quite seriously that we should go off together, first to Barcelona to her sister Isabelle, the wife of Jose Maria Sert, the Catalan painter and muralist, and then to the Muthaiga Club in Nairobi where we had met. As attractive and intelligent as she was, I was not prepared to be drawn into an affair with her - it might have been fun and an adventure but would have been far beyond my means to entertain her in the style to which she was accustomed.

Nina eventually divorced her 70 year old husband in The Hague. The very next day, in the same court in The Hague, Lady Deterding divorced her husband who was also about twice her own age. I continued to send Christmas greetings to Huberich and was surprised to receive greeting cards in 1937 and 1941 signed by both Charles and Nina. After her divorce Nina remained friends with her former husband of 11 years and they foregathered occasionally.

5-5-36

Princess Nina Mdivani Sues for Divorce

'STILL FRIENDLY,' SAYS LAWYER HUSBAND

Country House Taken in Sussex

THE "Evening Standard" learns that Princess Mdivani has filed a petition for divorce at The Hague against her husband, Mr. Charles Henry Huberich, the well-known International lawyer. The grounds are understood to include incompatibility.

Mr. Huberich said to-day: "We are still on the friendliest of terms despite the petition."

Princess Nina Mdivani is the sister of the three famous Mdivani brothers—the late

PRINCESS NINA MDIVANI

When her second husband, Denis Conan Doyle, died in 1955 she married his secretary, Anthony Harwood. At one of the parties she gave, Nina introduced me to her brother Prince Alexis Mdivani who was married to, and later divorced by, Barbara Hutton, the

Woolworth heiress. He was killed in a car crash in Spain whilst driving his Rolls Royce in a 90 mph dash to catch a train to Paris for his fellow passenger, Baroness Maud Thyssen. His estate of £2 million was divided between his siblings, leaving Nina about £400,000.

Pola Negri & Serge Mdivani

Nina's brother Serge married Pola Negri, the famous Polish actress and film-star and another brother married Mae Murray, also a famous film star.

Nina wrote the following letter to me from the Hotel Splendide in Piccadilly after we had we returned to London. I kept the letter as a relic of 'almost an affair':

Dear Mr Lott

I am forgotten and so soon – but I know you are terribly busy. I kept your violets very long on my little table near me and thought how nice it was of you to bring them to me. Please telephone to me Tuesday, before 10 o'clock in the morning, as I want to see you before I go again.

Nina Huberich

PS. Please don't feel in reading this letter full of faults as you felt the day of camel riding in Egypt.

London in 1927 and 1928

In my annual financial review in January 1927 I noted that the previous year had been my worst financially for a long time: 'I am appreciably poorer than at this time last year due to unfortunate speculation in rubber shares which have slumped in the last two months.'

However, this did not seem to cramp my style in entertaining and I continued dining out with friends three or four times a week. Amongst the many dinners which I hosted my diary notes that in February 'I took Leslie West and Carlos Brandes to the Piccadilly Hotel where I dined them both well with champagne, oysters, sole bonne-femme, cutlet, fruit and cream, costing a total of £4.10s'.

The following week I took Miss Skrine to dinner at the same hotel before we went on to the Welbeck Palace Hotel where 'I danced with half a dozen partners'. Although I was 44 years old this was 'my first experience of the kind' and I escorted Miss Skrine, Mrs Palmer, and another lady home to their place in Warrington Crescent, Little Venice, returning to my Club 'in the early hours of the morning'. The Van Dyck School used the Welbeck Palace Hotel for dancing classes, and it became one of our regular venues for dances on a Wednesday evening. On other occasions I changed into tails and took Miss Skrine to dinner and dancing at the Riviera Club (£1.17s. each) or the Savoy Hotel (£4 for the two of us).

Other evening venues we frequented were the Royal Palace Hotel, the Empress Rooms, Dartmouth House in Charles Street, and the Golden Square Club where we went with Malcolm Gunn and his partner and danced 'but only the waltz as the floor was rather crowded with Charlestoners'. Sometimes I would 'refresh at the Strand Palace Hotel before returning to the Club' generally between midnight and 1 am.

During the year there were advances in radio and television technology which I could see would change our way of life dramatically. The first public demonstration of television by John Logie Baird in his laboratory had been in 1926 and this was quickly followed by longer distance transmissions. On 8th April I wrote that 'the Beam system of wireless to Australia was put into commercial use yesterday. Some American journalists in New York were given a demonstration of wireless television from Washington, 220 miles away, with the voice of the event being transmitted simultaneously. There is no doubt that television will become as important in the future as wireless is today.'

The motor car industry was also expanding fast and Henry Ford, who had been making Model 'T' Fords for 18 years, set a new standard by introducing an 8 hour, 5 day working week. Several of my friends were now buying cars; Leslie West bought a Morris Oxford Coupé for £250, and Malcolm Gunn took me to Colchester one weekend in his A.C. Sports car where I picked up my Clyno Tourer from the car park and drove on to Woodgates. Clara and Bob Fitch arrived later in their new Morris Cowley. A year or two later a friend of mine bought a 2nd hand Morris Cowley for only £35. These early cars did not hold their value; my Clyno, although still running well, was already showing a few rust patches.

After returning from Kenya in the autumn of 1927 I slipped into my usual routine at the Constitutional Club; it was so very convenient and economical for meals and entertaining. Wines, including the fabulous 1921 Hock which I generally ordered, were available at very little above cost price. I dined well, even when on my own, and my diary records dinners of sole and marrow on toast or oeuf mornay and asparagus followed in the season by 'lots of strawberries and cream', then by cheese with a hock. Lunches were more casual; one lunch at Lyons cost me only 1s.7½d for beef steak and kidney pie with mashed potatoes, brown bread and butter, stewed prunes and cream and a large white coffee.

At weekends I went back to Woodgates where my father, then aged 78, was still farming and losing money at it whilst I guaranteed his ever-increasing overdraft at the bank. The aunts would come to tea, bridge, and supper after which I would take them home. And on Sunday mornings I would walk to Mistley and back (about 5 miles each way) to see Clara, Bob, and little John if they had not come over to Woodgates that weekend.

My father had long since sold his old car, a 'T' Model Ford, and had taken to doing some cycling. On his 80th birthday I gave him a new bicycle with a lower frame which made it easier for him to mount and dismount, but failing sight soon stopped his use of it. Sometimes I had a little pheasant shooting, walking around the farm with him and his gun-shy and utterly useless dog.

As well as my regular work on EAP&L business I spent many long hours in the office on the preparation of tenders for power plants, transmission lines or other infrastructure projects, sometimes until 10.30 or 11.30 at night and even until 2.15 am on the final day before one submission. The schemes on which we were bidding were many and varied and included projects for the electrification of Central and South-East England, the Grampian Power Scheme, electrification of the suburban lines of the Great Indian Peninsular Railway in Bombay, a Santa Fe to Panama Transmission line and the amalgamation of Montevideo Tramways.

Music was important to me and I enjoyed going to concerts at the Queen's Hall with my cousin Amy Lott to hear the London Symphony Orchestra under Felix Weingartner. One evening, after dining at the Piccadilly Hotel, we listened to a programme of works by Elgar conducted by the composer himself. It wasn't until four years later that I went to a sale of second hand pianos at Harrods and bought a Steinway upright grand piano for 88 guineas and had it delivered to Woodgates so that I could play it when I was at home at weekends. I eventually sold it in 1953 when I could no longer stretch an octave easily, and I used the proceeds to buy our first television set in order to watch the Coronation of Queen Elizabeth II.

Job Offers

In 1927 I had more than one opportunity to leave Balfour Beatty & Co. and improve my position. Before I left for Kenya, Tom Parry whose niece, Barbara Herring, I was destined to marry in 1942, dined me at the Chemical Industries Club in Whitehall and told me of a new and subsequently very successful cement company being formed – the Ketton Cement Co. He wanted me to become its Managing Director at a salary of £1,000 per year until it was producing cement when the salary would promptly increase. He was my sister-in-law Dot's elder brother, and it was Charles' success, both in managing men and the operations at the Kirton Cement works, that had decided him in my favour. Some 10 years before that Parry had introduced me to a job in a modern works in the heart of Sheffield. So this Ketton Cement opportunity was the second I had turned down; I did not see myself as a factory manager.

In September I was lunched at Simpson's in the Strand by Evan Parry (no relation of Tom's), a partner in the firm of Preece, Cardew and Rider, Consulting Engineers to the Government and particularly to the Colonial Office. After the meal, which turned out to be an interview, Parry asked me 'if I would consider an appointment as Director of Electrical Undertakings for the Ceylon Government at £2,500 per year'.

Now Ceylon was about to embark upon its first hydro-electric project, however, after a few days of enquiries and reflection, I entertained Parry to lunch at my Club and declined what had at first seemed an attractive move. I had learnt of political intrigue and corruption in Ceylon Government circles and had also discussed the offer with my Managing Director, Wm Shearer, with whom I was prepared to take another chance. I decided that a bird in the hand was worth, in this case, 2 birds (£2,500 pa) in the bush. Thus I made another of several career decisions which greatly affected my future – for better or worse. Recognising that I might be tempted by other interesting opportunities, Shearer, who had been phased by the resignation of one of his other engineers, raised my salary to £1,200 pa back-dated to April.

During the dark winter evenings of November and early December I wrote my annual Christmas letters to relatives and friends around the world. Of the 100 or so letters I wrote each year about 60 were sent first to friends overseas. I spent just over £100 on Christmas presents which included £5 in the Club Christmas box plus 10 shilling tips for several of the staff. To Mother I sent £50 plus some delicacies and Christmas crackers; I gave my 'driver' Painter £10 and sent boxes of chocolates to various lady friends and relatives.

Christmas in Paris

Over the Christmas holiday an engineering friend, W.H.J. Miller, and I spent a week in Paris. We 'did' Versailles and all the usual sights, walking miles during the day before going for nights out on the town in Montmartre at the Moulin Rouge and the Folies Bergère. For rather more cultural evenings we went to La Tosca at the Opera Comique and Wagner's Rheingold at the Grand Opera House. On Christmas Day we attended High Mass in La Madeleine and the evening service in Notre Dame where the cardinal was the focus of the elaborate ceremonial. The Roaring Twenties were lively years in Paris – the musical halls were flourishing, and the artist Soutine was capturing the serving classes in his paintings of the cooks, waiters and bell-boys of the city's hotels and restaurants.

1928

My accounts at the end of 1927 showed net assets of £6,324 (almost all in stocks and shares) and a salary of £1,140 plus £228 from my investments which gave me a net income of £1,251 after tax of £117. My expenditure that year was a little bit less, at £1,136, and I noted to myself that 'economies plus appreciation of investments are necessary to effect progress'. However, I was doing better than my brother Charles who told me that he was worth £4,500 and was hoping to increase that to £6,000 by the end of his five-year contract as manager of the Kirton cement works.

I spent New Year in Lincolnshire with Charles and his family at Breezemount in Kirton. It was 10 miles south of Scunthorpe where I was taken by his friend Eric Elmquist to see the 300 ton/hour breaker plant at the Appleby Iron & Steel works and the nearby power plant, with its MAN-Vickers gas engines and a 6000 kW BTH turbine, before I caught a train back to London.

As well as weekends with family and friends in the East Bergholt area I often went for dinner after work with my sister May and her family in Harrow. On the train coming back one evening, my diary notes that at Wembley 'we were joined by a weird crowd who go to the greyhound races – a sport recently introduced in England last summer'. I also spent a weekend with my nephew Jack Lott in Loughborough where he was studying at the Technical College. He showed me around the workshops, and we had a 12 mile walk to Stanford-le-Soar and Normanton-le-Soar before I returned to London on the Sunday evening train.

In January 1928, the deaths were announced of Thomas Hardy and Field Marshall Earl Haig, with both of whom I had had brief contact; and 14 people were reported drowned in their basements in Westminster when the Thames overflowed its banks.

The following month newspaper headlines told of an Australian, Bert Hinkler, who had flown solo from Croydon to Australia in a 30 hp single-seater aeroplane in 15½ days, beating the previous best time of 28 days. A few months later the first flights across the Atlantic (by von Hunefeld-Kohl and then Amelia Erhart) and across the Pacific (by Kingsford Smith and Ulm) were reported and the airline industry was born.

Love affairs and financial difficulties seemed to be dominating the lives of several of my friends. Leslie West's tales of woe increased with his continuing losses on the Stock Exchange and possible insolvency. Over our dinners together he told me of the brutality of his father and his frustrations with the volatile temperament of his fiancée whom he did eventually marry. Malcolm Gunn's brother's affairs had involved him badly and he was also talking of putting their firm into bankruptcy. Harrison Edwards, who had asked me to be his best man, called off his engagement not long before the wedding; and walking back to the Club with Carlos Brandes after dinner one evening, he told me that he was very much in love with a married lady from South Africa.

It was also a difficult time for me financially; the boom in the stock market periodically faltered and the fall in some commodity prices (rubber, oil, tobacco, and tea) resulted in my own portfolio incurring losses of over £700 in the first 4 months of 1928. Despite this I still had to guarantee Father's £250 overdraft at the bank in addition to the £750 I had loaned him and on which I had waived the interest. By the end of 1928 my net assets were down to £5,817 but, by cutting back on my expenditure, I managed to save £354 from my salary of £1,200 and £275 of investment income. When the market resumed its rise again in January 1929 I recovered some of my losses.

Earlier in the year I had had several recurrences of the malaria which I had caught in Kenya and was increasingly concerned about my health generally. I had put on almost a stone since returning from Kenya and was now over 14 stone and not happy with the distinct deterioration in my profile in a swim suit. I was also being treated for eczema in the ears by Dr Gray of New Cavendish Street who gave me several doses of X-rays to clear up the condition. Another specialist, Dr Mennell, fitted me with a finger splint to try to correct a fibrous growth which was pulling my little finger into the palm of my hand, diagnosed as Dupuytren's contracture. The splint was so painful that it kept me awake at night; he had advised against an operation which would disable me for 6 weeks and may not be successful. However, I decided later to have the operation which proved to be a great success.

Sharp pains in the groin, which the doctor diagnosed as probable appendicitis, had also caused me to take almost a week off work and have a few days bed-rest in the Club. These ailments, together with my losses on the stock market and the lack of any progress in my career at Balfour Beatty, resulted in me feeling somewhat depressed. Although still meeting friends and going out to dinner and the theatre two or three times a week, I was spending more evenings on my own at the Club and working long hours at the office without an assistant to do some of the relatively junior work. The fact that several of my friends were now either engaged or married probably did not help.

HMS Hood

'The Mighty Hood'

In April, at the invitation of my first cousin, Harold B. Sears, then Engr. Lt. Commander DSO, I went to Weymouth and thence by pinnace to board HMS Hood, a battle cruiser which, with Rodney, Renown and Repulse, was taking part in a Naval Review in honour of the King of Afghanistan. The review took place in 'thick weather' the day after my arrival on board and I was shown over the ship with its 160,000 hp engines and crew of 1,300. After the Review and speed runs at 25 knots past the Nelson, from which King Amanullah Khan was watching, we went to Plymouth.

That evening there was a special dinner for the guests, 8 of us including the Secretary of the Navy, given by the Admiral Dreyer in the wardroom. After the dinner with champagne and the gamut of wines, Harold and I paid a visit to the Warrant Officers' mess, there to be offered more and different drinks. At Plymouth I left the ship, again in a pinnace, after two nights aboard and caught an early train back to London.

'The Mighty Hood', as it was called, had been commissioned in 1920 and was the last of the Royal Navy's battle cruisers; the biggest warships then built. At Jutland, three of her sister ships had been blown up by long-range, plunging shells. Her armour should have been strengthened but never was. Between the wars the Hood 'showed the flag' to the Empire and the world. However, in an encounter with the Bismarck off Norway in May 1941, she was blown up by German gunfire. All except three of the crew of 1,418 men were killed by the explosion in the magazine. The Repulse and Renown, the former with my young godson, Harry Tayler on board, were torpedoed by the Japanese off Singapore; he luckily survived.

Holiday in Germany

In May I went for a week's holiday to Berlin via the Hook of Holland to stay with the family and friends of Carlos Brandes. In Berlin I was met by Carlos, Mrs Stella McNaught and Frau Maurice Talbot, our hostess whose husband had recently died, and we were driven to her summer home in Sackrow, near Potsdam. After several outings in Potsdam and Berlin and much entertaining, Carlos and I left and took a non-stop train to Hamburg. On this Sunday night train we were able to telephone Potsdam to thank our Berlin hostess, using headphones so that we had a three-cornered conversation. The call, transmitted by wireless, cost only 3 marks. The first trans-Atlantic telephone call, also by radio, had been made the previous year. After three nights at Blankensee near Hamburg with Carlos' German relatives, we headed back and boarded the new German liner SS Cap Acorna which had a full size tennis court on the top deck and a swimming pool on the bottom deck. I disembarked at Boulogne the next day and took a cross-channel steamer to Folkestone whilst Carlos stayed on board to go on to Brazil.

In an effort at self-improvement I decided to take a course in Pelmanism, designed to improve my memory, which it actually did. It also had the beneficial effect of improving my well-being and my self-discipline in food, work, and exercise. I managed to lose a stone in weight so that I was down to 13 stone when stripped before swimming.

During the unusually hot summer holidays I had spent a week at the sea-side at Dovercourt and Yarmouth where I took up swimming, and I began going to the pools in Marylebone and Great Smith Street to keep up the exercise when in London. Outings to the seaside at weekends and for summer holidays were the norm for most people in those days and the English seaside resorts such as Frinton, Walton and Clacton were flourishing. Few people could afford a foreign holiday.

For Christmas week I went to Bath and spent a few days at The Empire Hotel, swimming in the mineral waters of the Royal Baths before breakfast and going on trips to Bristol, Wells and Cheddar.

My parents John and Marion Lott on their Golden Wedding in 1924

Bob & Clara Fitch with John (5) and my mother at Woodgates c.1927

To Shanghai on the Trans-Siberian Express
Around the World in 78 days
1929

The year 1929 was for me another remarkably memorable one, starting with a business trip to Shanghai which took me around the world, and ending with a challenging business assignment in Southern India.

On 24th January, Mr George Balfour MP, Chairman of both Balfour Beatty and Power Securities Corporation, instructed me to go to Shanghai with a Mr Alfred Brooke-Smith as soon as our Russian visas could be obtained by a firm of Berlin travel agents. The agents sent a special messenger to Moscow to 'do the necessary' to obtain the visas and then delivered them by another messenger to us in London.

We were to represent a London syndicate of which the British Trusts Association, Power Securities Corporation and the Hong Kong & Shanghai Bank were the principal members. The syndicate had been formed to make a bid to purchase the Shanghai Electricity Department; one of the largest electricity undertakings outside the USA and one for which the Americans were known to be keen bidders.

Mr Brooke-Smith who was 10 years older than me was given Power of Attorney to act for the syndicate in Shanghai; he had once been Chairman of the Shanghai Municipal Council as well as Managing Director of Jardine Matheson & Co in Shanghai and was persona grata with all the key organisations there.

As Brooke-Smith was not an engineer I had been selected to accompany him and act as his engineering adviser and assistant.

But for the delay of 14 days in obtaining our Russian visas permitting us to enter the Soviet Republics in Europe and Asia, we might have left for China earlier, but I also had to obtain a new passport as my old one was completely full of stamps from my various travels in Europe and my 1924 voyage around the world. My feeling of being seen as a 'greenhorn' with a clean new passport soon wore off as the Russian, Polish and Chinese visas were added before our departure.

My passport photo – 1929

Whilst waiting for the visas I attended several meetings of the syndicate at one of which I was asked to submit, the next day, a skeleton draft of a Concession Agreement on which we could base our offer. The draft I presented was approved, almost without alteration. It was the result of another of the lucky strokes in my life, for I had found in the filing department of Balfour Beatty a copy of the Concession Agreement granted years before by the Shanghai Council to the purchasers of their Waterworks Department. And so, in a matter of hours, I was able to prepare a draft Agreement for the sale to the syndicate of the city's Electricity Supply Department. Not only did the syndicate use the draft but it was taken by the Power Committee of the Shanghai Council as the basis for tenders.

Our visas having arrived the previous evening, Brooke-Smith, his wife, and I left London on the morning of 6th February for Parkeston Quay and the Hook of Holland. I had 168 pounds weight of personal luggage including formal evening wear, my fancy dress outfit, and a complete set of tropical clothes for a possible assignment in Madras on my return journey.

We spent the first night in a most elaborately decorated wagon-lit across Holland to Berlin, arriving there the following morning. Here, with 12 hours to spare, we had an opportunity for a bath at the Hotel Bristol and to see the city under very wintry conditions. Europe was experiencing an exceptionally cold spell; even in southern England the temperature was zero Fahrenheit (32 degrees of frost) when we left, and it was several degrees below zero in Berlin.

The complicated business of registering our luggage right through to Southern Manchuria took hours but gave us time for a trip to Potsdam by car before boarding the train for Moscow via Poland. The train had only single glazed windows which were so covered in hoar frost that we could see nothing at all of the Polish towns or countryside. The spy-hole we made by breathing on the window froze over quickly before we could put an eye to it.

At the Russian frontier, where our baggage and passports were again examined, we transferred to a Russian train on their broader gauge, and this became our home for the next 8 days and nights during our journey across Siberia. It was noticeable that the Russian porters who transferred our bags refused a tip – a Soviet rule perhaps.

Moscow

We arrived in Moscow in the dark at 6 pm on 9th February, nearly 3½ hours late. We therefore saw very little of the city, except Red Square where we viewed Lenin's red granite tomb but did not go inside. Later, in Shanghai, a lady said to me: 'Oh, you should have seen Lenin; he is keeping ever so much better than Sun Yat-sen in Nanking – he is not keeping well at all.' Prof Vorobieff, who embalmed the body of Lenin by a special method in 1924, had apparently not expected the embalming to last more than a few months, but with control of the atmosphere in the glass canopy it is now likely to last almost indefinitely.

The temperature in Moscow was 30 degrees below zero (62 degrees of frost) and there was a distinct breeze blowing. With all my experience of winters living in the Canadian bush, I had never experienced quite such biting cold. We started our sightseeing around Red Square in a horse-drawn sleigh, but the cold was so painful that we changed to a rather ramshackle and wildly driven car in which we toured the rest of the city and looked into the magnificent church of St Saviour, built at fabulous cost after Napoleon's retreat from Moscow. Although it was a Saturday afternoon there was a large congregation attending the service.

My old Canadian cap of Persian lamb pulled down over my ears and a rabbit-fur collar I had bought for my overcoat in Berlin served me in good stead. However, we soon retired to the Grand Hotel close to Red Square to thaw out by running around a table in the hotel lounge and beating our hands. We had dinner at the hotel before boarding our train again at 10 pm. After a shot of vodka as an aperitif I chose hare soup, roast goose with cut apples and a baba au rhum desert. The hotel's rich furnishings of the Czarist times remained, including the elaborate chandeliers in the large dining room where an orchestra was playing classical music. However, Moscow generally had a lean and hungry look about it and the majestic, bearded commissionaire in richly coloured livery seemed to be a relic of earlier days.

Trans-Siberian Express

In pre-Revolution days a journey on the Trans-Siberian Express was considered one of the most luxurious train journeys in the world. Sadly, most of its glories departed when the Soviet Government confiscated all the rolling stock of the International Wagon Lits Company. However, with the exception of a distinct crudeness in the dining car equipment and service, and also the poor condition of the telescopic connections between the cars, we found little to complain about. There were, of course, no baths on the train so I had to employ the method, learned in the trenches in France, where we achieved an all-over wash using only a pint mug of water. I had a sleeping compartment to myself but shared a lavatory and wash basin with my next-door neighbour – opening my door automatically locked his. Our only complaint was that the heat was too great, but the windows were double glazed so that we could at least see the countryside throughout the journey.

The Trans-Siberian Express train

Before the Revolution, the Trans-Siberian train had been frequented by businessmen and officials but during our journey we saw very few travellers using the route; visas had become increasingly difficult to obtain for non-Communists. We were careful to avoid suspicion and took no photographs, writing our diaries at night when not under observation.

The evenings were usually spent playing bridge. Meals in the dining car were good and the menu was in four languages; Russian, German, French, and English. When entering Russia we had had to pay a heavy premium for the roubles required for the journey but in spite of this a 4-course meal cost only 3/6d plus 4d for vodka and 10d for Narzan mineral water.

Passengers who could not afford to eat in the dining car had opportunities at the longer stops of having hot meals in the elaborate station restaurants, decorated with candelabra and rubber plants, where the heat and the smell of steaming fur-coats was almost overpowering. Butter, eggs, and milk were also obtainable on the ice-covered station platforms and boiling water for tea could be drawn from taps protruding from well-lagged boilers on the platform.

The temperature throughout the 4,800 mile journey across Russia and Siberia rarely went above zero Fahrenheit. We reached Irkutsk on the Angara River close to Lake Baikal early on the ninth morning. Our sleeping car, which had developed an over-heated axle, was detached from the train and, without our being disturbed, was shunted into a running shed where it was lifted by crane whilst a fresh set of wheels was fitted; the whole operation delaying us only 2 hours. It was interesting to see suburban trains crowded with early morning workers arriving in Irkutsk, giving the station the atmosphere of a London terminus.

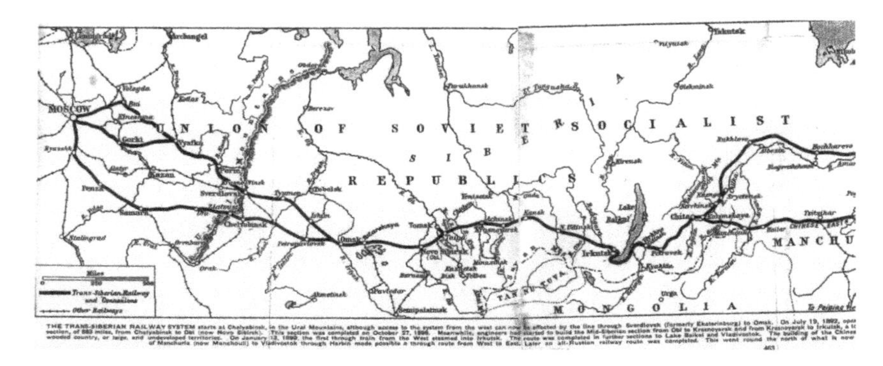

The route of the Trans-Siberian Express from Moscow to Irkutsk

From Irkutsk we experienced 205 miles of wonderful railway engineering around the southern tip of Lake Baikal, the deepest, oldest and one of the largest fresh water lakes in the world; it is 330 miles long from north to south and has an area of 11,580 sq. miles. At its maximum depth of over 5,000 ft it is the deepest depression on the earth's surface, being 3,800 ft below sea level. In the early days of the Trans-Siberian Railway the crossing of the lake was by ice-breaking ferry until the freeze-up when the ice became thick enough and a track with exceptionally long sleepers was laid so that trains could run over the ice. However, the emergency of the Russo-Japanese war of 1904 compelled the

Lake Baikal

construction of a line around the southern tip of the lake involving 42 tunnels totalling 4½ miles through solid rock.

After some climbs to over 2,000 ft the train was halted until the Russian 'chef du train' had checked that the hand-brakes were working properly on each car before the descent. The hand-brakes were operated by the car attendant who also looked after the wood-fired boiler that heated the car. In spite of the wintry conditions and the lengthy stops at all important stations to change engines, refuel with wood and take on water for the steam locomotive and sleeping cars, the train averaged 25 miles per hour, and we arrived at Manchouli, the frontier in those days between Russia and Manchuria, only 4 hours later than scheduled.

Manchuria

After passing through Customs we changed into a Chinese Eastern Railway (CER) train with the aid of Chinese porters who, although efficient, demanded large tips unlike their Russian counterparts. The Chinese Eastern Railway had been built across Manchuria by Imperial Russia to link Chita with Vladivostok in the Far East. Our very modern train, which had been built and was still owned and operated by the Russians, was to take us the remaining 1,015 miles to the port of Dairen in Southern Manchuria where we were to board a Japanese ship for Shanghai. Three or four years later the Russians sold the railway to the Japanese who had then wrested Manchuria from the Chinese.

Our greatest surprise was in the dining car where, on every table, there was a hot-house plant, purple and blue cinerarias in full bloom, with pot palms and fruit on a sort of buffet at the end of the car. At dinner we chose dabchicks for the main course and the bill for the three of us, which I still have, including a vodka aperitif, a bottle of French wine and finally a Cognac served with the coffee, came to a very reasonable £2. 0. 8d.

Donald of China

Reaching Harbin, the 'Paris of the East', we had almost 3 hours to spare and were entertained in a modern flat to caviar and claret by two wealthy friends of the Brooke-Smiths. From Harbin I shared a two-berth sleeping compartment in the almost new and richly veneered coach with a free-lance Australian journalist, William Henry Donald. Donald had been a friend and secretary to Sun Yat-sen, the first President of the Chinese Republic, whom he had assisted when he overthrew the centuries old ruling dynasty of the Manchus in 1912. The biography 'Donald of China', published in 1948 two years after his death, describes his extraordinary career. Besides acting as unpaid Foreign Minister to China's first revolutionary government, he was the trusted adviser to successive Presidents and a close friend of Chiang Kai-shek and his wife.

My two companions knew Donald well and during the day we listened to his tales of the recent history of China and the part he had played in it. He talked of his relationship with the 'Old Marshal', Chang Tso-lin, Manchuria's ruling war-lord, and his drug-taking son the 'Young Marshal', Chang Hsueh-liang, whom he later cured of his opium habit. Donald spoke of the murder, only six weeks before, of Chang and his fellow general, Yang, in the Young Marshal's house. He knew that the two powerful war-lords had been plotting a revolt. Greatly impressed by the courage and 'timber for leadership' of the Young Marshal (still in his twenties) Donald decided to stay and help him in Mukden, the capital city of Manchuria, refusing all requests of the Chinese Government in Nanking to resume his work as their adviser.

Later, Sir Frederick Whyte, formerly first President of the Legislative Assembly of India and now acting as political adviser to the Chinese National Government, went to Mukden to try and persuade Donald to return to Nanking but failed in his mission. A few days after this we found Sir Frederick in our hotel in Shanghai entertaining large parties of Chinese.

At Chang Chun we changed trains again, this time boarding a Japanese train on their South Manchuria Railway. The railway had been the locus and partial casus belli for the Russo-Japanese war and was an important factor in the 1929 Sino-Soviet conflict and the Second Sino-Japanese war. Our train was very comfortable and up-to-date; not only did it have a restaurant car, but also a library, an observation platform with deck chairs and a barber's shop. It was too cold to go onto the sun-deck and so we lounged in the comfortable Pullman style parlour car. The obsequious Japanese attendants, wearing white gloves, always bowed to the passengers and polished the outside handrails before we alighted from the train onto a station platform.

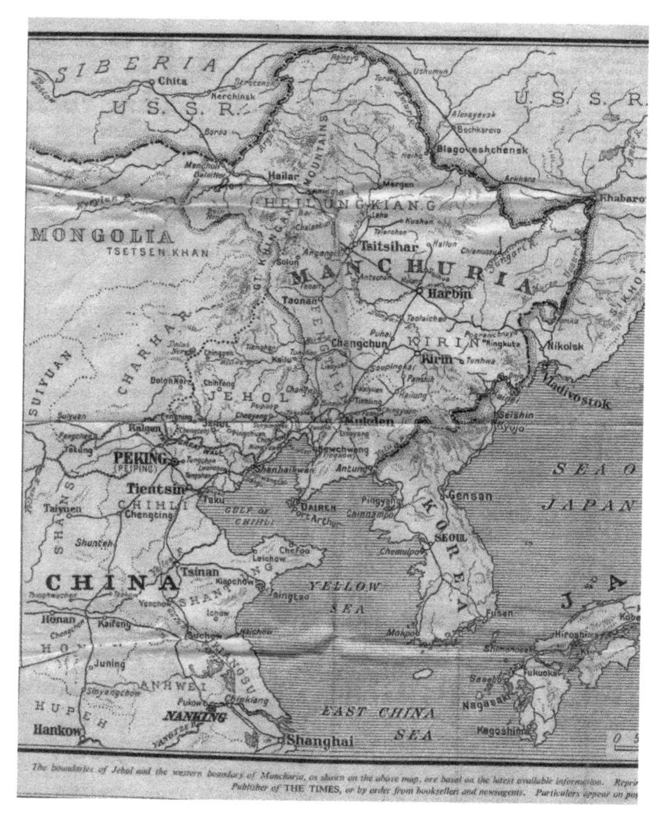

The route of the Chinese Eastern Railway to Vladivostok and the South Manchuria Railway from Harbin to Dairen

South Manchuria Railway

We arrived at Dairen, the terminus of our train journey, on the 13th day out from London. That night we enjoyed a long-desired bath in a modern Japanese hotel in which each room had a private bath and telephone. The next morning we boarded a small Japanese steamer for Shanghai, stopping on the way at Tsingtao long enough for us to accept hospitality at a beautiful house and take a drive to the forts and to the top of the peak for a magnificent view.

Leaving Tsingtao at noon on 20th February we were delayed for 24 hours by fog in the mouth of the Yangtse River below Woosung. Whilst there we had a narrow escape from being rammed by a Blue Funnel Liner which just steered clear in time. As the fog lifted in patches the following day and we sailed on to Shanghai, we saw that we were part of a flotilla of sixteen other ships which had been held up by the fog in the densely crowded waterway.

Shanghai

Shanghai at last on 23rd February - a day late after 16 days of travel. I settled into my suite of three rooms in the luxurious Majestic Hotel at £3.10s per day. This hotel reputedly had the largest ballroom in the world, shaped like a clover leaf, with meal tables around the slightly raised edge. I danced there on several evenings and, at a fancy-dress ball, I wore my Bedouin Sheikh's costume again before going on with others to a Russian carnival dance.

I spent 24 days working with Brooke-Smith, plus a stenographer and office boy, in our temporary office in the newly built Hong Kong & Shanghai Bank building. Brooke-Smith was an excellent boss, extremely punctual and meticulously accurate in detail. We visited the Riverside Power Plant, its boiler houses, pump houses and its two new 20,000 kW Metro-Vickers machines not yet commissioned and were also shown some of the city's substations. I collected technical and commercial data and assessed the valuation and depreciation of the plant for later transmission to London by cablegram. I had to check the long coded cablegrams we sent, sometimes after midnight, which cost the syndicate a total of about £1,000. To these, which I handed in at the cable office each evening, we found the coded replies from the London syndicate awaiting our arrival at the office the following morning.

Shanghai in 1929

During the next three weeks I was introduced to many of the British residents and took particular trouble to remember their names and faces for the inevitable future contacts with them in the

Shanghai Club with its 132 ft long bar which was packed on Saturdays at noon, or in the Country Club where we sometimes dined and spent our breaks from long hours of work, relaxing with a whisky soda and reading the papers. I was greatly helped in this memory test by the fact that I had completed half of the 12 lesson Pelman Course of Memory and Mind Training before being selected for this assignment.

There are several references in my diaries to the 'white' Russians I met in Shanghai, all of them members of Russian families who had fled for their lives from the Bolshevik's Red Army. Wealthy Chinese often employed white Russians as guards to protect them from kidnapping which was a daily occurrence in Shanghai; ransoms up to £20,000 being demanded. A Police Report published in the Shanghai newspapers on 9th March listed 34 armed robberies, 5 murders, 4 pickpockets and 13 snatchers in the city during the week.

One of the Russians, V.S. Bebenin, a deputy superintendent of the Shanghai CID, had become a personal friend during our three day voyage from Southern Manchuria. He had left Russia through Siberia and Manchuria, riding or walking by night and hiding by day and had changed his name from Kossineff. A few of his Russian compatriots ran restaurants or clubs in Shanghai, whilst others found jobs as waiters or were forced to beg on the streets like the poorest Chinese – a truly pathetic sight. Several years later Bebenin turned up unexpectedly at my London club, a very distinguished looking man in a smart outfit. On my way home from Shanghai I visited his sister, Miss Kossineff, in Tokyo where she was teaching music.

On the occasional evening Bebenin took me to a Russian restaurant where the food was good but the surroundings rather crude. We would then go on to Ladaw's dance hall, not getting back to my hotel until the early hours. Dance halls had become popular in Shanghai in the 1920s and were places where Chinese tycoons and gangsters mingled with pretty girls and foreign adventurers in a modern atmosphere, only a decade after the idea of men and women dancing together would have been considered scandalous.

Shanghai in March was nearing its best, with frosty mornings and the temperature rising to 75 degrees during the fine early spring days; the birds were singing and the trees budding. Although there was a general untidiness, the streets were much cleaner than London; old women in large straw hats over their caps were continually sweeping up, day and night. Nanking Road was noisy, narrow, and congested with crowded streetcars, motors driven at high speed running great risks and rickshaws also ignoring pedestrians. There were no horse-drawn vehicles, except a few pony-drawn Victorias used by brokers who found them faster and more convenient. Pavements were narrow, less than 3 feet wide in many places, and at the street corners Sikh policemen controlled the traffic effectively.

Our work ended on 19th March with a meeting with the Power Committee. After they had received and examined our 'accepted' cheque for £1,000,000, which had to be produced as a token of our good financial standing, they opened our tender in which we offered £6.6 million or £7.2 million if some terms could be altered in the Concession Agreement. However, an American Syndicate's bid of over £10 million was chosen and so our journey to purchase this huge electricity undertaking proved fruitless.

On receipt of the disappointing news, London sent a cable instructing me to 'return home by the earliest convenient booking'. The quickest route would have been by rail via Siberia and Europe, but this would have involved a long delay in getting Russian visas again. The usual alternative was to take a P&O steamer via the China Sea and Indian Ocean, through the Suez Canal to Marseilles from where one could go by train to the Channel and take a ferry to Dover.

Instead, I booked a passage on the RMS 'Empress of Asia' to Vancouver via Japan, and thence by train across Canada to

Montreal and New York for an Atlantic crossing back to the UK at a total cost of £120. This took 33 days, saving 1 day over the route via Suez and thus relieving my conscience. My request for a superior berth across the Atlantic and lower berth on the train across Canada only cost me an additional £20.

Passage to Japan

Embarking at Shanghai on 22nd March we reached Nagasaki the following morning. There I witnessed what was reported to be the speediest coaling of a ship in the world at that time. Japanese men and women formed a human conveyor, delivering the coal in little baskets from 26 square-ended barges. On the barges, which had been lined up stern-wards to the ship, men filled each basket with two shovelfuls. The operation went on hour after hour without noise, except that of the coal falling down the chutes to the bunkers.

Nagasaki had a beautiful land-locked harbour with hills rising steeply from the city. The gaily decorated streets were packed with motor cars and bicycles. Almost all the men wore Japanese costumes but with felt caps or hats.

RMS Empress of Asia – from Shanghai to Vancouver via Japan – March 1929

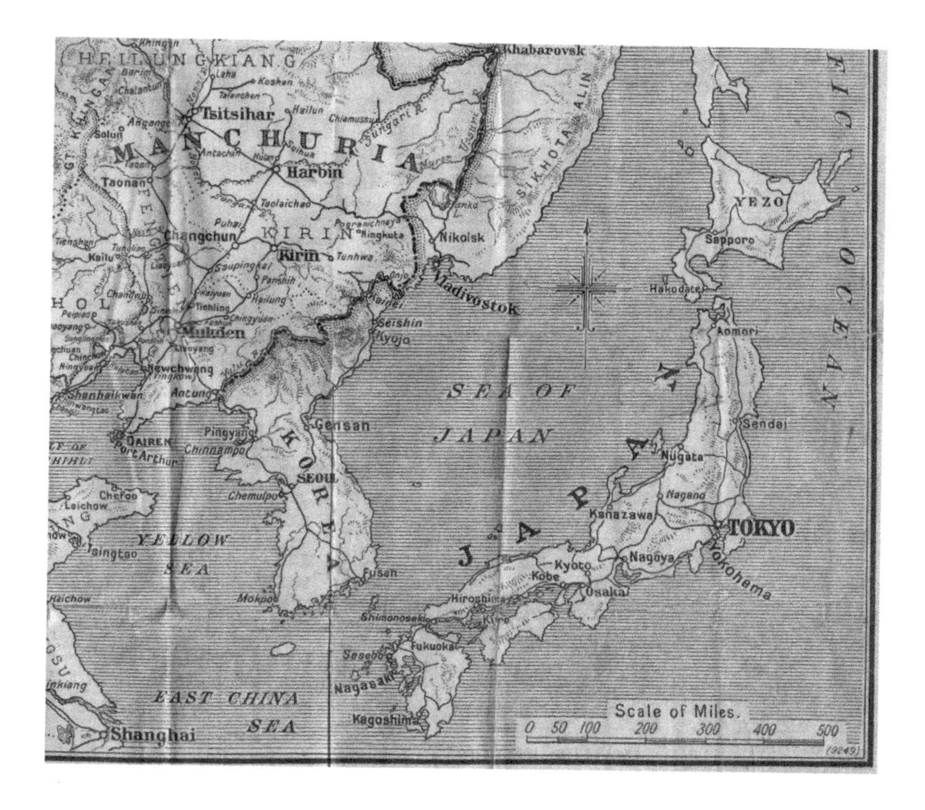

From Nagasaki we reached the Shimonoseki Channel to enter the Inland Sea of Japan. Unlike my previous experience of this beautiful 250 mile stretch of water, rain and mist shrouded the islands. I disembarked at Kobe and took a train to Tokyo, seeing no motor cars or domestic animals throughout the 12 hour journey but noticing scores of pretty children in beautiful Japanese costumes returning from school, all carrying umbrellas.

Tokyo

In Tokyo I spent two nights at the Imperial Hotel which had been my headquarters during my 1924 visit. I found Tokyo a city of contrasts: beauty and ugliness; hygiene and filth; extreme politeness and extraordinary rudeness; pretty women and unattractive men, the former in the most artistic clothes of well-chosen colours, the men literally spoiling the scene, their Western hats crowning the last relics of Japanese clothes.

The streets were a maze of untidy overhead wires strung from drunken-looking poles which leant under the weight of cables and transformers; a tangle of service connections at each pole. Street lights were kept on all day, probably for lack of a means to switch them off. Earth roads and sidewalks resembled the devastated towns of France, with pot-holes of mud so that a passing motor car squirted any nearby cars or pedestrians. Cotton masks were worn over nose and mouth by many of the lower and middle class. The steel buildings under construction revealed great depths of girders and much bracing to make them safe in earthquakes.

Rabindranath Tagore

I left Tokyo on 28th March by the fast inter-city train and rejoined the ship at Yokohama, now a new and ultra-modern port, rebuilt from the ruins I had seen there five years earlier when it had been devastated by the 1923 earthquake.

After a pleasant start to the voyage we encountered a strong wind from the north, the sea became rough, and I was laid up for two or three days with sea-sickness due to the heavy pitching and rolling of the ship.

An interesting fellow passenger on the voyage across the Pacific was (later Sir) Rabindranath Tagore of Bengal (1861-1941), the famous, white-bearded Hindu polymath, poet and philosopher and winner of the Nobel Prize for Literature in 1913. He read to us on the ship several of his poems, some in Bengali and some in English. Although I was not normally fond of poetry, I could not help enjoying his rendition of them.

We made a short stop at Victoria and arrived in Vancouver on the afternoon of 6th April. I had dinner with my old friend C.B. Pearson at the Hotel George before boarding the CP train and making my way across Canada to New York, stopping in Kamloops, Winnipeg, and Montreal to visit friends and relatives on the way. In Kamloops I was met by Charlie Green who took me to see his ranch during our day's stop-over there. He had been the 22 year old groom at Wenham Place when my Aunt Agnes, then aged 42, caused a scandal by marrying him in 1906 and they had immediately emigrated to Canada.

I spent a busy two days in both Winnipeg and Montreal looking up many old friends. It continued snowing during the journey to Montreal and the lakes were still frozen. In New York I was entertained by Curt Pfeiffer whom I had met on my previous round the world cruise; after dinner we went to Roxy's new Super-Cinema and I saw my first talkie film 'Three Different Eyes'. The synchronisation and production were excellent and realistic except in the close-ups. The talkies had improved since 1928 when the first ones were produced with much music and little dialogue.

Dr Felix d'Herelle

I left New York on 16th April on the CP 'Empress of Australia' bound for Southampton. Crossing the Atlantic I shared a table in the dining saloon with Dr Felix d'Herelle (1873-1949), a French Canadian microbiologist who had discovered bacheriophages, viruses that infect bacteria. He was famous for his success, especially in India, in reducing mortality from cholera and had been appointed Professor of Protobiology (the study of bacteriophages) at Yale University.

The meals on board were generous and there was always a varied menu to choose from, as can be seen from the luncheon menu. On the night before we docked in Southampton on 25th April we were treated to an elaborate 'Dinner au Revoir'.

After saying goodbye to the dozen or so passengers with whom I had dined and chatted during the voyage, I caught the 4 o'clock train to London and went straight to the Constitutional Club to collect my mail and settle in for the night.

The next day at the office Shearer had 'nothing but praise for my work on the trip to Shanghai and hoped that the experience would do me good'. He even promised me a bonus of £200.

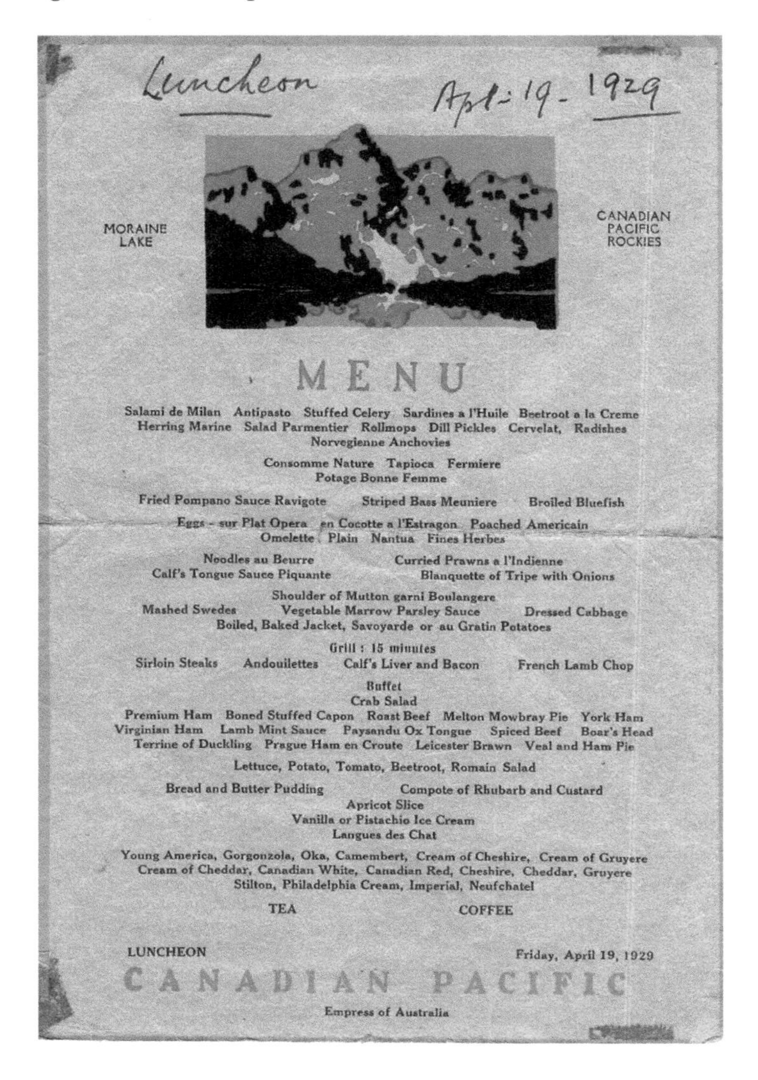
Luncheon Apl-19-1929

MORAINE LAKE

CANADIAN PACIFIC ROCKIES

MENU

Salami de Milan Antipasto Stuffed Celery Sardines a l'Huile Beetroot a la Creme
Herring Marine Salad Parmentier Rollmops Dill Pickles Cervelat, Radishes
Norvegienne Anchovies

Consomme Nature Tapioca Fermiere
Potage Bonne Femme

Fried Pompano Sauce Ravigote Striped Bass Meuniere Broiled Bluefish

Eggs - sur Plat Opera en Cocotte a l'Estragon Poached Americain
Omelette Plain Nantua Fines Herbes

Noodles au Beurre Curried Prawns a l'Indienne
Calf's Tongue Sauce Piquante Blanquette of Tripe with Onions

Shoulder of Mutton garni Boulangere
Mashed Swedes Vegetable Marrow Parsley Sauce Dressed Cabbage
Boiled, Baked Jacket, Savoyarde or au Gratin Potatoes

Grill : 15 minutes
Sirloin Steaks Andouilettes Calf's Liver and Bacon French Lamb Chop

Buffet
Crab Salad
Premium Ham Boned Stuffed Capon Roast Beef Melton Mowbray Pie York Ham
Virginian Ham Lamb Mint Sauce Paysandu Ox Tongue Spiced Beef Boar's Head
Terrine of Duckling Prague Ham en Croute Leicester Brawn Veal and Ham Pie

Lettuce, Potato, Tomato, Beetroot, Romain Salad

Bread and Butter Pudding Compote of Rhubarb and Custard
Apricot Slice
Vanilla or Pistachio Ice Cream
Langues des Chat

Young America, Gorgonzola, Oka, Camembert, Cream of Cheshire, Cream of Gruyere
Cream of Cheddar, Canadian White, Canadian Red, Cheshire, Cheddar, Gruyere
Stilton, Philadelphia Cream, Imperial, Neufchatel

TEA COFFEE

LUNCHEON Friday, April 19, 1929

CANADIAN PACIFIC

Empress of Australia

England in 1929

Appendicitis and convalescence

During the return journey from Shanghai I had suffered a great deal of pain in my stomach and so, when I got back, I consulted Mr Wilfred Trotter, a Harley Street specialist who diagnosed a 'grumbling' appendix and recommended I had it removed, even though I might not be spending much more time abroad in the wilds. He referred me to Dr Purves in Lincoln, and so I checked into the Red House nursing home there where I had it removed in May.

The three weeks compulsory rest that this incarceration entailed was most welcome and I took a further two weeks off work, staying first with Charles and Dot at Kirton and then with my parents in Woodgates. Whilst I was in the nursing home there was a General Election in which the Conservatives lost over 120 seats to Labour, allowing Ramsay MacDonald back into Downing Street to lead a minority Labour government for the second time. There were also reports on the radio of a battle in the Yangtze near Woosang, within 20 miles of Shanghai, between Chinese Government forces and a pirate fleet that had been terrorising the area. Twenty pirate boats were sunk and over 1,250 pirates killed, drowned, or captured.

The Summer of 1929

During the extremely hot summer evenings, when the temperature rose to 85 degrees, I generally went for a long walk after dinner before turning in. Sometimes, on Wednesday evenings, I left the city at 5 pm and took a train to Clacton, Frinton or Walton for a night out. I had a swim or a walk along the front, went to a dance at the Blue Lagoon in Clacton or the Sea Spray Lounge in Walton and stayed overnight in a boarding house where bed and breakfast cost 3 shillings or 3/6d (three and sixpence). After an early morning swim or walk along the front I caught the 8.00 am train back to London and was back in the office by 10.00 am. Breakfast on the train was excellent - grapefruit followed by haddock, bacon and sausage, with marmalade and 'wonderful' buttered toast to finish.

My life in London resumed with regular visits to the theatre and evenings dining with old friends as well as the new ones I had met on my trip to Shanghai. I had a few more dancing lessons at the Hotel Somerset with Miss Skrine to perfect my slow fox-trot and sometimes gave her dinner afterwards. One evening we dined at Frascati's and went on to the Astoria to dance until midnight. She was the nearest I came to having a girl-friend in London. I enjoyed her company, and we spent many evenings together, mainly dining and dancing, but our relationship did not develop much beyond her being my dinner date and dancing mistress.

My more regular dinner companions were my men friends, Harrison Edwards, Malcolm Gunn, Leslie West, and Charles Painter. In August, I took Painter to the Tivoli to see 'Bull Dog Drummond', my first talkie film in England. Gloria Swanson was the star in another emotional talkie which we saw at the New Gallery. One evening Malcolm and I gave a little supper party at the Troc for two lady friends, Miss Russell, and Miss Winifred Moss, after which I escorted Miss Moss home to Argyle Mansions in Beaufort Street, Chelsea.

Back in East Bergholt at weekends I sometimes met up with Reg Kemble, a distant cousin; he would join us for dinner and bridge at Woodgates and we would go for walks and sometimes drive to Felixstowe or Dovercourt for a swim or a game of tennis – we had good games and were both quite equal. There were the usual family visits and I sometimes took Mother and Father and the aunts for a day out in the car to see relatives or go to the seaside at Dovercourt for tea. The car, having just done 9,000 miles, needed some new inner tubes and I sent one of the tyres back to Dunlop as it had lost its tread. Father finished harvesting the corn at the end of August after a long hot summer. September was also hot and dry; rain at the end of the month brought an end to a 37 day drought, the longest for 70 years.

As well as working on the Maragua-Tana scheme for EAP&L and the Pykara scheme in India, one of my projects in the office was the Central Scotland Electrification scheme which involved a trip up to Glasgow, Pitlochry, and Kinloch Rannoch to inspect some of the equipment and the towers which I thought had 'beautiful lines with Eiffelised legs'.

I was feeling very fit again and went swimming and for long walks after busy days in the office. I had presented a challenge cup for a swimming Gala at the Hoxton Baths, not far from Old Street, and acted as timekeeper for their annual competition.

The Great Wall Street Crash - October 1929

Despite 'corrections' in March and May 1929 the stock market continued its inexorable rise and the Dow Jones put on another 20% between June and September; it had risen in value tenfold over the previous nine years. Commodities were also doing well again, and rubber prices had doubled, so in July I sold £500 worth of rubber shares and invested in two or three other companies, not realizing what was about to happen. Over lunch in September Leslie West boasted that he had just put £235 in the bank after making a good profit on Rhodesian Minerals. He was a happy man again having told me at length at our previous lunch a couple of months earlier of the woes of a married man, both financial and domestic. He said that 'staying away from home for 5 nights a month made for success at home'. However, at our next rendezvous I heard once again his usual tale of temperaments, incompatibility, and extravagance.

The boom on the London market came to an abrupt end in September and was followed by the Great Wall Street Crash on Black Thursday, 24th October. Thus began the Great Depression which would last for 12 years and affect all Western industrialized countries.

For some reason the fall in the market did not appear in my diary until the following year when I regularly noted the record low prices of rubber, copper, and other commodities. I took two weeks holiday in October starting with a long weekend in Lincolnshire with Charles and Dot. Whilst in Kirton I bought a game license so that I could join Charles on a visit to the Days at Manton for a shoot in the afternoon. There were 6 guns, and we came back with 7½ brace of pheasant, 5 brace of partridge, 5 couples of rabbits and 4 of hares; 43 head in all. After dinner, bridge, and a chat over supper at Manton we made our way back to Breezemount. Charles showed me around the cement works and the lime quarries on the Monday and I returned to East Bergholt on the Tuesday.

The next day I drove to Brentwood where Painter met me and drove us to Eastbourne via the Tilbury-Gravesend ferry and Tunbridge Wells. I put up at the Cavendish Hotel in Eastbourne and, after joining me for lunch and a swim, Painter returned to London by train. Over the next week I took tennis and swimming lessons in Eastbourne and also went up to Perivale to the West London Shooting School for lessons in clay pigeon shooting. I usually went for a swim before breakfast in the morning, and in the evenings, after dinner, I joined in the dancing at the Hotel. There I met and danced with Kathleen Davy and her friend Esther Scott and spent several evenings with the two girls, Malcolm Gunn joining us from London as my guest for the weekend. When I took him to the station on Sunday evening my diary notes that 'I motored about looking for petrol of BP brand'. I had 'lent' two gallons of petrol to the wife of an Indian Army officer who had joined us the night before. She had left the hotel at midnight and was concerned that she might run out of petrol on the way home.

When I was told, on the day of the Great Crash, to go to India 'tomorrow week' or by the earliest available boat, Mr Shearer's choice of me for this assignment disappointed my rival on the engineering staff of the firm, Eric Bergstrom. The object of my trip was to negotiate a cost-plus construction contract valued at about £500,000 with the Madras Government. Under a 1925 agreement with the Madras Government, Power Securities Corporation Ltd, whom I was to represent, gave up a concession for the exploitation of all the water-power on the Pykara River in return for the promise of a contract to construct the first hydro-electric development on the river, harnessing a 3,094 ft waterfall, the 5th highest head of water-power in the world at that time, and to build the initial HT transmission lines. My job was to arrive at the fair percentage to be paid to us on the actual costs of the project to cover our work on the design, supervision, and head-office expenses and to make a reasonable profit.

I had several detailed briefings from Shearer and Valentine and left for Paris on 6th November on the Golden Arrow from Victoria Station. After crossing the channel from Dover I boarded a similar Golden Arrow train at Calais and had identical seats for the quick journey to Paris; the whole journey from London had only taken 6½ hrs. I checked in to the Hotel du Louvres for 50 francs a night and went to meet Simone Gueschwind, dining with her at the Rôtisserie de la Reine Pédauque near the Gare St Lazare. On the way I lost my letter case containing my money and my passage ticket to India, having left it in the taxi. After a sleepless night and two hours at the Prefecture de Police the next morning, with my customary exceptional luck, I recovered it just in time to catch my Paris-Rome de Luxe Express for Naples.

BRITON'S BILLFOLD FOUND IN TAXICAB

The steamship ticket and the $1,600 in cash that Mr. H. C. Lott had intended to make last for a long, long trip would have paid for just one taxi-ride—if it had not been for Mlle. Henriette Salle, of the rue de la Procession, Chatou.

Mlle. Salle hired the cab immediately after Mr. Lott had left it. She found a billfold containing the ticket and money, and turned it over to police. The ticket gave the loser's address as Balfour Beatty and Company, 56 Queen street, London.

I subsequently received a Christmas card from Charles and Nina Huberich from the Hague attaching a newspaper cutting describing the event and saying: 'We hope that the good luck referred to in this clipping will continue in 1930 and the years thereafter'.

Nina had added a cutting comment on the card saying: 'Do you forget your friends in the same way?' She remained upset that I had not pursued our friendship more actively and enjoyed an affair with her.

Having caught my train and reached the Italian city of Genoa, I saw the Customs officials removing everyone's baggage for inspection. My baggage included a shot-gun and so I hastily jumped off the train taking my bags with me, gave the gun to Cook's local agent to return to London, went through customs and caught the next (slow) train to Rome and thence to Naples where I was just in time to board the SS City of Hong Kong bound for India.

The voyage from Naples to Bombay took 16½ days at about 310 miles per day. I was fortunate in being up-graded from a three-berth cabin to a single berth cabin on the top deck. There were several army families with their children on board going to India, including Lt.Col. and Mrs Strover, musical friends of my sister Clara. In the Straits of Messina we passed through torrential rain and thunder storms and were battered by hailstones as big as marbles, but after that the weather improved. On the voyage there were the usual games of bridge, deck quoits, treasure hunts and dancing to gramophone records in the evenings and I again won a prize for the best fancy dress wearing my Bedouin Sheikh's costume which I always took with me for such occasions.

Once we had passed through Suez and were in the Red Sea the night-time temperature in my cabin rose to 83 degrees and was considerably higher during the day. I started the day with a regular swim in the pool on deck at sunrise and spent the rest of the days reading, writing letters, chatting, and relaxing.

Contract Negotiations with the Government of Madras
The Pykara Falls Hydro-electric Scheme
November 1929 to February 1930

Upon arrival in Bombay on 24th November I was met and entertained by business friends before I left by train to cross the Deccan to Madras. Although the fastest train on the route, it took 33 hours to cover the 790 miles, averaging a little over 20 miles per hour.

At Madras I was greeted by Major (later Sir) Henry G. Howard, Chief Electrical Engineer of the Government of Madras. He put me up at his lovely house for the first few days during the very tough contract negotiations which we had; a struggle more difficult than any I had experienced in my business career to date.

During discussions with Howard I found it necessary to jot down many of his remarks and comments, some of them almost threats. These detailed notes stood me in good stead in 1931 when I had to do battle with him again on the same contract.

After business hours however, he was an agreeable companion and seemed genuinely glad of my company at his home and at the European clubs where we spent our leisure hours - the Madras Club in the city; the Adyar Country Club in its incomparably beautiful setting by a river where I remember the spectacular sunsets; and the Ooty Club.

The Ootacamund Club

The last-named club, in the hill station of Ootacamund, was my home and base for several visits to the nearby Glen Morgan dam and Pykara Falls and for my reconnaissance trips through the jungle on the route of the HT transmission lines. The descent of over 3,000 ft from the top of the Falls to the proposed site for the hydro-electric power station was down 3½ miles of path and took 4 hours. I found this descent more tiring to my leg muscles than the return climb by the very crude path that in those early days paralleled the future pipeline.

During some of my reconnaissance trips along the transmission lines from the Falls I was accompanied by a young Indian engineer, Mr Satyanarayana Murthi, whom I found a pleasant and intelligent companion. On one particularly gruelling day we walked towards Kotagiri, up and down the Nilgiri hills, through plantations of pepper, coffee, tea, camphor, lemons, pomolos and teak trees, over Adderley Ridge and down from an altitude of 6,500 feet to the Coonoor River at 1,300 feet – a descent of over 5,000 feet from cold weather to sticky tropical heat in a few hours. I was advised to carry a shot gun as protection against mad jackals but did not need to use it. The following day involved a mixture of driving and walking, being carried across the Coonoor River by coolies, a trudge through jungle from transmission tower sites 107 to 127 and across numerous streams and gullies until we reached the Bhavani River where we had lunch. After lunch we were ferried across the river and had a painful 3½ mile drive and walk into Mettupalayam at the base of the Nilgiri hills. I was so thirsty and dehydrated that on arrival I drank four cups of tea, a bottle of beer and a bottle of lemonade. At Mettupalayam station I boarded the train from Ooty; my kit and bearer were on board and we travelled overnight to Madras where I checked into a hotel, changed, and went to Howard's office.

Howard, an ambitious engineer who was knighted a few years later, wanted his department to build the hydro-electric scheme and it galled him to realise that my firm had the rights by its 1925 Agreement with the Madras Government to manage and supervise the engineering works on a profitable basis, having given up a potentially valuable concession to finance and develop the electricity supply over a larger area of the Province.

My negotiations, first with Howard, then with the Secretariat, and finally with Sir Krishnan Nair (the member of the Provincial Cabinet responsible for electricity supply) lasted 78 days, many of the later days spent in great suspense as to the outcome of my efforts.

Lord Irwin, Viceroy of India

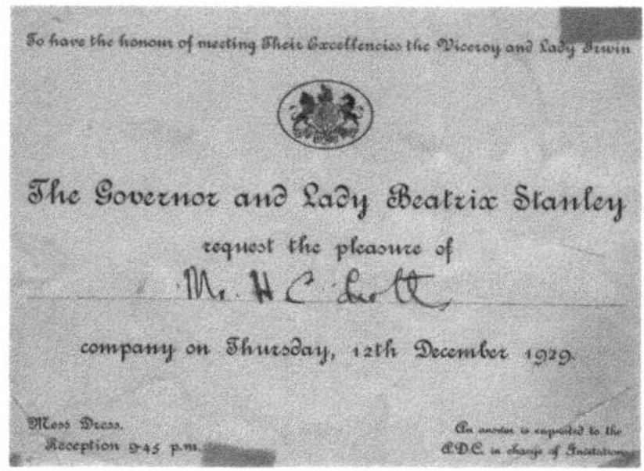

To have the honour of meeting Their Excellencies the Viceroy and Lady Irwin

The Governor and Lady Beatrix Stanley
request the pleasure of
Mr. H C [illegible]
company on Thursday, 12th December 1929.

Mess Dress.
Reception 9-45 p.m.

An answer is requested to the A.D.C. in charge of Invitations

Invitation to the Ball in the Banqueting Hall

The long, tough reconnaissance tramps through the jungle contrasted with the formality of the social functions I attended in Madras City. Socially the period was marked by several highlights apart from normal entertaining at the three old established clubs. On 12th December, His Excellency the Viceroy of India, Lord Irwin, who later became Earl Halifax, and the Vicereine came to Madras to visit the Governor Sir Herbert Stanley. Their arrival at the railway station involved, for all of us senior Europeans, attendance in top hats, morning coats and striped trousers – scarcely a sensible garb in the sticky tropical heat. Having been forewarned of the event I had been measured for my morning suit before going up to Ootacamund.

Their Excellencies were driven to Government House in a high State Landau with footmen and outriders in scarlet livery, escorted by the Governor-General's bodyguard of mounted Indian Army soldiers who looked like our Horse Guards in the bearing and the magnificence of their uniforms. That evening we attended in full evening dress with decorations a reception in the Banqueting Hall of Government House given by His Excellency the Governor and Lady Beatrix Stanley for the Viceroy and Lady Irwin. I went with the Howards from their dinner party for ten of us. After the State Lancers, the general company, including many brilliantly clad Maharajahs with diamonds in their noses and wearing many jewels, danced until midnight.

The press reports the following day described the event as a brilliant reception with a large and representative gathering of about 1,200 guests. 'There were distinguished Indians from remote mofussil districts gorgeously arrayed in the splendour of Indian costumes, high officials, naval, military and civilian, in uniforms that vied with the Indian dress in splendour, and charming ladies in the garment of modes which indulgent fashion today permits.'

Amazingly, even in Government House there were no WCs, only the beastly thunder-boxes which were emptied at short intervals by Indians of the 'sweeper' caste. This same primitive custom obtained at my hotel, Spencers, the best in the city. Every time I made use of a thunder-box my Indian bearer shouted across the courtyard to the sweeper to come and empty it. Water-closets had not come to this third largest city in India, even by my last visit in 1931.

After the formalities in Madras I left my luggage with Howard and took the train back to the hills, to Coimbatori, the second largest city in the State and known as the Manchester of South India due to its cotton and textile industries. There I put up at Mrs Simon's boarding house, met Satyanarayana Murthi again, and we motored out towards the route of the transmission line and walked along it, over a ridge dominated by the Perur Pateeswarar Hindu Temple. That night 'I slept delightfully in the open over the porch, clear and starlight; with a mosquito net of course.' The next day we went by train to Mettupalayam and had breakfast with Surgeon Louis Williams and members of the Malaria Commission of the League of Nations who were visiting the area, after which we took the Mountain Railway back up to Ootacamund.

I was warmly welcomed by Truscott, the Resident Engineer in Ooty, and his family with whom I spent several evenings. They also kindly invited me to join them for their Christmas dinner party at Woodside. During December and January I was making notes on my reconnaissance missions and taking photographs which would be important for our final design and implementation of the Pykara scheme. I also had to go back and forth several times between Ooty and Madras for negotiations with Howard and officials of the Government and the Public Works Department over the details of the Agreement between Power Securities Corporation and the Government of Madras.

Howard was becoming increasingly impatient and 'discouraged by the grave disadvantages' he considered were involved in our cost-plus contract which he thought would raise the project cost by 3½ to 5%. For my part I was cabling London with my recommendations and requesting their instructions on various points, getting frustrated at their slow response, and typing out amendments to the draft agreement as they were negotiated.

During the negotiations I stayed again at Spencers Hotel and usually started the day with a 5 mile walk before working long hours on paperwork, typing reports, letters, and amendments to the Agreement, and exchanging cables with London. I met various local officials and visiting businessmen in the hotel and the Club but, after a harassing day, I was happy to dine alone and spend the evenings relaxing and reading the illustrated English papers at the Madras Club. Occasionally I would meet and play tennis with D.B. Marsland, a young representative working for ICI in Madras, and we would go out for dinner or to a cinema where we saw Bebe Daniels starring in the film 'Swim Girl Swim'.

Another invitation to a Ball at Government House arrived and I went in full evening dress with decorations after dining with the Howards again. Their party included Miss Norrie Keene and her brother Hughie, a police officer, and George Ionides as well as the Government Finance Secretary, H.A. Watson. On two or three occasions I also received invitations to dancing and bridge at Government House Guindy, a spacious and elegant country house on the outskirts of Madras.

On 5th February I wrote in my diary: 'This business of negotiations resembles a game of chess for which the stake is thousands of pounds and in which the moves take place on an average of one a week.'

I had put some pressure on the Madras Government by informing them that I had been instructed by Balfour Beatty to leave India on 14th February to attend a Tribunal in Kenya and this may have helped to get the negotiations over the finishing line. During the final three weeks of tediously slow and stressful negotiations with the Government on the wording of several clauses in the Agreement, I received advice and encouraging cablegrams from London.

I refused to accept any time penalty in the contract nor responsibility for exchange rate fluctuations and finally, on 11th February, Sir Krishnan Nair and the Cabinet were persuaded to accept the terms of the contract including our 10% fee. I received a cable from Shearer with the message: 'Congratulations upon successful conclusion of difficult negotiations.' All the approvals including that of the Governor General were forthcoming and, my Power of Attorney having been accepted by A.E.S. Thomas, the Government Solicitor, I signed the Agreement with Mr Leach, the Secretary to the Government, said my goodbyes to everyone and left that evening for Bombay.

Shearer wrote to me on 15th February:

'We all realise the difficulties which you have had to encounter in connection with the final adjustment of the Agreement with the

Madras Government and are confident that you have dealt with the matter, in view of all the circumstances, on sound and diplomatic lines. It is obvious that the opposition to the contract with us was substantial and was not confined to one particular individual. We therefore recognise the diplomacy and tact which you must have exercised to bring the issue, in the face of all the opposition encountered, to a successful conclusion, and we congratulate you on completion of the Agreement.'

'We trust that you will not be long delayed in Kenya, as naturally your presence here is required at the earliest possible date in connection with the arrangement of the Pykara situation as the information – technical and otherwise – which you have acquired will be of considerable value to us in initiating and carrying through our obligations under the contract.'

In accordance with my instructions from London I had booked a passage from Bombay to Kenya, where I was to give expert evidence to a Tribunal on my proposed scheme to harness the rapids of the Tana River. In Bombay I was once again entertained by business colleagues, including a lunch at the Bombay Yacht Club, before boarding the SS Ellora, a small 5,200 ton ship of the British India line bound for Mombasa. Apart from Captain C.J. Halls and his Chief Engineer, there was only one other European passenger on the ship – all the rest were Indians.

As we left coconuts were thrown into the water for good luck. I cannot recall a voyage smoother or more enjoyable than this slow 10-day trip across the Indian Ocean. The sea was relatively calm, and we saw no other vessels except a small sailing boat near Mombasa and shoals of flying fish. The ear trouble which I had had for two years and which recurred in Madras disappeared. I had an exceptional feeling of contentment after the tension of the negotiations and was now completely relaxed in mind and body. No report on my negotiations was necessary and I had a delightful visit to Kenya to look forward to.

British India ship SS Ellora

Before reaching Mombasa, the ship called in at Zanzibar where I went ashore and walked through the narrow streets, through the European, Indian, and native bazaars to Victoria Park. There were no beggars to be seen and the streets were spick and span. Many of the buildings had magnificent wooden doors with carved lintels and centre-posts and panels studded with pointed brass knobs. Heaps of cloves were laid out in the sun to dry and there were coconut trees everywhere. I hired a car to see the ruins of the old palace of the Sultan of Zanzibar and visited the local power station where there were two large 330 kW DC Willans & Robinson diesel engines and two smaller sets.

335 BRAKE HORSE-POWER DIESEL ENGINE
WILLANS AND ROBINSON, LIMITED, RUGBY, ENGINEERS

The next day will be remembered for a 'jaunt' in the ship's rowing boat with the skipper and two or three young ship's officers, to a lovely uninhabited coral island where we spent the day swimming in the warm shallow water, sunbathing, and walking along the beautiful white sand beach seeing crabs galore and lizards and heaps of taper shellfish. We did not return to the ship until 9.30 that evening when my cabin temperature had fallen to 85 degrees, having been as high as 95 degrees the previous day.

A day on the beach in Zanzibar with officers from the SS Ellora

It was still extremely hot and sultry on 25th February when we arrived in Mombasa where disembarkation was delayed by a small-pox case amongst the passengers. I was met at the port by J.H. Odam, the new General Manager of EAP&L, and G.G. Bompas. They took me to see the power station where great changes were taking place before we went to lunch at the Mombasa Club with Stanley and Coverdale and then to the station where we caught the train to Nairobi.

I have already described that visit to Kenya and Tanganyika. After six months away, I arrived back in London on 1st May 1930, having left for the Pykara negotiations in Madras on 6th November 1929.

Settling back in England in 1930

My first experience of television was on 5th June 1930 when attending the Annual Conversazione of the Institution of Civil Engineers, a colourful event of the London season attended by many diplomats and other guests as well as engineers and their wives. We saw 'the tiny flickering picture, about an inch or so across, of a man's face; the man at the other end of the long library was talking and making grimaces.'

World Power Conference in Berlin - 1930

Later, in June, I had an interesting break in routine from the London office when I travelled to Germany to attend the World Power Conference in Berlin at the Kroll Opera House. I went with a Swiss engineer friend Chas. A. Burnier. Besides listening to the papers and discussions using head-phones to hear the simultaneous translation of speeches made in German or French, we visited the manufacturing works of several large companies and were entertained at a number of social functions arranged for the hundreds of guests from all countries.

The German Government hosted the opening function at the Berlin Zoo at which a dinner was served with drinks of hock-cup or beer, followed by dancing and strolls through the well-lighted Zoo.

Photo of delegates at the AEG Works during the
World Power Conference, Berlin – 1930
I am standing with my briefcase in the front row,
second from the left

Another memorable evening was a festival banquet in the Berlin SportPalast, the largest meeting hall in Berlin, where 3,000 of us dined whilst thousands of performers, athletes with uniformly sun-tanned bodies, entertained us with physical displays and drill on the huge arena below us. During the banquet addresses to the delegates were relayed from San Francisco, London, and New Jersey by means of telephone, radio, and cable. Lord Derby, speaking from Aldershot, addressed the Conference and the Electric Light Association Convention in San Francisco simultaneously. He was followed by Guglielmo Marconi and then Thomas Edison, the great American inventor whose inventions included the phonograph, the movie camera, and the long-lasting incandescent electric light bulb.

I remember one of the Conference lectures in particular; it was given by Albert Einstein, but despite listening to the English translation through headphones 'I understood nothing of it'.

Burnier and I made visits to the AEG Works and the research laboratories of the Charlottenberg High School to see electrical testing at 1 million volts, and during the weekend break in the Conference the two of us went to the holiday resort of Bad Saarow on the Scharmutzelsee for swimming in the hot springs, sun-bathing and a tour of the lake in a small steamer.

Touring the Schamutzelsee in a small steamer with Burnier

Returning from the conference in Berlin to the Hook-of-Holland I met on the train the young John Reynolds. He was a commercial artist and son of Frank Reynolds, for some years the Art Editor of Punch. Besides his famous advertisement-sketch for Shell, 'Crikey, That's Shell, that was', he contributed a weekly full-page humorous sketch for the Bystander. He also illustrated two comic books '1066 and All That' and a book about 'The Horse'. As we talked it quickly transpired that we had both emigrated to North America (he to New York) with only a few pounds in our pocket and without a job to go to. He

had lived there by his pencil for about 18 months before returning to England.

He wrote to me on 29th June soon after we had returned to London:

Dear Colonel Lott,

You have probably forgotten entirely who I am. I was the young man that sat opposite you in the Hook express.

I should very much like to see you again and have dinner or something. If you feel like it, please either ring me or write me a note.

Please don't bother if you are too busy or too little interested.

Sincerely yours, John Reynolds (The man that reminded you of someone else)

We arranged to meet, and I entertained him at my Club after which, in evening dress, we walked to the House of Commons. I sent in my card to my Chairman, George Balfour MP, who put us in the Strangers' Gallery where we listened to a debate in which Winston Churchill took part. Balfour then showed us around and entertained us on the Terrace.

Besides being a member of the Constitutional Club I was also a member of the Royal Automobile Club in Pall Mall which I had joined mainly because of its beautiful swimming pool and excellent restaurant. When Reynolds dined with me there we always preceded the meal with a swim. I recall one evening dining with him at Quaglino's, a particularly fashionable haunt where dinner cost us 10/6d each and a bottle of the 1921 Hock cost 14/-.

I invited Reynolds to be one of my guests at a special dinner party which I gave at the Berkeley Hotel for Mr and Mrs Shearer, Ruth (27) and Hugh Balfour (25) - children of George Balfour - and Lady Cox, who had become a friend when she and Sir Percy Cox had been in Baghdad in 1920-23; he as the first High Commissioner in Iraq. I arranged for my taxi-driver friend Painter to collect Lady

Cox in a hired Humber Snipe and bring her to the hotel where we foregathered for a dinner. I had already selected the menu of melon, salmon trout with Burgundy sauce, chicken cutlets with asparagus tips and, at my request, mango ice-cream; it was the first time they had served it.

MR. JOHN REYNOLDS

MISS JOYCE KONSTAM

We went on to a musical play at His Majesty's Theatre followed by supper and dancing at the Savoy. Supper consisted of grapefruit or caviar, sole bonne femme, quails on toast, and Japanese salad with mayonnaise. The dance floor was crowded, and HRH the Duke of Gloucester was there once again looking jovial, sunburnt, and thinner than I expected. Painter took Lady Cox home and returned to take me back to the Club at 2.30 am. The evening was a great success and cost me about £30 (≈ £1,950 today).

Reynolds' death on Christmas Day 1935 at the age of 27 was both a shock and great grief to me. He was engaged to Miss Joyce Konstam, the sister of Mrs 'Bunny' Austin. They had been out driving and visiting friends when she saw that he looked ill. She drove to a friend's house to call her father and came back to find he had disappeared. He had gone to find his own car which he drove to some woods where he was later found dead in the back of the car. He was a sensitive and highly strung man, prone to overwork and had recently been under some pressure; nevertheless none of his friends had noticed any problems and his apparent suicide was unexplained.

In August on one of my weekends at home I played the beautifully toned 3 manual organ in Great Wenham church and gave a short recital afterwards. I was keen to maintain my musical interests and renewed my subscription of 5 guineas for the series of ten winter concerts at the Queen's Hall given by the London Symphony Orchestra with some of the most famous conductors including Bruno Walter and Sir Thomas Beecham. I often took along my cousin Amy Lott, herself a professional musician, and one evening we heard the young Yehudi Menuhin perform brilliantly on the violin.

Ever since my schooldays I had suffered from an inferiority complex, especially in sports and ball-games, and I continued to spend money on lessons and coaching in golf, tennis, shooting and swimming as well as dancing. I enrolled for a dozen golf lessons at an indoor school in Kensington as well as for more tennis lessons during a week in Eastbourne in the summer. I also continued my shooting practice with my 12-bore shot-gun at the West London Shooting School at Perivale; it was expensive, but it helped to increase my confidence before attending a weekend shoot as the guest of William Shearer who had hired the shooting at Lord Waring's place at Foot's Cray in Kent.

Samuel Waring was a pioneer of household furnishing and decoration and founder chairman of Waring & Gillow. He had bought Foot's Cray Place from the Walsingham family in the late 19th Century and was given a baronetcy in 1919 for his work during the Great War when he organised factories for the production of aeroplanes and other war materials. A prominent supporter of the Boy Scout movement he gave his Foot's Cray estate to the people of Sidcup in 1931.

Whilst working directly under Shearer I was fortunate that he treated me as a friend. Not only did we exchange hospitality at parties at the best hotels, but he invited me as a guest to his house in Chislehurst for occasional dinners and for the weekend shoot.

I had become a keen and regular swimmer, frequently using the public baths in Marshall Street and Great Smith Street after work and also the Lavington Street Baths where the Balfour Beatty

Swimming Club met. I had become a committee member of the Club and had lessons in swimming and diving from young Trenowth, the best swimmer in the Club. When at home in East Bergholt I liked to go for a swim at Dovercourt or in the River Stour near Brantham Mill, regardless of the time of year, and I maintained this discipline always taking the temperature of the water with a thermometer on a string before diving in. During Christmas 1931, which I spent at home with my parents, I went for a lonely swim at high tide in the Stour estuary at Wrabness; my diary notes that 'the water was not cold, as last night's air temperature was 42 degrees'.

To improve my dancing I paid Gee Skrine for more lessons and continued to take her as my partner to dinner dances at the Savoy, the Piccadilly, the Astoria and the Grosvenor House hotels and the Kit-Cat Restaurant. Her brother Frank had been appointed by the Government as the tutor to the Sultan of Brunei and his younger brother. I met both of them at a dinner party which she gave for the Sultan at her flat in Ruskin Manor, Denmark Hill. I was fond of her and we enjoyed evenings together which normally ended with me taking a taxi and dropping her off at her flat before returning to my base at the Constitutional Club. However, one evening, when I had a particularly bad head-ache, she insisted on being taken home first and did not let me off at the Club which was not far from the Savoy where we had been to a dinner-dance. Her lack of consideration that evening was one of the factors which put me off taking the relationship any further.

My brother Charles and I continued to help our father by financing and guaranteeing his activities at Woodgates Farm. Father loved farming in the old fashioned way, and we helped him to carry on even after he had practically lost his sight. I had a fairly good income and in spite of 'pouring money down the drain' I was able to indulge in the pleasures of life, becoming a connoisseur of good food and wine, eating at some of the best restaurants, drinking good wine, always in moderation, and entertaining my friends generously. I agree, however, with the remark of a famous novelist who said that 'The spice of life is in contrast. To eat partridge all the time, as the French say, is to lose one's palate for game.'

The comfortable life I was living in London was in great contrast to many of the experiences I had had earlier in my career. I had lived in comparative poverty during my student days in the city; the two years of apprenticeship at Marshall's of Gainsborough had involved hard and dirty manual work for 60 to 64 hours a week; I had roughed it for 2 years, winter and summer, in a tent in the northern Canadian bush; and I had experienced tough and terrifying conditions in the trenches in France, especially during the long-drawn-out battles of the Somme in 1916 and Passchendaele a year later.

Admittedly there had been occasional luxuries during my service in Mesopotamia; the 10-week voyage from Bombay to Vancouver in the luxurious CP liner in 1924; and the journeys under first-class travelling conditions to and from Africa, India, and China with Balfour Beatty.

Now I attended many Lucullan feasts in the banqueting halls of the ancient and wealthy Livery Companies in the City, including the Mercers, the Fishmongers, the Patternmakers, and the Goldsmiths. In October I attended the Centenary Dinner of the Royal Geographical Society at which the Prince of Wales presided and gave a long speech, and the following week I presided at the first dinner of the Old (Dorchester) Grammarians to be held in London.

On 14th November 1930, to celebrate the 'coming of age' of Balfour Beatty & Co., a dinner was held at the Savoy Hotel at which our Chairman, George Balfour JP MP, was the Guest of Honour. It was a large and distinguished gathering and, in proposing the toast of the guest, Mr Shearer said that 'Mr Balfour possessed three outstanding qualities – courage, industry and imagination. He had been a pioneer in the electrical development of Britain and, at a time when finance for electrical developments had been almost impossible to raise, he and his colleagues had gone out and compelled investors to take an interest in those undertakings. He had the clever quality of surrounding himself with capable young men who had helped to build up the business from small beginnings.'

My work in the office was interesting and varied and I prepared reports for Shearer on infrastructure projects for India, Argentina, Australia, Nigeria, Albania, Estonia, and Latvia and even a financial proposition for the then undeveloped Cape Canaveral in Florida.

The memoranda which I wrote, after considerable research and analysis, enabled Shearer and the Board to determine whether or not to invest in a project and to give reasoned responses to the promoters seeking risk capital for some of these out-of-the-way schemes. At the same time I remained responsible for providing technical advice and support to the East African Power & Lighting Company as they continued to develop new schemes to meet the growing power demand in their territory. The proposed schemes on which I produced reports included:

- *Hydro-Electric Scheme in Latvia to supply power to Riga.* The Latvian Government was offering a 40 year Concession Agreement to the company to finance, build and operate a 30,000 kW hydro scheme at Dole on the River Daugava with a total of 900 miles of overhead transmission lines to supply electricity to all the public authorities in Riga. I concluded that the scheme had attractions and would provide a tax free 7 to 10% return on capital.

- *Grain Elevators in the Argentine Republic.* Although I concluded that there was a great need for grain elevators in the Argentine and profit could be made from financing and constructing them, I advised against a scheme put forward by Mr J.P. Grosscurth, an independent gentleman from Paris who was clearly interested in developing a grain trading business for himself and his friends in the Argentine Government.

- *Western Australian Government Electricity Supply.* The WA Government was looking for a company to take over the management of, and possibly even purchase, the City of Perth electricity generating facilities to improve their efficiency and add to the capacity. After a meeting with C.H. Merz, founder of Merz & McLellan, and Sir James Connolly in London, I prepared a letter for Balfour Beatty to send to the WA Government offering our assistance if the Government appointed a local firm of consulting engineers to work with us on the technical and legal issues involved.

- *Salt Monopoly in Albania and Electricity Supply in Tirana.* The Director General of the Industrial & Trading Society of Albania (SITA), which had the monopoly of salt production and refining, was seeking finance and a technical partner to take on the 20 year Concession being offered by the Government to supply electricity to Tirana and its local industries. BB offered to assist if the Concession period was extended and the return on the new Debentures was increased above the proposed 6%.

Ten of my good friends got married in 1930, including Harrison Edwards, Cyril Skinner and, in Kenya, Hubert Stanton and Bompas, but I remained single and enjoyed my independence. My salary had risen to £1,400 pa and my total expenditure during the year amounted to £955; so, despite some extravagancies, I was still living within my means and managing to save a little too.

A Difficult Year - 1931

1931 proved a disastrous year for me financially and I lost £1,200 which I had invested at my broker's suggestion in the Cyprus Asbestos Company. Although a very well-run operation, it went into liquidation when the price of asbestos fell below the cost of production.

The Great Crash had hit my investments badly and my net worth fell from an estimated £6,000 in 1925 (≈ £366,000 today) to only £2,150 in December 1931 (≈ £139,750) after writing off the loan to my father of £750. However, despite a fall in my dividend income I still managed to save about £500 a year from my salary and expenses of £1,600 pa and by the end of 1933 my net worth had recovered somewhat to £4,210 (≈ £303,000), partly due to the 10% fall in value of sterling over the previous 10 years which had enhanced the value of my overseas holdings.

In January Father had had an eye operation which was not successful; he had glaucoma and was gradually losing his sight. The operation did not improve his sight and he had difficulty reading and even playing bridge. During my weekend trips home after work on Saturday I did what I could to help him with his accounts and paperwork. I normally took the midday train from Liverpool Street to Colchester or Manningtree and was met at the station by Rogers (from the garage in East Bergholt) who would come with my car to pick me up. It was my habit to have lunch on the train and, after one particularly poor lunch, I wrote to the Superintendent at Liverpool Street Station complaining about the quality of the food they served. Not long afterwards I noticed a wonderful improvement and my diary records a subsequent 5-course lunch costing 3/6d and consisting of:-

- Iced Cantaloupe
- Salmon Mayonnaise
- Hot Lamb - or Cold Meat and salad
- Gooseberry Tart with fresh cream
- Cheese and biscuits.

During the winter of 1930/31 I decided to move back into central London where I took a room at the Connaught Club for £3.3s.0d a week. However, once the weather improved in April, I moved back to the West Side Country Club in Ealing where I could practice my golf and tennis, all the while maintaining my membership of the Constitutional Club where I frequently lunched and dined.

Austin Tourer – 16 hp & 6 cylinders

My 1926 Clyno Tourer had been giving a bit of trouble and I decided to sell it in May and buy a new 6 cylinder, 16 hp Austin Tourer for £310. Despite my attempts to smarten up the Clyno for sale I only received £37.10s. for it, having purchased it for £260 five years earlier. Improvements in the design and manufacture of motor cars meant that there was little demand for older models and their value declined rapidly.

Painter had helped me choose the new Austin and came with me to collect it and drive it back to Woodgates. A month later, when it had done 500 miles, I took it back to Mann Egerton for a recommended tune-up and oil change, then after 1,500 miles it had its first service. Painter and I had tested its petrol consumption which, at 18.3 miles per gallon, was a bit below the advertised performance. When he and I attended the Motor Show later in the year I noticed that the cheapest car was a Rover at £89, with the engine at the back.

My grandfather's cousin, Elizabeth Lott, died in May; she was in her 96th year. Her sister Anna Cecelia Haward (née Lott), who celebrated her 100th birthday later in the year, died in 1934 at the age of 103. I knew them both as they lived at Chattisham Hall, not far from my parents, and were regular visitors to Woodgates.

Back in London I had an attack of vomiting and continuous vertigo (probably labyrinthitis) the cause of which Dr Eager said he was unable to identify. I suspect that it was caused by stress and a touch of anxiety due to over-work, too much entertaining and filling 'every minute with sixty seconds of distance run' as Kipling put it in his poem 'If'. Anyway, the doctor gave me an injection of morphine sulphate, presumably to relax me, and told me to drink bicarbonate of soda to settle my stomach. The attack passed and by the time of my 48th birthday on 16th July I was in good shape again, recording in my diary that I felt nearer 32 years old and far more active than I was at that age.

Occasionally, instead of going home, I would go with a friend for a weekend break to a hotel outside the capital. My diary records visits to the Cavendish Hotel in Eastbourne with Burnier where I had more tennis lessons; to Paignton with D.L. Morgan for golfing practice, and to Bath with Malcolm Gunn where we swam in the Roman Baths. We had plenty of fresh air and exercise during our days out and after dinner on the Saturday evenings we went to dances at the hotel or other nearby venues. During the summer I took two weeks holiday and explored the Norfolk Broads in a motor cruiser with Richard Bray and Eric Masterton. For holiday reading I had taken R.W. Service's book 'Why not grow young'. I had been a fan of his since my days in Canada; his lyrical poems and ballads: 'Songs of a Sourdough', 'Rhymes of a Red Cross Man' and 'Ballads of a Bohemian', told of his days in the Yukon and the gold rush of 1898, earning him the nick-name the 'Canadian Kipling'.

Towards the end of the year my old Baghdad friend, Lt.Col. John Mousley, was posted to Hong Kong where later my god-daughter Ethelyn Ada Mousley was born. Before his departure I was entertained by his mother-in-law Lady (Arthur) Peake and met his sister-in-law Mrs (later Lady) F.O'B. Wilson of Kenya. I had met F.O'B in Nairobi years before.

In November I invited three old school acquaintances, Hill, Hodder, and Pike, to the annual dinner of the Old Grammarians at which I presided and gave a short speech. I attempted to fire the imaginations of the younger members at the dinner by speaking of the great pleasures I had had in my travels, starting with a passage across the Atlantic at 36 hours' notice on the 1905 Atlantic Cable Expedition, followed by my 7 years in Canada, 4 years in France during the War, 4 years in Mesopotamia, and then time spent on business in Kenya, India, Japan, China & Russia. I had visited 21 countries and each place had its own 'room' in my 'House of Memories', filled with people, pictures and souvenirs and kept alive by the many photographs I had taken and the detailed diary which I had kept since 1900. I said that people who felt themselves as somebodies in Dorchester might receive a rude shock to their vanity when they came to London. 'I was a much more important person when, as a boy of 15 I played the organ at Fordington St George church, than I am today.' The subsequent report in the Durnovarian magazine kindly said that 'my genial chairmanship was instrumental in dispelling the awkwardness which youth and (comparative) age feel in each other's presence'.

A few days later I was invited by Harrison Edwards to a dinner at the Fishmongers' Company where the ancient ritual of 'wiping the back of your ears' with eau-de-cologne from a lordly dish, to stimulate the Alderman's nerve and supposedly whet the appetite, was observed before the second half of the multi-course banquet.

Sir Milsom Rees in 1931

The following week I changed into 'tails' again to be entertained by my young friend John Reynolds and his fiancée at their ultra-modern flat in Great Cumberland Place, complete with butler, after which JR took me to a theatre.

My office work at this time included discussions on a projected cement factory for Mombasa with the promoters who included James Cumming, Erik Alquist a specialist on cement plants and Sir Milsom Rees the King's throat specialist, whom I met on several occasions when he invited me to meetings at his house in Harley Street to discuss the project over lunch or tea.

I was conscious of not putting on too much weight and, as an antidote to my fine dining habits and otherwise sedentary lifestyle, I walked a lot both in London and at weekends in East Bergholt. When my daily check on the weighing machine at the Constitutional Club showed that I was 4 lbs over-weight at 13 stone 8½ lbs, I wrote in my diary that 'something has to be done about it.' Curiously enough my weight at the time of writing this, 28 years later in 1960, is about the same in my clothes.

For regular lunches near the office I used to go with Valentine, A.J. Selleys, and Peter Parsons to Deacons where we sometimes finished with coffee and a game of Matador (a form of dominoes). When not out on the town in the evening I would generally dine at the Club and stay there reading or writing letters, going for a long walk before turning in.

The early 1930's were times of great political chaos. The shadow of the Great Depression darkened everything and left many parts of Europe very much worse off than they had been twenty years earlier. When the Government collapsed in Britain in August 1931, King George V asked the leaders of the main parties to form a Government of National Unity comprising 4 Labour members, 4 Conservatives and 2 Liberals. Banks had collapsed in America and Germany and the pound took such a steep drop in September 1931 that England had to abandon the gold standard which seemed to mark the beginning of the end of the British Empire. The country recovered to some extent by drawing out gold from India and Egypt, both still under its control, but this seriously deflated their economies.

India also appeared to be on the verge of a revolution with increasing violence between Hindus and Muslims. Ghandi attended a Round Table Conference on India in London in 1931 and told the British Government that he wanted 'complete independence for India and for India to have co-equal status within the British Empire.' He was not even prepared to contemplate Dominion status, but the British were not yet ready to hand over India to the Indians. I saw signs of these problems later in the year during a very welcome break from my office routine when Shearer asked me to go back to Madras to sort out a problem with our project there.

Negotiations on Pykara in Madras - 1931

A crisis had developed in Madras over our construction contract on the Pykara Hydro-electric scheme. My old adversary, Major Henry Howard, had threatened to throw our resident construction superintendent off the job and to finish the work himself using his own departmental resources. After a discussion with my directors we decided to send him a cable instructing him to hold his hand and await our representative.

I was given orders to go to India as soon as a passage could be booked and to call his bluff. So on 30th July I left Victoria Station on the Pullman for Folkestone. After a 1 hour wait in Boulogne I caught the Bombay Express for Marseilles and boarded the 15,000 ton P&O liner SS Comorin for Bombay. One of my fellow passengers was Lt.Col. C.A. Brown, on his way to Singapore; he talked at length about a new book, 'The Mysterious Universe', by Sir James Jeans which discussed Max Planck's quantum theory and Einstein's theory of relativity. Suez was hotter and sticker than ever; my cabin temperature rose to over 100 deg. and even the sea temperature was 91 deg. In Aden, Brown and I took a taxi to Golden Mohur Bay for a refreshing swim and made a short visit to the (Tawila) Tanks on our way back to the ship.

The Indian Ocean was rougher than on my last visit and I was hors de combat with sea-sickness for a few days, hardly eating at all. I arrived in Bombay on 14th August after two weeks at sea and immediately took the train to Madras. We stopped for lunch at Kalyan, climbed the Ghats to Poona (the Metropolitan-Vickers electric locomotive powerfully climbing the 1:40 gradient) where we had tea before turning in for the overnight journey to Madras. It was a much quicker journey than my previous one in 1929.

I was met in Madras by Major Howard who had no inkling as to who our firm's negotiator would be, and I had a month's desperate struggle with him to uphold our contract rights. My detailed record of his remarks during my previous visit in 1929-1930 whilst the contract was being drawn up proved a powerful weapon in my hand, although I decided to retain the one and only British barrister in Southern India to represent us in case of a show-down leading to a law suit or arbitration.

In order to establish the facts I went up to Ooty, checked into the Club, and spent four weeks based there working with Lyell, our Resident Engineer, and his team inspecting the progress of the works at Pykara, going down the penstock line to the powerhouse and observing the work on the foundations for the substations and the transmission line towers. I urged two more shifts on the concrete foundations in order to speed up the work and had a serious talk with Menon, our Assistant Resident Engineer, who complained of the inefficiency of the stone cutters and of a strike of the coolies on the transformer yard works. Heavy rain had delayed the work and there had been a small landslide.

Despite the problems, I concluded that the project could still be completed on time and within budget and went back to Madras to make our case to A.G. Leach, Secretary to the Government and the Public Works Department. During my negotiations I requested and was granted an interview with the Governor of Madras, Sir Herbert Stanley, to reinforce my arguments with Howard who, outside office hours, was as friendly as in 1929/30, entertaining me at his clubs and in his home. The fact that the Government of Madras later preferred to pay us £10,000 rather than go to arbitration showed the rightness and success of my mission.

The train back to Bombay arrived early on 19th September and, after collecting my ticket from the offices of Mackinnon Mackenzie, I left that afternoon on the P&O liner SS Kaisar-i-Hind for home. As on the outward voyage I spent much time swimming in the pool rigged up on the open deck, choosing to occupy it at tea-time and very early in the mornings when it was deserted.

At Aden I went ashore with the Maharajah of Cutch and his son before we embarked on our hot passage through the Red Sea.

I went ashore again in Malta – it was my first visit to that island, and I enjoyed a car ride through the old town, visiting St John's Cathedral and museum.

Valetta, Malta, and (rt) the S.S. Kaisar-i-Hind docked in the port

After leaving Malta we sailed to Marseilles, arriving on 2nd October. There I transferred from the ship to a train, arriving back in London via Calais the following day. After collecting my letters from the Club I went home to East Bergholt for the weekend.

SS Kaisar-i-Hind

Fine Dining in London in 1932

A highlight of February 1932 was another Livery dinner, this time as a guest of the 750 year old Mercers' Company in their beautiful banqueting hall lined with Grinling Gibbons carvings. Each of the 13 panels included the Madonna (of the Company's crest) at different stages of her development, from a young to an old woman. After the 'gorge-ous' (making puns was one of my failings) meal I was introduced to Lord Baden-Powell and his brother Major B-P. I asked the former who he thought would be his successor as Chief Scout; he replied: 'Only God knows, and he won't tell'. We talked about the ban on Boy Scouts in Italy and Russia and also discussed flat roofs for buildings, one of his hobbies. I told him of my letter to the Times criticising rather scathingly 'the barn-like roof with attic windows' of the new Bank of England building. Like me he agreed that valuable ground space should be transferred to the roof of a building and thought that it would only be a matter of time before one could make use of roof gardens rather than having to dive into basements for coffee. I had always admired him, the organisation which he had founded and his philosophy; he believed that courage is not something a person summons up for the performance of a single act - it is something he lives his entire life by. When at Charterhouse School his favourite game was football. He shone as a goal-keeper for reasons entirely in keeping with his character. When his goal was in danger he would let out a blood-curdling yell of challenge and defiance which would put the attacker off his kick.

Lord Baden Powell

More city dinners followed in the Spring including the annual dinner of the Institution of Civil Engineers which I always made a point of attending; this time it was at the Savoy Hotel. After dinner I had a chat with Sir Alexander Gibb about our Pykara Scheme and contract. He was one of the leading consulting engineers of the day who had established his own firm. On other occasions I met Dr Oscar Faber, Charles Merz and William Halcrow, all founders of similarly famous consulting firms.

The annual dinner of the Old Students' Association of the Central Technical College was held as usual at the Colony Club and my old chemistry Professor H.E. Armstrong FRS was there, 'querulous and protesting that engineers and scientists do not count for anything in public life'.

The Colony Club where the Old Students' Association held their dinners

Nigeria - 1932
Survey of Government Electrical Installations

In July 1932 I was again given an unexpected but very welcome overseas assignment; this time to accompany Major Marks to Nigeria; he was a director of some local tin companies and had good contacts there. Our job was to tour Nigeria and report on all the electricity undertakings owned and run by the Government, with a view to Power Securities Corporation making an offer to purchase the concession to expand the existing generating plants and finance new ones. The Colonial Office in London agreed to sponsor my inspection on condition that they were given a copy of my final report.

Leaving England on 27th July for Lagos on a diesel-engined ship of the Elder-Dempster Line, we were able to go ashore for 6 hours at Madeira where I enjoyed a swim in the marvellously warm, clear blue water. We called in at several ports along the African coast and had only a brief stop at Bathurst in the Gambia, but we had 7 hours ashore in Freetown, Sierra Leone, and also landed at the twin cities of Takoradi - Sekondi and at Accra on the Gold Coast (Ghana).

On arrival in the capital Lagos on 11th August I received and accepted a personal invitation from His Excellency the Acting-Governor and Commander-in-Chief of Nigeria, Mr George Hemmant, to stay as his guest in Government House for as long as my work kept me there. Hemmant had previously been Colonial Secretary in the Straits Settlements in Singapore. As a host no-one could have been kinder or more thoughtful and this applied equally to Mrs Hemmant who had travelled out on the same ship and had sat at the Captain's table with me. Having noticed my liking for the sweet course at meals, she gave instructions to the Government House chef to provide a sweet as well as a savoury whenever I was present. Later, on my return to Lagos one day after a strenuous day-trip to Abeokuta, 65 miles out, she ordered H.E. to change early for dinner.

Government House, Lagos, where I stayed as a guest of the Governor

His Excellency also arranged my membership, paying the subscriptions and giving me vouchers at the local Golf Club and the Ikoyi or Country Club explaining that he could not always accompany me.

Beside my daily work which involved interviews with Government officials, collecting data and accounts from their offices, and close inspection of power plants and distribution systems, followed by typing up my notes on return to Government House, I was one of the guests at the Governor's dinner parties of which there were seven on consecutive evenings, some of them followed by dances at one of the clubs.

At the weekend a few of us practiced our golf on the lawns of Government House where some gardeners were assigned to collect our balls and return them to us. When they were not keeping up with us the Governor called out: 'Send for some more gardeners.'

After one dinner I accompanied the Governor and Mrs Hemmant to a club dance, together with the Aide-de-camp and the Private

Secretary. When we arrived the dancing stopped, the National Anthem was played, and everyone waited until the Governor was seated with his party in the front row. After this little ceremony, dancing and complete informality resumed.

The evenings generally ended with me accompanying the ADC and the Private Secretary, 16 and 18 stoners respectively, in a drive in the Government House car to one of the two nearby Atlantic beaches where we practised on surfboards in the heavy surf, returning in the early hours to bath, wash off the sand and salt from our bodies and fall into bed. My enthusiasm for this sport gained me the title of 'king of the beach' and, a month later, provided the raison d'être for the farewell beach party which the Governor and his good lady threw on the eve of my departure. But more about that later.

Evenings at Government House began with cocktails in the lounge accompanied by 'small chop' as the hors d'oeuvres were called. We then went in to dinner at which the gamut of wines was served including sherry, champagne, port for the Royal toast with brandy to finish. Whisky sodas were served later during games of bridge. A similar pattern was followed at the private houses to which I was invited. His Excellency and Mrs Hemmant were the principal guests at two of the seven outside dinners I attended, which generally included the Government House circle of senior officials: the Chief Secretary Mr (later Sir) Alan Burns, the Solicitor-General Mr Howard who was Mrs Hemmant's 'boy-friend', the Director of Marine, the Director of Public Works, the Post-Master General and the Director of Railways. The Chief Electrical Engineer and his wife were also invited to one of the parties, probably because he was my principal informant in my business enquiries.

After a fortnight of this hectic social life I left by train for my tour around the country. First stop was Ibadan, 120 miles from Lagos, with its population varying between 120,000 and 240,000 during the year; there was as yet no electric light and only a few oil lamps in the town.

Three days later, on the train between Ibadan and Kaduna, I was pleased to entertain to lunch a young English missionary, 22 years old, who was getting only £10 a month and had had no leave for over 31 months. Thus I was able to repay the hospitality which I had received 20 years earlier from a similar young missionary in Canada, at Fort Alexander at the mouth of the Winnipeg River, where he was working amongst the Indians as the only white resident. We, MacGibbon and I, had had our food stolen from our up-turned canoe by husky dogs. The young Canadian was himself on very 'short commons' which he shared with us, refusing to accept any money, except as a donation to the mission.

In Kaduna, the capital of the Northern Province, where there was only one small electric power station, I stayed for 5 nights at the home of the Resident Electrical Engineer. At all other provincial towns, by arrangements made in London before I left for Africa, I was the guest of the local Branch Manager of the British Bank of West Africa for there were no hotels for Europeans in the country.

My next stay was at Kano where I spent 4½ busy days. It was unlike any other Nigerian city; although practically in the desert it was very picturesque. The population was 102,000 and there seemed to be more goats and vultures than human beings. The men were tall and athletic, not negroid in face, lips, or hair, and they gave a dignified salute holding their spear (actually or in imagination) vertically. Many of the staff of the Government Stores saluted by bending down, almost touching the ground with their hands.

At Kano I enjoyed (and occasionally suffered) more hospitality with elaborate and excellently cooked meals and unlimited drinks. Mosquitoes were troublesome in the evenings and my servant Garuba had to go to the hospital suffering from bronchitis and an attack of malaria.

Leaving Kano by train on 8th September I stopped off at Kaduna again where I dined as a guest of the Lieutenant Governor of the

Northern Province, G.S. Browne CMG, meeting Colonel W.R. Meredith DSO, Commandant of the West African Frontier Force, who had been a fellow passenger from England. After the meal, a Government car took me to Kaduna Railway Station to continue my journey to Bukuru, on the plateau 4,000 ft above sea level.

At Bukuru I was the guest for almost a week of Capt. H.W. Boyes, a tin-mining engineering consultant. It was planned that here I could relax a little and prepare my notes and data from the first half of my mission. Boyes' bungalow was large and most luxuriously furnished. The lounge, with its 14 easy chairs, abounded in silver trophies, cups, salvers, etc. All the English weekly and monthly magazines and the daily papers were displayed on a long table. Boyes lived utterly regardless of expense. Of his staff of several well-trained servants, four waited at table at meals. His head-boy, Yaro, twice married and already a father, looked and probably was only about 20, but he was as capable as any English butler with just as much responsibility. Boyes was also employing Mr Foley's head-boy during his master's absence on leave.

In the lounge, as soon as a servant saw a cigarette finished, he rushed up immediately with a large silver box and with a match alight. A dinner party for 12 involved no trouble for the host; just an order to kill a turkey for one of the half dozen courses. On the table were lovely cut-glass, shaded electric lamps and roses as decoration. Excellent wines at the meal were followed by 1842 Cognac (Hedges & Butler). After dinner we played snooker, Newmarket (a card game of the matching type) and bridge.

Besides a visit to Jos, the principal town on the tableland, I saw the dam and hydro-electric power station of the Nigerian Electric Supply Co., a non-government undertaking for which my firm were technical advisers; we later became their consultants for the development of new dams and generating plant. I also inspected some of the tin mines, all significant users of electric power, and was entertained to lunch and a swim in the deep pool at one mine by Mr Cothay, an eccentric English engineer.

Pressed by Boyes, I gave a lecture to his cadre of budding RE Officers on my experiences in the Great War, with special reference to transport at the front and the problems with light railways in the mud of the battlefields. I had prepared my notes for this lecture on the train going up-country after receiving from Boyes a telegraphed request which allowed no refusal. It was the first lecture which I had ever given and so I made my apologies at the outset; however, I had prepared properly, and it seemed to be well received.

Along the roads in the Highlands and working in the fields were the Pagans who have been described as some of the most contented people one could hope to meet. According to an article I read 'they appeared to want for nothing at all and wore no clothes, except that the women, if they remembered, picked a tuft of leaves to wear behind, with stalks uppermost, and also, but more rarely, a bunch of half-a-dozen leaves in front. The men were tall and well-formed, in contrast to their women-folk who seemed to be naturally shapeless. The men wore even less than the women – just a 'finger-stall' of plaited yellow straw – but they didn't wear it on their finger. This showed up against their black skin. Nothing else was worn, but the men carried a pipe and wallet containing their home-grown tobacco, and sometimes they carried a spear or bow and arrows.'

The Pagans seemed to have no need of textiles of any kind, not even a blanket, although the nights on the plateau could be cold. They slept without clothes on a bed of hardened mud in their mud huts. It was to the credit of missionaries that they had not changed the habits of these happy primitive black people by forcing them to become 'respectable'. Mrs Pagan was said to be one of the most moral and contented of her sex to be met with in Africa. Besides seeing them walking in single file along the roadside, I saw them at work in some gardens and fields.

On 14th September I was driven from the Plateau about 7 miles from Rayfield (alt.4,400 ft) down the escarpment to a railway station at Jagindi (alt.1,700 ft) some 435 miles inland from Port Harcourt. The road was good enough for us to drive at 50 mph in some places, but my native driver rarely exceeded 40 mph.

I left Jagindi by train for Enugu, travelling the 282 miles in 16½ hours. For some reason which I cannot now remember I walked the last stretch with a railway foreman. We crossed the new Benue River Bridge, which was costing £1 million, and then walked the remaining 1¼ miles to Makurdi station where we arrived dripping with perspiration. The long bridge had only recently been completed and the rail track was not yet operational.

I was met at Enugu by my next host, Mr Hutson, the manager of the local bank, whose house was extremely well equipped with a Frigidaire, electric light and running water in the bathroom. Then, having written my name in the visiting book of the senior Government official, the Secretary of the Southern Province, Mr W.E. Hunt CMG, I met his staff.

At Enugu, besides intensive study of the local electricity supply arrangements which were run and staffed by the Railways, I visited the local Udi Colliery and a grotto in Iva Valley. Except for a formal dinner party at the official home of the Secretary, my entertainment was much less formal and more enjoyable than anywhere else in Nigeria except Lagos. I had a few swims in a beautifully sited pool and watched a football match, played in the heat of the day between some veterans over 38 and a younger team whom they beat. A 'small chop' party in the evening was followed by a dance at the club before a 'sausage and mashed potato party' which ended in the early hours.

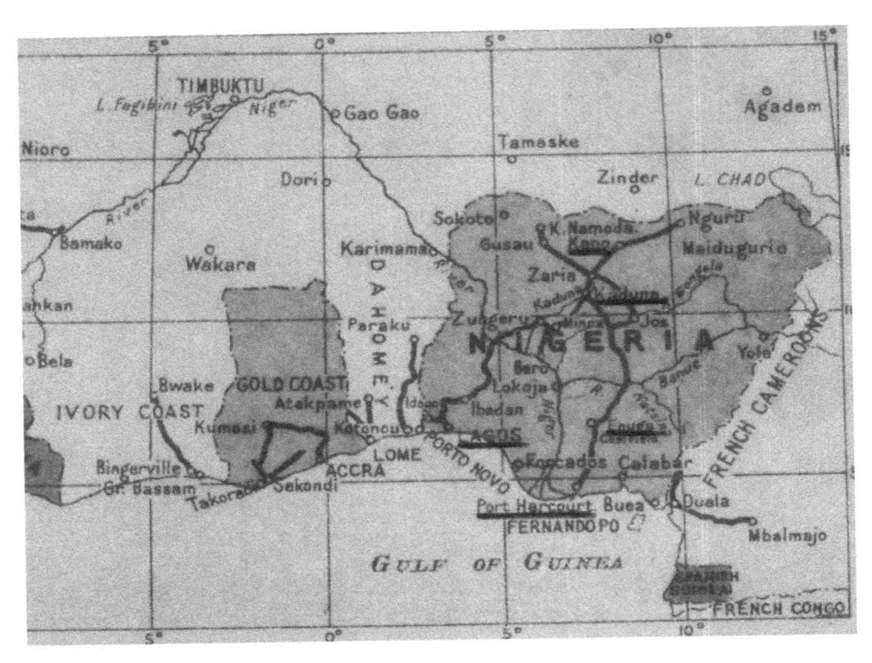

A map of the Nigerian Government Electricity Undertakings

After two more days of interviews and data collecting, and after my usual early morning swim, I left Enugu on 20th September by train for Port Harcourt where I was again the guest of the local bank manager, a Mr Cowe, who had lived on this coast for 26 years and only once had needed to go to hospital, with dysentery. There was only one other European on the train and a noisy Christian local couple, one of them loudly declaring the efficacy of prayer 'except to make a black man white'.

It is appropriate to mention here that, on advice I had received in London, I did not attempt to repay the hospitality of my various hosts with money, but with a case of spirits – a dozen bottles of whisky or gin delivered to them from the local stores just after I left.

In Port Harcourt I inspected the small electric power station, 594 kVA of steam-driven plant housed in an elaborate building, and the distribution system. This was the last of the four Government Electricity undertakings which I visited. After two days there I left for Calabar, involving a train journey to Aba, a 78 mile car journey to Cron, and finally three hours in a wood-fired stern-wheeler down the river to Calabar.

Arriving at Calabar on the evening of 23rd September my inspection of the town and local industries took two days. A dinner party at the Residency followed by a dance at the club was the principal break. My diary tells of a parrot, belonging to my host, saying very clearly 'Women, I hate 'em like Hell - and so to bed, slightly foxed.' My return to Port Harcourt retraced my journey there by steamer, car, and train.

Back at Port Harcourt I stayed one more night with the bank manager before embarking, with my native servant Garuba, on the RMS Appam, a ship built in 1912 for the British and African Steam Navigation Company and now operated by the Elder Dempster Line between Liverpool and the West African ports. We left Port Harcourt on the morning of 28th September and arrived in Lagos the following afternoon. There I was met by the Military Private Secretary, Major Tom Bovell-Jones, with a Government House car and a lorry for my servant and kit.

On the following two evenings the Governor gave dinner parties, the second one being followed by a visit to the Saturday night dance at the Ebute Metta Club in beautiful outdoor surroundings with an almond tree conspicuous in the lights with its rich red leaves.

I remember particularly a social event on the Sunday when ten of us left Government House in a launch for an all-day picnic near the Lighthouse, trolleying part of the way. Preparations for lunch had already been made by the Private Secretary (PS) and the ADC who had taken the kit, tables, and chairs and 12 servants. Before and after the substantial cold meal, I and others had some exciting surfing as well as swimming and sunbathing on the sandy beach.

By swimming for nearly two hours in the afternoon, the PS and I missed tea but refreshed on whisky sodas instead. We all returned in the dark, bathed and changed, 'tremendously tired' after a most enjoyable day.

Another memorable meal on the evening of 4th October included caviar, sole creamed with mushrooms, followed by ice-cream pudding. We played mah-jong afterwards, although contract bridge generally followed dinner on most evenings. At bridge one evening, my diary records, 'I gave a misleading call of 3 Hearts on 8 to A,K,Q and nothing else. I should have called 4 Hearts as I had not 1½ tricks besides Hearts.'

I should perhaps mention that my selection for this Nigerian assignment had depended partly on my ability to play contract bridge and to dance. My chief, who knew that I would be staying in Government House and would have to join in the social activities, had asked me in the presence of Major Marks: 'Lott, are you good at poodle-faking?' My answer apparently satisfied Major Marks who was to be my senior and companion at the start of the trip.

Dinner on 6th October was followed by a trip to the Lagos Club to see a film. The audience waited until the Governor had arrived with our party; all stood up when he entered and again when he left the Club. As the Representative of the King he was accorded royal honours in public.

Howard, the Solicitor-General, gave a dinner party on 7th October and we all played roulette after the meal. I lost only 8 shillings on my stakes of 1d, 3d and 6d. On another occasion, when dinner was followed by mah-jong, I lost 3 shillings at 1/- per 1000.

After talks with the Director of Public Works and the Administrator of the Colony of Lagos on 8th October, I went with the Government House group to a formal lunch. That evening 14 of us were entertained to an outdoor dinner party by Mrs Oliver, a fellow passenger from the UK and wife of the senior manager of the Balfour Beatty Welfare Association. There was 'a gentle breeze, a half-moon and white fleecy clouds, with palm trees as a back-cloth.' After dinner we all went to a dance at the Golf Club where I danced with all 5 of the ladies, but 'the waltzes were too quick and the floor too slippery'. At 1.15 am, on our return to Government House, the PS suggested that we go on to Victoria Beach for surfing with Bovell-Jones, changing into our swimming gear as we motored to the beach. It was nearly high tide and really quite dangerous. Others from the dinner party arrived later, including Mrs Hemmant and her 'boy-friend' Howard. He and I had to help Mrs H in the wild seas, holding on to her hands.

Later that day the PS and I went back to the beach, this time to Casuarina Beach, where we spent a couple of hours in the water swimming and surfing. One especially strong wave threw me onto a fallen tree and tore my chest and costume, but it did not stop us going for a third swim in the evening at low tide when the runs were shorter. During the evening, His Excellency repeatedly pressed his invitation for me to stay a further 2 weeks and accompany him and Mrs Hemmant on a trip to the Cameroons which I sadly had to decline.

The mornings often started with 12 holes of golf in the hour before breakfast. Some days we played a round after tea and had a drink at the Golf Club before returning to Government House to change for dinner.

Although the evenings were filled with elaborate dinners and social activities, I had a lot of work to do during the day, gathering and analysing all the data I needed to complete my analysis and report. After another long hot day of work on 11th October, I joined the Government House circle (HE and Mrs H, the PS and ADC) at a bridge party at the Lagos Club. I partnered the Postmaster General, Hebden, and lost 11/6d at 6d per 100. We returned with several guests for supper at Government House where the menu consisted of soup, salmon cream, cold pheasant with ham (cooked in white wine, beer, and stout respectively) and rum cream followed by a savoury, all accompanied by sherry, white wine cup, port and finally brandy. After all this, several of the party went to Victoria Beach where, again, I had to help Mrs H in the treacherous sea. The evening ended at 12.15 am with the usual bath to wash off the sand and salt.

During this my second stay in Government House I had been allotted the Prince of Wales' room in which HRH had slept during his recent official visit to Nigeria. Besides the special bedroom furniture and an enormous mosquito net surrounding the bed, there was a wonderful writing table which served me well each day for writing and typing up my notes.

On my last evening in Nigeria I was given a 'grand finale' by my host who, in view of my love of surfing, had arranged a beach picnic party. After cocktails and small chop about 15 of us left Government House in cars for Victoria Beach. I changed from shorts and shirt into swimming gear on the way. His Excellency did not venture into the water and left me to give my hostess, Mrs H, a lesson in surfing. Most of us were in and out of the water several times during the night and were offered Drambuie or cherry brandy each time we emerged from the surf. It was a very warm night and there was no need for towels to dry off. About 11 pm the servants laid out a cold supper of turkey, ham, and sausages for us, serving us with whisky sodas and beer, followed by liqueurs.

After supper I walked up and down the sandy beach talking business with His Excellency, it was after all the purpose of my trip to Nigeria; he seemed to be enjoying the lapping of the waves around his trousered legs. Finally, another long spell on surfboards before we returned in the cars at 1.15 am for a bath and bed.

Before leaving Government House on 15th October, I phoned the ship RMS Accra to put two bottles of champagne on ice so that, in accordance with local custom, I could offer a drink to the several friends who came aboard to say farewell. The ship left at noon 'at long last' my diary records, for I had a splitting headache.

On the voyage home I was greatly impressed at Accra with the magnificent physique of the Kroo boys, recruited from the Fanti coast, who paddled to the ship in surf-boats loaded with cocoa. Clad only in loin cloths or less, they seemed the happiest of men, enjoying their work and their physical strength. They reminded me of the Kurds in Baghdad whom I saw carrying colossal loads, even one man carrying a piano down the street. We took on more cocoa at Takoradi, this time from open lighters, with more Kroo boys controlling the electric cranes under a Kroo boy leader.

We had two hours off in Monrovia, the capital of Liberia, where the Postmaster General came on board to sell stamps to the passengers. A stop for three hours in Freetown, Sierra Leone, was the only other break until 23rd October when we went ashore in Las Palmas. There I acted as host to Mrs (later Lady) Burns and also Dr and Mrs Davis in taking a launch ashore and a car drive up to the Cathedral, climbing to the top before going to Quinneys in the Monte Brigida Hotel for tea.

During the voyage I had the use of the empty cabin-de-luxe as an office where I worked on my notes and my report. However, after Las Palmas the sea became steadily rougher until a westerly gale as we approached the English Channel did a lot of damage on board. Tremendous waves broke two thick plate glass windows and flooded several cabins in which trunks and all loose cases were thrown about with a terrific din. I was one of the unlucky ones but felt too sick to help the stewards to cope with the situation. The ship was hove to during the storm until the windows were repaired. I was hors de combat in fact until we reached shelter in the lee of Lands' End when I had just enough time to pack before disembarking at Plymouth on 28th October, three months and a day since I left England. I took the train to London where I went straight to the Club, my London pied-a-terre.

I make no apology for having described my time in Nigeria in such detail for it was one of the most crowded and colourful of all my varied experiences. It was also the last overseas assignment which I had with Balfour Beatty. From then on I was destined, as I approached my second half-century, to live a much less exciting life with practically no relief from London office routine until I retired 23 years later at the age of 72.

Not long after returning from Nigeria I attended a dinner of the Kosmos Club and, as was the custom, I had to give a brief account to the other members of my visit. I had covered a distance of 1,450 miles by railway, a few hundred miles by road and a short distance in a stern-wheeler. I compared my impressions of the country, whose population of 19 million made it second only to India in population amongst our colonies, with my observations in Kenya.

The Nigerians seemed to be advancing towards civilisation much faster than their Kenyan brothers, where all skilled work, clerical work and even driving motor-cars was done largely by Indians or Sikhs. In Nigeria, the native servant would drive his master's car and could earn up to £500 per year compared to a maximum of about £120 in Kenya. A salary of £250 was quite common for a Nigerian cashier or secretary. Most skilled work in Nigeria was done by a native who, unlike his Kenyan counterpart, was often also a clever trader.

I also noticed that, compared to East Africa, there was an absence of animals in the bush and fewer birds. During the rainy season when I was in Nigeria there was almost a complete absence of bothersome insects except a few mosquitoes and sand flies. Nigeria seemed to me to be a country of negatives – no hotels, no animals, no insects, no birds, no enmity between natives and Europeans, no scandals, and no water-closets.

The walled city of Kano, home of the Hausas, was to me almost as interesting as Baghdad which I thought it resembled in some ways.

The mangrove forests, covering thousands of square miles and forming islands in the many mouths of the Niger River, seemed an almost inexhaustible resource of high calorific wood for fuel, unexploited except for tanning from the bark.

The End of my First Half Century – 1933

My first job back in the London office was to prepare my report on the Electricity Supply in Nigeria and its prospects. One copy was passed to the Colonial Office as they had stipulated when sponsoring my visit. In my report I severely criticised their consulting engineers, Preece, Cardew and Rider, for the extravagant design and size of all the Government owned power plants, and the use of underground cables instead of overhead poles. As a result, electricity was far too expensive and literally millions of people in the larger towns were unable to afford a supply.

In Europe Hitler, who had stated his intention of annexing Austria, was made Chancellor on 30th January 1933 and Nazi storm-troopers were let loose all over Germany, beginning a reign of violence and terror. In 1935 he defied the Treaty of Versailles and introduced military conscription, openly creating a German air force, and increasing the German army to thirty-six divisions.

Winston Churchill warned an uneasy Parliament that Britain was entering a corridor of deepening and darkening danger. However, despite the gathering storm clouds, London court and social circles carried on much as before under King George V and Queen Mary. These might have been called the 'dancing years' in London. Former social barriers had been gradually broken down since the war, and that once all-exclusive body known as 'Society' had merged steadily and imperceptibly into that association of international celebrities known as 'café society'. The 1930's were the golden years of films, night clubs, and the irreverent lyrics of Cole Porter and Noel Coward – private lives were becoming increasingly public.

My life in London resumed its previous pattern and the first social occasion worthy of note was a dinner with my bosses who were entertaining Sir James Connolly and the Chief Engineer of Perth

(Western Australia) Electricity Supply Co. at Quaglino's, one of the smart London restaurants. After dinner we were taken to the theatre and finally to the Savoy Hotel where we had a light supper of kippers and champagne.

I was disappointed that Balfour Beatty did not send me on any more overseas assignments after 1932, and for the rest of my career I remained largely office bound, providing Valentine and Shearer with the benefit of my experience and engineering support. The company was dominated by Scotsmen and I was not part of their 'club'; there were only three of us Englishmen in senior positions and none of us were directors.

However, being at home in England did have the advantage that I was able to keep an eye on things at Woodgates where my parents were getting increasingly old and infirm and in need of support and assistance. It was probably also time for me to give up my nomadic life-style and settle down in England to a more stable social life in my fifties.

It was clear that my parents could not manage any longer on their own; my mother had been seriously ill and, although recovered, she was much weaker. I agreed with my brother Charles that we should arrange for his niece by marriage, Barbara Herring, to move into Woodgates as their 'companion' and help to manage the household. Although she was young, she was very capable and had had experience in a similar role with some old folk in Lincolnshire. Mother was naturally against the idea at first and did not like the thought of someone coming in to take over the running of her house.

Miss Herring arrived in April 1933, soon after her 25th birthday, and settled in quickly. The following weekend I came home to find Mother 'very bright, although still an invalid'. She said, 'You couldn't help liking Miss Herring; she is a fascinating person with a good deal of sense.' The success of our choice was reinforced a couple of weekends later when Mother, who was in excellent form, spoke of Miss Herring as 'one in a thousand; isn't she a charming little thing?' and to Father she said, 'You and I are now having the time of our lives'. It was a huge relief to me and, after one weekend at home in June, I noted in my diary that 'Woodgates was the happiest house in England and the centre of it was my parents radiating cheerfulness, bonhomie and humour.'

My mother no longer needed Nurse Edgar who had been looking after her and she let Miss Herring take over the responsibility of running the house which she did very capably with great care and sensitivity, quickly becoming part of the family, joining in games of bridge, and coming with us when we went on family outings.

Thus my first half century ended in 1933 and with it the majority of my colourful adventures which have been the main subject of these memoirs. Over the next few years I continued to live in London during the week and spent most weekends at Woodgates, eventually falling in love with Barbara who was looking after my old parents so well.

Although I remained extremely fit and active, the rest of my life was less colourful. I have not written about the later years leading up to and during the Second World War, my marriage to Barbara in 1942, and my family life thereafter with our only son, Brian. However, they were very happy years and, at the age of 59, I was extremely lucky to have found a young wife to keep me active and with whom to enjoy the second half of my life.

After my retirement from Balfour Beatty in 1956 at the age of 72, I set about compiling these memoirs from my diaries and the mass of papers and photographs which I had accumulated over the years. I finally finished adding to them in 1974 at the age of 90.

In the following Appendix I have included some reflections on fine dining and my collection of menus from around the world, which formed the basis of two or three talks I gave in my retirement. I have also added some notes on my habit of letter writing, with extracts from a few I received, including a remarkable letter from my Kenyan friend, Hubert Stanton, on the trials and tribulations of catching wild animals and delivering them to zoos around the world.

The other hobby which I continued to pursue during my retirement was genealogy. I had acquired from my father a considerable number of parchment wills and other family documents from the 18th and 19th centuries and had inherited an interest in the family history. Thus I became the family archivist and, with the help of a researcher, Ms Lilian Redstone, and a distant cousin, Charles Partridge, I added to the family history and the family tree, tracing six lines of my ancestors back to the 17th century.

Barbara Herring in 1933

Barbara Herring with Aunt Alice at Woodgates

With my wife Barbara and son Brian c.1950

Post-script by Brian Lott

Throughout his life, until he died aged 91, my father maintained an active correspondence with all his old friends around the world. Each Christmas he wrote or typed, about 100 personal letters until, as the years went by, the number sadly dropped off as he outlasted most of his old friends.

In one letter he wrote: 'One day, when he is about 70, Brian might be interested in these memoirs and might possibly edit them for publication'. Over the past few years, in my spare time, I have been doing just that on a word processor, not primarily for publication, but more importantly for the future family record and the interest of my children and grandchildren and their descendants for whom the world will be so very different.

My father titled his memoirs 'Some of the Highlights and a Few of the Lowlights of the Colourful Life of an Engineer' focusing largely on his overseas travels and adventures. All of that which he wrote is included in this edited version. However, having read his diaries from 1900 to 1933, I decided to add some more details with a few more of his comments and observations, to fill out parts of his story. My purpose was to make the story less a travelogue and more a personal biography, adding historical notes to put it into the context of the day.

In parallel, I have been adding to my father's work on the family history and the family tree with my own research, transcribing all the old parchment wills and extracting details from them to add to the story of each generation. In this I have had the help of Jane Sherwood, a distant cousin, and Stella Colwell, a Flatford historian, both of whom have added considerably to our knowledge of the family. Jane's 'sleuthing' amongst the censuses and the records of births, marriages and deaths in the National Records Office has unearthed an enormous amount of information on our immediate family and cousins during the 1800's.

I paid Stella Colwell to undertake the tedious transcription of John Lott's Journal and Farm Accounts which contains fascinating details of the activities of the family at the Valley Farm and Willy Lott's Cottage in the early 1800's. This has also provided her with input to a book she is writing about Flatford at the time when Constable was painting there.

These documents will hopefully provide the family with a readable and as complete a history as possible of our family and its origins and will enable me to consign all the original documents and family archives which I have inherited to the Essex and Suffolk Records Offices for the benefit of future researchers, saving my children the problem of what to do with them when I am gone.

Appendix 1
'Eating Out' and my interest in Menus

I always enjoyed dining out and made a point of keeping copies of the menus of the many dinners I attended. The banquets and dinners of the Livery Companies and also of the Institution of Civil Engineers were always accompanied by the gamut of wines. Quite often cocktails were followed by a punch, then Sherry or Madeira with the soup. The white wine with the salmon might be a Hock, Moselle, or Graves, after which Champagne was often served. The meat course would be accompanied by a Claret or Burgundy and then Port, Brandy, Benedictine, or Whisky would be on offer.

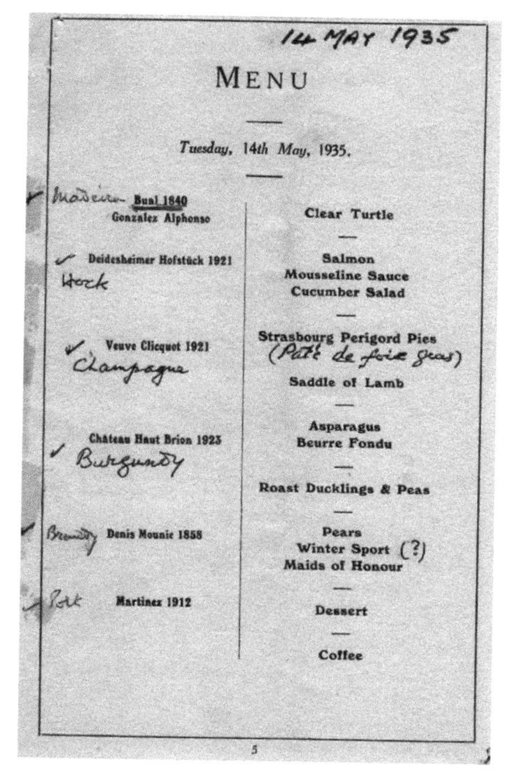

14 MAY 1935

MENU

Tuesday, 14th May, 1935.

Madeira Bual 1840 Gonzalez Alphonso	Clear Turtle
Deidesheimer Hofstück 1921 Hock	Salmon Mousseline Sauce Cucumber Salad
Veuve Clicquot 1921 Champagne	Strasbourg Perigord Pies (Paté de foie gras) Saddle of Lamb
Château Haut Brion 1923 Burgundy	Asparagus Beurre Fondu
	Roast Ducklings & Peas
Brandy Denis Mounie 1858	Pears Winter Sport (?) Maids of Honour
Port Martinez 1912	Dessert
	Coffee

5

Mercers' Company dinner menu – May 1935

I was invited to the Mercers' Company dinners by my old friend Lt.Col. W.B. Lane, four members of whose family became Masters of the Company in the 1920s and 30s.

Their menu shown here was typical of the banqueting menus of the Livery Companies at that time. An almost identical menu was used by the Institution of Civil Engineers for its annual dinner in the Guildhall on 24th March 1937 when Sir Alexander Gibb was President and HRH the Duke of Kent was the Guest of Honour.

My invitation to the Patternmakers' Banquet in Vintners' Hall in February 1938 came from my boss, William Shearer, who was the Master Patternmaker that year. George Balfour, H.S. Beatty, E.M. Bergstrom, and others from Balfour Beatty were also present as was the Master of the Vintners, J. Sell Cotman, who must have been a descendant of John Sell Cotman (1782-1842), the Norwich School artist one of whose works I inherited.

During these City dinners music was generally played by a small orchestra or a military band and after dinner a selection of songs was sometimes sung. The climax of the entertainment was the Post Horn Gallop performed by two horn players at opposite ends of the hall. As the final phrases of the piece rose higher and higher the two horn players took it in turns to finish on an ever higher note until one conceded defeat and the hall erupted in clapping.

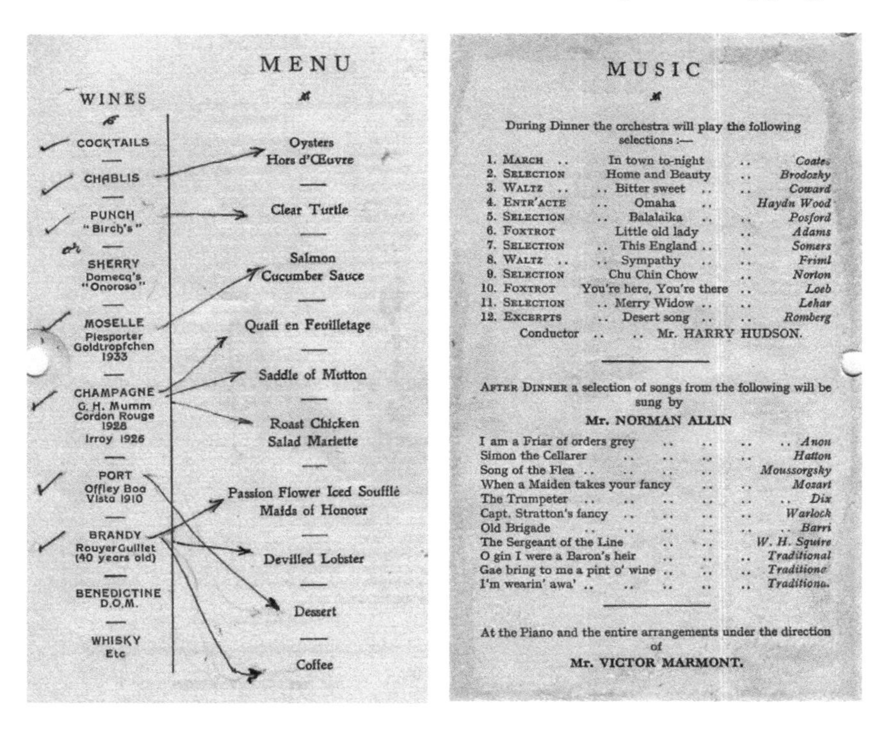

MENU

WINES

COCKTAILS

CHABLIS

PUNCH
"Birch's"

SHERRY
Domecq's
"Onoroso"

MOSELLE
Piesporter
Goldtropfchen
1933

CHAMPAGNE
G. H. Mumm
Cordon Rouge
1928
Irroy 1926

PORT
Offley Boa
Vista 1910

BRANDY
Rouyer Guillet
(40 years old)

BENEDICTINE
D.O.M.

WHISKY
Etc

Oysters
Hors d'Œuvre

Clear Turtle

Salmon
Cucumber Sauce

Quail en Feuilletage

Saddle of Mutton

Roast Chicken
Salad Mariette

Passion Flower Iced Soufflé
Maids of Honour

Devilled Lobster

Dessert

Coffee

MUSIC

During Dinner the orchestra will play the following selections :—

1. March ..	In town to-night	..	*Coates*
2. Selection	Home and Beauty	..	*Brodozky*
3. Waltz ..	.. Bitter sweet ..	..	*Coward*
4. Entr'acte	.. Omaha ..		*Haydn Wood*
5. Selection	.. Balalaika ..	..	*Posford*
6. Foxtrot	Little old lady	..	*Adams*
7. Selection	.. This England ..	..	*Somers*
8. Waltz ..	.. Sympathy ..	..	*Friml*
9. Selection	Chu Chin Chow	..	*Norton*
10. Foxtrot	You're here, You're there	..	*Loeb*
11. Selection	.. Merry Widow ..	..	*Lehar*
12. Excerpts	.. Desert song ..	..	*Romberg*

Conductor .. .. Mr. HARRY HUDSON.

After Dinner a selection of songs from the following will be sung by

Mr. NORMAN ALLIN

I am a Friar of orders grey	.. *Anon*
Simon the Cellarer	*Hatton*
Song of the Flea	*Moussorgsky*
When a Maiden takes your fancy	*Mozart*
The Trumpeter	.. *Dix*
Capt. Stratton's fancy	*Warlock*
Old Brigade	.. *Barri*
The Sergeant of the Line	*W. H. Squire*
O gin I were a Baron's heir	*Traditional*
Gae bring to me a pint o' wine	*Traditional*
I'm wearin' awa'	*Traditional*

At the Piano and the entire arrangements under the direction of

Mr. VICTOR MARMONT.

The menu and music for the Banquet of the Worshipful Company of Patternmakers held in Vintners' Hall on Tuesday 22nd February 1938

My interest in elaborate menus led me to collect newspaper cuttings of a few notable dinners:

- During King Edward VII's last days 'On the evening before he went abroad, King Edward gave the last in a series of dinners which he had recently instituted at the Palace for men of distinction in various fields. He was seen to do justice to: Turtle soup; Salmon steak; Grilled chicken; Saddle of Mutton; Several snipe stuffed with foie gras; Asparagus; Fruit dish; An enormous iced concoction and a Savoury. Normally his dinner seldom consisted of fewer than twelve courses and he adored rich and elaborate dishes. Preferring champagne to claret, he was a moderate drinker. The scale of his smoking on the other hand, was as immoderate as that of his eating. He rationed himself to one small cigar and two cigarettes before breakfast, but he smoked thereafter a daily average of twelve enormous cigars and twenty cigarettes.'

- The royal banquet given by the Shah of Persia in Persepolis in October 1971 to celebrate the 2,500th Anniversary of the Persian monarchy was legendary: 'The meal was cooked and served by a staff of 180 drawn from Maxim's in Paris, the Palace Hotel, St Moritz, and the Hotel de Paris, Monte Carlo, working under the supervision of M. Vaudable, the owner of Maxim's. The menu consisted of quails' eggs stuffed with golden imperial caviar (Champagne and Château de Saran); mousse of crayfish tails (Haut Brion Blanc, 1964); roast saddle of lamb with truffles (Château Lafite Rothschild, 1945); sorbet of Moet at Chandon, 1911; fifty peacocks with tail feathers restored encompassed by roasted quails and served with nut and truffle salad (Musigny Conte de Vogue, 1945); fresh figs in cream with raspberries and port wine (Dom Perignon, 1959, reserve vintage); coffee and cognac Prince Eugene.'

- At the dinner which Lord Palmerston had with the Speaker of the House, Mr Dension, in his 81st year (1864) 'He ate two plates of turtle soup; a very ample serving of cod and oyster sauce; a pate; two very greasy looking entrees; two slices of roast mutton; then the largest slice of ham which disappeared in time for the butler to enquiry 'Snipe or pheasant, my Lord?' He immediately replied pheasant and went on to eat pudding, jelly dressed oranges and half a large pear.'

- In December 1962, an article in the Financial Times entitled 'Menus Grow Longer in the City' noted that: 'The number of courses eaten by guests at the bigger London hotels has been greatly reduced compared with the more leisurely meals of the 1930's. The trend is towards the four-course menu. In the City, however, a serious attempt is being made to return to the 6-7 course meal. As a result, the sorbet (popularised by Edward VII when Prince Regent – less for its own merits than for the Russian cigarette served with it and smoked before the loyal toast) has made a reappearance between fowl and meat. Soup is on the decline, and guests now often start with a fish course such as sole or lobster. And, where soup is still in demand, the popular choice is fish soup such as Richmond bisque (eel soup). Oysters too have declined in popularity, only one tenth of the number being eaten compared with before the war. For the main course guests want beef if they can get it. At the Dorchester for instance, fillets of beef are soaked in white wine and sherry overnight and served with mushroom sauce. The charge per head for a first-class hotel dinner varies from about 30 shillings for something fairly simple to five guineas for the lavish grouse dinner. Drinks often double these prices and are where the caterers make their money.'

Years later, in my retirement, I gave a talk to the local Women's Institute on 'Eating Out' and described the wide range of dining experiences I had had and the changes in menus over the years. I described:

- frugal meals during my student days in London;
- outdoor meals in the Canadian construction camps;
- a lunch with Sir Douglas Haig under a hedge during the Great War;
- dinners in the mess in Mesopotamia;
- two banquets with Faisal when he was appointed King of Iraq;
- meals on the Trans-Siberian Express and on the round-the-world ocean liners;
- dinners at top London hotels; and finally
- banquets in the halls of the City Livery Companies.

Appendix 2
Letter writing and letters from friends

Throughout my travels and also when staying at the Club in London I kept in touch by letter with all my old friends and colleagues around the world, writing or more often typing long missives to them with my news and comments on matters of the day. I also wrote, often critical letters, to newspapers and the BBC about matters which I considered to be important, abhorring the negative effects of publicity or bias in reporting. The list of friends to whom I wrote at Christmas stretched to more than 100; each letter was personal, not the round-robin letters sent by many people today. My friends were generally not such diligent correspondents, but when they did write, they did so with much interest and appreciation.

One such was my Russian friend in Shanghai, Vladimir Bebenin, with whom I spent lively bachelor evenings at night clubs when I was there in 1929. He married a Russian girl soon after I left Shanghai and in 1934 responded to one of my letters saying:

'This matrimonial affair turned out unsuccessfully; very short lived, budget breaking, and caused me a great deal of unhappiness, hence the reason for my not visiting London. However, on the way back to Shanghai at the beginning of 1930 I met another unhappy soul and while consoling each other we eventually married in February 1931, and thus we remain. My wife is English and most charming. We get along splendidly and up to now we are quite happy but unfortunately cannot afford children. As you can imagine my hectic bachelor habits are a closed book, but the energy is still there and so I commenced to learn to read and write Chinese. This should give you an idea of the energy there is to spare. In fact I am becoming such a sober person that when I do have an occasion to drink I suffer frightful hang-overs which was unheard of in the past. It may seem strange that I have never forgotten our meeting and have always hoped that our paths might cross again sometime. I am most interested to know if you have met with new adventures and how life is treating you in general.'

My dancing mistress, Gee Skrine, wrote in September 1934:

'It is topping of you to send us such a lovely wedding present; it arrived safely today from Mappin & Webb and is perfectly lovely. Thank you very, very much. But I am so disappointed that you cannot come and dance at my wedding. I shall be sending along a piece of the cake, which is the next best thing I can do. I am so sorry to hear that you have so many complications in life just now *(a reference to the problems I had looking after my old parents)* and expect I shall be letting myself in for such things too. I shall be continuing my work, which will necessitate my spending about one week in every month in Town, but otherwise shall be living in Manchester. I do so hope that you will come and have dinner with me and a little chat some evening when I am in London. Yours very sincerely, Gee Skrine.'

A letter from Frau Emma Talbot said that her flat in Marienbad had been broken into by burglars who had stolen her 5 fur coats. She wrote that:

'Business in Berlin is rotten, but I believe it's the same all over, even in the USA. ... I do hope whenever you come to Berlin you will always come and see me in Sacrow - you can spend a weekend, also loving swimming in our beautiful lake.

With kindest regards and may all your wishes go in fulfilment.

Yours very sincerely. Emma.'

The following letter from Carlos Brandes, asking me to allow him to postpone repayment of my loan to him, was sent by Graf Zeppelin from Rio de Janeiro in September 1933:

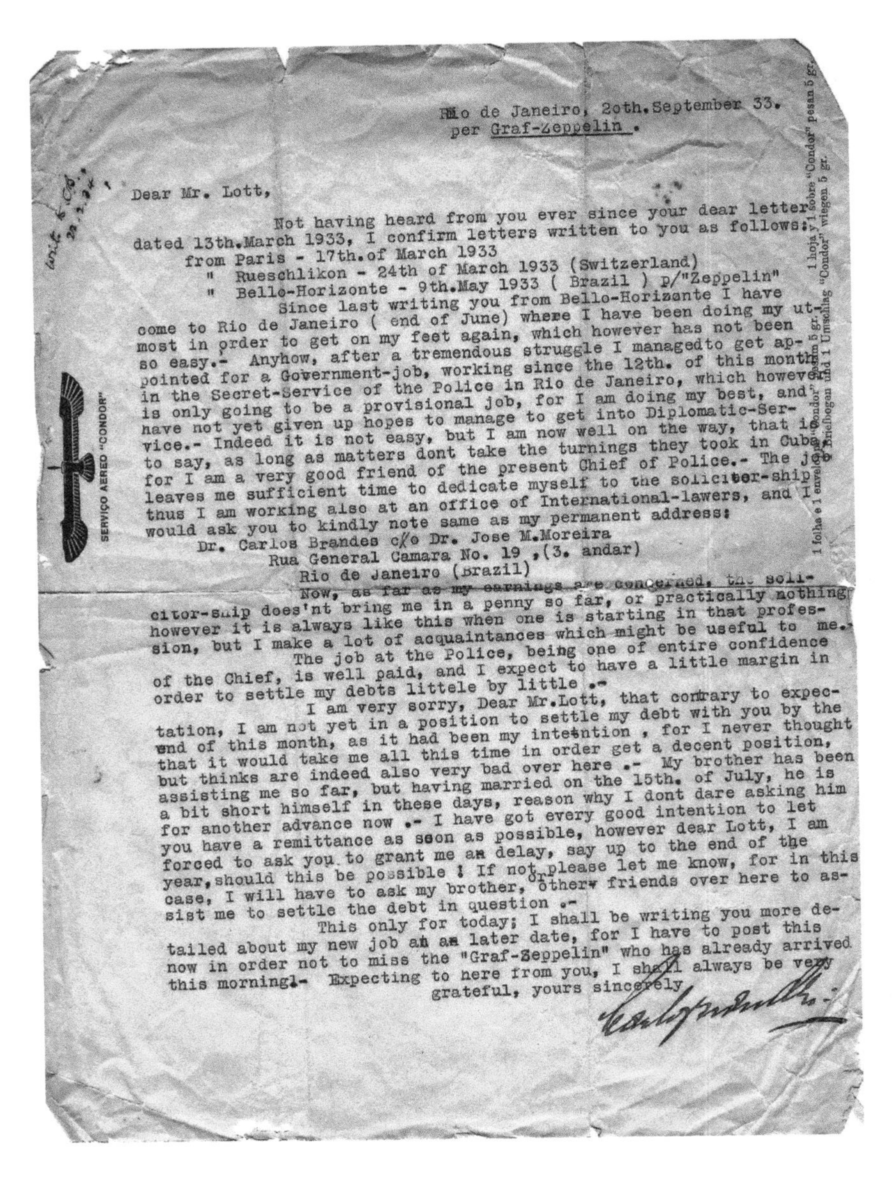

SERVIÇO AEREO "CONDOR"

Rio de Janeiro, 2oth.September 33.
per Graf-Zeppelin .

Dear Mr. Lott,

Not having heard from you ever since your dear letter dated 13th.March 1933, I confirm letters written to you as follows:
from Paris - 17th.of March 1933
" Rueschlikon - 24th of March 1933 (Switzerland)
" Bello-Horizonte - 9th.May 1933 (Brazil) p/"Zeppelin"

Since last writing you from Bello-Horizante I have come to Rio de Janeiro (end of June) where I have been doing my utmost in order to get on my feet again, which however has not been so easy.- Anyhow, after a tremendous struggle I managedto get appointed for a Government-job, working since the 12th. of this month in the Secret-Service of the Police in Rio de Janeiro, which however is only going to be a provisional job, for I am doing my best, and have not yet given up hopes to manage to get into Diplomatic-Service.- Indeed it is not easy, but I am now well on the way, that is to say, as long as matters dont take the turnings they took in Cuba, for I am a very good friend of the present Chief of Police.- The job leaves me sufficient time to dedicate myself to the soliciter-ship and thus I am working also at an office of International-lawers, and I would ask you to kindly note same as my permanent address:
Dr. Carlos Brandes c/o Dr. Jose M.Moreira
Rua General Camara No. 19 ,(3. andar)
Rio de Janeiro (Brazil)

Now, as far as my earnings are concerned, the solicitor-ship does'nt bring me in a penny so far, or practically nothing however it is always like this when one is starting in that profession, but I make a lot of acquaintances which might be useful to me.-

The job at the Police, being one of entire confidence of the Chief, is well paid, and I expect to have a little margin in order to settle my debts littele by little .-

I am very sorry, Dear Mr.Lott, that contrary to expectation, I am not yet in a position to settle my debt with you by the end of this month, as it had been my intention , for I never thought that it would take me all this time in order get a decent position, but thinks are indeed also very bad over here .- My brother has been assisting me so far, but having married on the 15th. of July, he is a bit short himself in these days, reason why I dont dare asking him for another advance now .- I have got every good intention to let you have a remittance as soon as possible, however dear Lott, I am forced to ask you to grant me an delay, say up to the end of the year, should this be possible ! If not please let me know, for in this case, I will have to ask my brother, or other friends over here to assist me to settle the debt in question .-

This only for today; I shall be writing you more detailed about my new job at a later date, for I have to post this now in order not to miss the "Graf-Zeppelin" who has already arrived this morning!- Expecting to here from you, I shall always be very grateful, yours sincerely

Finally, I will close these memoirs of my first 50 years with extracts from two letters from my 'White Hunter' friend, Hubert Stanton. His remarkable and vivid story of catching and transporting animals to a zoo in Buenos Aires reminded me of those days I spent with him on safari in Kenya in 1927-30 and highlighted the complete contrast between his life in Kenya and mine now in London.

He wrote the first of these letters in April 1936 from aboard a ship 'nearing Rio de Janeiro':

'... I don't know where my last letter left off; but anyway I've been going fairly steadily ahead with the trapping since I saw you in London and have been having a fairly steady flow of abominable luck – or perhaps it's more a question of mismanagement.

Hubert Stanton - 1930

I landed that big Buenos Aires (BA) order and from then on, probably feeling wealthy too previously, everything went wrong. The order was for a pair of elephants, a pair of giraffes, one rhino, one eland, one waterbuck and one oryx. Of all these animals I had only three giraffes on hand, but as all three were already booked by other zoos, I had to start the BA order from scratch.

I felt sure of the giraffe, never having failed on seven previous ventures, and the elephants I intended to buy from the elephant farm in the Congo, and so I started out last August for the rhino and antelopes. This meant a big camp near Rumuruti, about 160 miles NNW of Nairobi. After five months of that and having built every conceivable trap and snare I could think of, I didn't catch a thing. Under contract with the BA Zoo I had to have the animals on board a steamer to Mombasa by 15th March 1936.

In November I had arranged with a man in Kitale to get all the necessary structures for a giraffe drive and in January Jane and

I went up to our old trapping grounds to try for the giraffes; there were plenty there and the man engaged there had made a good job of the structures. We failed utterly to get any and had to give it up and returned to Rumuruti to clear up there.

In late January I sent my younger brother Rudolph to the Congo to bring down the elephants which I had already negotiated for. He flew to Juba and motored from there to the elephant farm and was to have started the 250 mile trek with the elephants so as to reach Rhino Camp on the Nile by 16th February to catch the river steamer on that day. It is a fortnightly Uganda Railway service and connects with the through service to Nairobi and Mombasa.

I had by this time managed to buy an eland and an oryx and, as the people who had booked the three giraffes (Rangoon and Bristol Zoos) hadn't sent their deposits, I decided to let BA have two of them as their money had been sent long ago. I had all the shipping arrangements ready for the consignment to leave Mombasa on 24th Feb, minus of course the rhino and water-buck, but I had had the contract made so that I wasn't penalised if I was short on the order.

A few days after my brother had left for the Congo, I had a wire from him saying that the farm people had warned him that it was impossible to do the 250 mile trek with the elephants in that time (he had 15 clear days for it) and what was he to do about it? I wired back telling him to catch the boat leaving Rhino Camp on 1st March. In the meantime I had to alter all the shipping arrangements at Mombasa to a steamer leaving on 14th March.

You can imagine how pleased I was with things in general by this time, particularly when a few days later an air-mail letter arrived from my brother saying that another £90 was needed, chiefly because of extra Government taxes and the enforced delay. But this is all a mere flea-bite to all the trouble still in store.

On 13th February I received a wire saying my brother had died on 6th February, just the day before he was to have started on the 250 mile trek to catch the boat on 1st March.

I was at Rumuruti when that arrived at noon ; within an hour I was on my way by car to Nairobi (160 miles) leaving a mass of arrangements for Jane to close down the traps and camp. I arrived in Nairobi that evening and caught a plane the next day for Juba and then had all sorts of trouble en route, including a return to Kisumu, after we had left it 1½ hours behind, because of engine trouble. We didn't reach Juba until the night of 15th. By an early start in a hired car, I managed to reach the elephant farm on the night of 16th. On the 17th I had to go to Niangara, where my brother died, to fix things up there and returned to the farm the same night. I started the long trek on the 18th; that gave me just 12 days in which to do the journey. By dint of perseverance I completed the 250 mile journey in 10 days, but it was awful walking in the rain without equipment.

Anyhow, I got the elephants safely through to Nairobi arriving there on 6th March. I found that, in the meantime, the oryx had died. Jane and I left Nairobi on 12th March with the animals: 2 elephants, 2 giraffes, 1 eland, 1 leopard, 1 hyena and 1 lynx, the last three being a speculation.

I had discussed the height of the giraffe crates with the railway authorities before leaving and was told that I could set the crates to a height of 12 feet from the truck-floor level. Actually I set them an inch less than that allowed, and this was checked by the railway people before leaving. On arrival at Athi River bridge the tops of both the giraffe crates were caught by the superstructure and broken, and only by luck the giraffes were not damaged. It was impossible to proceed further as the giraffes could put their heads and necks out and be caught by obstructions at stations en route. I decided to cut off all the animals' trucks - 6 in all, including fodder trucks - at Athi River station. I managed to get a very expensive lorry-ride back to Nairobi and arrived there at 7 pm (still the 12th) and arranged for materials and carpenters to go out to Athi River that same night.

At 11.30 am on 13th, with the crates repaired, we continued our journey to Mombasa by goods train. Early on 14th I went to inspect and feed the animals at one of the stations and found that the leopard had chewed through his cage and escaped. Anyhow, we reached Mombasa at 9 am and there one of the elephants was found in a dying condition. We loaded all on board the American Line steamer 'Robin Goodfellow', except the dying elephant.

I got the veterinary doctor onto him, but it was no use; he died that day. Then came the job of removing the carcase and dismantling the crate – a magnificent structure 12 feet long, 9 feet wide and 6½ feet high. I won't go into the details of that Saturday when everything had to be on board by 1 pm or double rates would apply. It was hotter than hell, alternating with heavy rain squalls. It all sounds rather like a fairy story, but there it is, and here am I (7th April) still on board the Robin Goodfellow bound for Rio de Janeiro. We should reach there by the 10th and then tranship for Buenos Aires and return to Kenya by the first possible means.

The elephants were insured from the commencement of their journey in the Congo for £400 each and were covered for £700 each when on board ship at Mombasa. Had that brute delayed his collapse for one day I would have been £300 better off. Funnily he showed no signs of anything untoward the previous night. Of course I get a good walloping financially over this order, but one cannot expect it to be always fine. Jane, I need hardly say, has been grand throughout; we should have been together on the trip, but no lady passengers are allowed on this line and that was the crowning disappointment in having to alter our shipping dates. Did anyone have a more consistent run of ill-luck and disappointments?

I want to get back to Kenya and have another go at those rhinos – they have been so canny in avoiding the traps. Actually they were on the traps more than a dozen times (a large mesh-net affair that would lift them off the ground) and baulked at the last few inches that would have caused them to brush against a thread and release the trip.

In the next letter, dated 31st October 1936 from Nairobi, Kenya Colony, Stanton wrote:

'In the light of subsequent events I very much wish I had been armed with a letter from you to the Rio Chief of Police – you mention him as a personal friend in your letter.

The hoodoo of ill-luck did not cease with the writing of my last letter posted to you in Rio. The voyage had been fine, and the animals thrived and behaved splendidly. A week before reaching Rio, I wired a shipping company there to arrange the on-carriage of the animals to Buenos Aires, giving them every possible detail about the animals, the size of the crates, etc. At no time have I ever been in such a hopelessly desperate situation as I found myself in in Rio.

Instead of being there 3 to 4 days, I had to spend 10. Instead of it costing me £100 to £150 they filched me to the tune of £360. I appealed to the British and Argentine Consulates, but the thing had gone beyond their capacities and I had to go to their Embassies instead. If it wasn't for the British Embassy I believe that I would still be in Rio and certainly all the animals would be dead. I have never seen such appalling administration (or rather lack thereof) and such complete corruption. I had expected something of this nature, but I had no idea that such as state of affairs could exist. The authorities in Rio could not point out a single irregularity in connection with the consignment or me arriving in Rio for trans-shipment. Everything required by their law had been carefully done by the Shipping Co. and myself at Cape Town through the Brazilian consul there.

But the fact remains that unless bribes to a legion of officials were paid, and further, that those same officials and business people were absolutely certain that one had no funds left, there was not a hope of doing anything. Even after giving your money you never knew where you were and were just as likely to be in the same fix as ever unless you had some influence behind you.

Rio is one of the loveliest towns I have ever seen but during my whole time there I never visited a single place which was not connected with my attempts to leave it. Meantime the animals were in a pathetic situation, wedged between the quay and a coal siding with railway engines working day and night, passing within a few feet of them and the drivers taking deliberate delight in blowing their steam whistles to make the animals startle and rear in their crates. Add to this that the ships alongside the quay within 10 yards of the animals were loading coal during all those 10 days. The atmosphere was dense coal-dust most of the time and sometimes it rained and so drenched the animals and their bedding; the contractor, partly paid in advance to make some covering for the animals, of course did nothing of the kind. During the off-loading at Rio, all done by Brazilian stevedores, they overturned one of the giraffe crates. Why the animal wasn't killed is a mystery, but she got off with 'barked' legs; it was horrible.

Thank goodness our contract with BA only obliged us to deliver the animals 'on board steamer at any quay, wharf or pier' in BA harbour. If it wasn't for that the whole circus would have had to start again there. It was of great help that the animals were for the Government Zoo, but even they had their work cut out getting the animals off the boat and to their Garden. I have never seen such appalling inefficiency and lack of facilities.

I had taken a lynx and a hyena on spec to BA; all the other animals had been ordered and paid for except these two. All were landed safely at BA, but the lynx was ill, and the Zoo authorities agreed to take it at £25, and the hyena at £35, but as the lynx died two days after landing I had to forfeit the £25. The post mortem at the Zoo showed poisoning, probably a little Brazilian prank as it became ill when leaving Rio.

On reaching Durban I had word from Jane to say that the giraffe for which she had made arrangements for despatch to Bristol had killed itself while en route from our house to the station in Nairobi. At that stage our animals were uninsured, so it was a complete loss. Bristol had, as we usually require, sent their money (£350) in advance and we therefore had to return it, leaving us with only £70 on my return to Nairobi.

Since then we have been here at Rumuruti carrying on with the rhino venture. I believe, after much experimenting, we have at last struck a method of catching rhino which holds out hope of success. Anyway we caught two fully grown eland a few weeks ago in the first trap of this new type. As we didn't want the eland we let them go and all was successfully completed without damage to eland or trap. Now we are busy constructing more traps of the new type.

Early in January (1937) we hope to be sending off another consignment to BA comprising an elephant, a rhino, a water-buck and an oryx. I have to buy all these animals, on overdraft of course, but that is a procedure that I don't like to advertise. This time Jane or I will take them as far as Durban and tranship them there to a German Line ship bound direct for BA. If you have any influential friends in Durban I should be glad to have a letter of introduction.'

It is sobering to realise that this is how many of our zoos around the world were originally stocked with animals from the wild.

Appendix 3

Results of our Tender for the Electricity Department of Shanghai March 1929

PROPOSED SALE OF THE ELECTRICITY DEPARTMENT

Three Tenders Received from British and American Syndicates; Broad Outlines of Offers Made

COUNCIL'S TERMS FOR CONSUMERS' PROTECTION

Tenders for the proposed purchase of the Shanghai Municipal Electricity Department were sent in yesterday, and broad outlines of them were immediately made available for publication. The three groups who submitted tenders to the Electricity Special Committee (1929) based upon the above Memorandum of Franchise were:—the Hon. R. D. Denman; British Trusts Association Ltd.; and the American & Foreign Power Company, Inc.

The tenders were opened by the Chairman of the Council in the presence of the representatives of the tenderers and the Electricity Special Committee. Those present were:—

S. Fessenden, Chairman of Council.
A. W. Burkill, Chairman of Electricity Special Committee (1929)
Arthur Bassett, Member of Electricity Special Committtee (1929)
F. N. Matthews, Member of Electricity Special (Committee (1929)
O. G. Steen, Member of Electricity Special Committee (1929)
T. Saito, Member of Electricity Special Committee (1929)
T. H. U. Aldridge, Engineer-in-Chief and Manager.
J. T. Ford, Treasurer and Comptroller.
H. Gordon Wright, Secretary to the Committee.

AND:

The Hon. R. D. Denman, Lord Meston's Group.
Mr. P. W. Massey, Lord Meston's Group.

Mr. A. Brooke-Smith, British Trusts Assocaition, Ltd.
Mr. H. C. Lott, British Trusts Association, Ltd.

Mr. S. W. Murphy, American & Foreign Power Co. Inc.
Mr. H. F. Jackson, American & Foreign Power Co. Inc.
Mr. V. Meyer, American & Foreign Power Co. Inc.
Mr. F. R. Davey, American & Foreign Power Co. Inc.

The following offers were made:—

First: The Hon. R. D. Denman's offer for leasing:—

In brief the scheme is that a S. M. E. Company lease the undertaking on terms of paying for the interest and Sinking Fund Instalments on all the Council's Electricity Loans plus a fixed rent of Tls. 2,000,000 per annum. After the payment of a 9 per cent dividend on the Company's ordinary shares, three-quarters of the surplus profits go to the Council and one-quarter to the Company. A sliding scale of benefits to consumers is included, which operates after 10 per cent. is paid, not on the whole capital of the Company but on the ordinary shares only."

Second: British Trusts Association Ltd:

Offer (A): Fifty-one million Taels—under the terms and conditions of the Memorandum of Franchise.

Offer (B): £7,200,000. Sterling.—conditional upon certain amendments to paragraphs 8 and 13 of the Committee's Memorandum of Franchise.

Offer (C): An offer to lease on terms to be mutually agreed upon.

Third: American & Foreign Power Company, Ltd, Inc.

Eighty-one million Taels—under the terms and conditions of the Memorandum of Franchise.

These offers will be taken under consideration by the Electricity Special Committee who will make their recommendations thereof to the Council.

Appendix 4

My Evidence to the Tribunal on the Maragua-Tana Power Scheme March 1930

THE MARAGUA - TANA POWER SCHEME.

Further Evidence Before Tribunal.

EVIDENCE BY EXPERT.

Unequivocal Support for the Project.

The hearing of evidence by the Special Tribunal appointed by Government to enquire into the question of the Maragua-Tana Power Scheme drew to a close yesterday, when the last of the witnesses gave his evidence before the Tribunal, sitting in the Supreme Court.

The witnesses included Mr. A. C. Tannahill, representing the Association of E.A. Chambers of Commerce, and Mr. T. Fitzgerald, Postmaster-General, who explained the position of Government in regard to concessions.

Expert evidence was given by Mr. H. C. Lott, advisor to the E.A. Power and Lighting Company. He was very definite in his advocacy of the Maragua-Tana project, as opposed to other suggested schemes.

GENERATING COSTS.

A sitting of the Tribunal appointed by Government to consider the proposal for the establishment of the Maragua Tana Power scheme was held in the Supreme Court Nairobi yesterday, when some extremely interesting and highly instructive evidence was recorded.

On behalf of the Associated Chambers of Commerce Mr. T. C. Tannahill the President, was granted permission to amplify the memorandum which had been submitted by that body.

Dealing firstly with the power of Government to control the price of power, he said that his Association felt very strongly that everything possible should be

(Continued on page 9.)

A VICTORIAN CHILDHOOD
and
COLLEGE LIFE IN EDWARDIAN LONDON
(1883-1907)

Volume 1
of
THE COLOURFUL LIFE OF AN ENGINEER
The Memoirs of Harry Chickall Lott MC

The story of Harry Lott, a young engineer growing up in England 120 years ago, provides a fascinating and thought-provoking contrast to daily life today. After a childhood in an Essex farmhouse, Harry went to school in Dorchester where his father became a partner in an iron foundry. A scholarship to the Central Technical College led to student life in London when Edward VII came to the throne and steam cars, omnibuses and the Twopenny Tube were replacing horse-drawn carriages.

Harry gained practical engineering experience at Marshall's of Gainsborough before emigrating to Canada in 1907, aged 24, after seeing the country on the 1905 Atlantic cable laying expedition.

EMIGRATION
and
THE ADVENTURES OF A YOUNG ENGINEER
IN CANADA

(1907-1914)

Volume 2
of
THE COLOURFUL LIFE OF AN ENGINEER
Memoirs of Harry Chickall Lott MC

Life in Canada before the First World War is vividly described by Harry Lott, who arrived in Montreal in 1907 as a 24 year old engineer with £10 in his pocket and no job to go to. He worked as an inspector on the construction of bridges, dams, transmission lines and early reinforced concrete buildings in five Provinces before returning to England in 1914 to join up for WWI.

Fascinating stories of life in Montreal and Winnipeg and two years in construction camps in the backwoods of Manitoba, canoeing expeditions and moose hunts, are interspersed with historical background details and engineering descriptions of the projects he worked on.

THE LIFE OF A PIONEER AND ENGINEER
ON
THE WESTERN FRONT

(1914-1919)

Volume 3
of
THE COLOURFUL LIFE OF AN ENGINEER
Memoirs of Harry Chickall Lott MC

A personal story of the humour, horror, and routine of the daily life of an officer and his men in the trenches and billets near the front line in World War I. The main events of the War in France are summarised, including the battles of the Somme and Passchendaele where Harry was wounded, making this a very readable history of the conflict of just over 100 years ago.

Harry left his engineering career in Canada to join up in England and went to France in 1915 as a 2nd Lieutenant in the Royal Sussex (Pioneer) Regiment. Mentioned in Despatches three times and awarded the Military Cross in 1917, he was promoted to Major in the Royal Engineers where he commanded No.5 Army Tramway Company. After the Armistice in 1918 Harry caught Spanish Flu' and returned to Loos for the battlefield clearance in 1919 before being transferred to the British Army in Mesopotamia.

MESOPOTAMIA
(1919-1924)

THE STORY OF AN ENGINEER WITH THE BRITISH ARMY OF OCCUPATION

Volume 4 of THE COLOURFUL LIFE OF AN ENGINEER
Memoirs of Harry Chickall Lott MC

A fascinating glimpse of Iraq 100 years ago and the activities of the British Army of Occupation. Based with the Royal Engineers in Baghdad and Basra, Harry was responsible for the supply of electricity, water, and ice to garrisons and local residents throughout the region, employing up to 8,000 men before reducing the staff and the cost to the Exchequer of the British presence.

The Arab Revolt, dinners with King Feisal, constructing facilities for the newly formed RAF, and working with Sir John Salmond are described, interspersed with river trips, tennis and garden parties at the Makina Club, and shooting trips for sand-grouse in the desert and for duck and wild boar in the Marshes.

Lightning Source UK Ltd.
Milton Keynes UK
UKHW021317040721
386529UK00007B/69